MIND THE GAP

MIND THE GAP

Navigating Transitions in
Life with Mindfulness

Beverley McGuire

PUBLISHED BY THE UNIVERSITY OF NORTH CAROLINA WILMINGTON | WILLIAM MADISON RANDALL LIBRARY

DOI: https://doi.org/10.5149/9781469672991_McGuire

ISBN 978-1-4696-7298-4 (paperback)
ISBN 978-1-4696-7299-1 (ebook)

Cover art: Higher Octave (2015) by Michele de la Menardiere, used by permission of the artist. (www.delamenardiere.com)

CONTENTS

First and foremost, I would like to acknowledge Anne Pemberton, to whom I dedicate this book. She was an exceptionally kind and caring colleague, who was so transparent about her own struggles and shortcomings—which is exceedingly rare in academic environments—that she inspired and held space for others to do the same. With me and Jacquelyn Lee, she cofounded Mindful UNCW: a campus-wide initiative to increase mindfulness practice among students, faculty, and staff at our university.[1] She was the Associate Director of Research and Instructional Services and Library Assessment at UNCW's Randall Library, where she had been a librarian and faculty member from 2003 until her death in 2021. She began practicing mindfulness as an undergraduate psychology major, and she continued using it to address her mental health struggles as she worked on healing from trauma, depression, and anxiety. She incorporated mindfulness holistically into her personal and professional life, viewing mindfulness as a way of life. Although I began writing this book in 2019 and envisioned it primarily for an audience of first-year students, after the COVID-19 pandemic and Anne's sudden death in the summer of 2021, I decided to widen the scope of the audience to include those experiencing other kinds of change and transition. Her death brought about a huge gap and tremendous sense of loss, but I have found solace and significance in publishing this book through UNCW's Randall Library with her former colleagues.

My own experience as a first-year student and as a First Year Seminar instructor originally fueled my desire to write a book that engages and equips students with the skills to meet transitions with curiosity and care. As a first-year student, participating in Structured Liberal Education (SLE)[2], a residential program designed to cultivate interdisciplinary and critical thinking through the study of literature, art, religion, and political theory, had a significant impact on my college experience. Teaching First Year Seminars about Eastern conceptions of the self at UNC Greensboro and mindfulness at UNC Wilmington has also informed my approach in this book, and my own and others' first-year students are its primary audience.

This book also connects with my own area of research, especially mindfulness, moral attention, and Asian religions. As a participant in the Public Theologies of Technology and Presence program (PTTP)[3], a three-year program sponsored by the Luce Foundation that examined ways technologies reshape human relationships and alter how people are or are not "present" with each other, I studied the impact of digital technology on moral attention—the capacity to discern and attend to the morally salient features of a given situation.[4] With the encouragement of the director of the program, Steven Barrie-Anthony, I decided to write a book for a popular audience—my own students—rather than other academics. I wanted to develop my students' moral attention: to make them "finely aware and richly responsible," in the words of Martha Nussbaum.[5]

Many mentors, friends, colleagues, and family members inspired me to write this book. Suzanne Greenberg, Marc Mancall, Jonathan Reider, and other SLE instructors fostered a vibrant first-year learning community of thoughtful reflection and lively conversations about important cultural, philosophical, religious, and political issues during my first year at Stanford. Martin Aylward and Mark Coleman, who trained me as a mindfulness teacher, modeled how one might bring mindfulness into secular settings, including higher education. Michele de la Menardiere allowed me to use her art for the cover of the book, and Erica Noles contributed her essay "How to Take Reading Notes" as an appendix. Rebecca Stultz, Erica Noles, and Erika Hanson shared their insights and observations as fellow First Year Seminar instructors at UNCW. Christine Pesetski and Kelsey Axe reviewed the manuscript. Lucy Holman, Allison Kittinger, and Stephanie Crowe from UNCW's Randall Library and John McLeod from UNC Press facilitated the publication process. Last, but not least, I would like to thank my parents, Gary and Sims Foulks, as well as my spouse, Michael McGuire, for their enthusiastic support. I am also grateful for my children, Haley and Connor, who persistently remind me—or rather, insist—that I take breaks from writing and play with them instead!

Finally, I would like to acknowledge that the University of North Carolina Wilmington, where I teach and who published this book, is located on the traditional territory of the Catawba people which has served as a site of meeting and exchange among many Indigenous peoples for thousands of years. I honor and respect the diverse Indigenous peoples connected to this territory that we now occupy—the state of North Carolina—including the Coharie,

Lumbee, Meherrin, Occaneechi Saponi, Haliwa Saponi, Waccamaw Siouan, Sappony, and the Eastern Band of Cherokee. This land acknowledgment is to pay respect and honor the elders of the Indigenous People and Nations both past and present.[6]

Notes

1. "Mindful UNCW."
2. "Structured Liberal Education."
3. "Public Theologies of Technology and Presence."
4. My research was featured in an article by a fellow PTTP participant: see Samuel, "It's Hard to be a Moral Person."
5. Nussbaum, "'Finely Aware and Richly Responsible.'"
6. "Honor Native Land: A Guide and Call to Acknowledgment."

"Mind the gap!" This was a perennial reminder that I heard in London's underground subway stations, warning passengers to be mindful as they stepped over the gap between the platform and the train. As a student studying abroad at Oxford University during my junior year in college, I would go to London on weekends to visit museums and art galleries, or to see a show in Leicester Square. I heard the phrase "mind the gap" so often that it worked its way into my subconscious. During the cold, wet winter months that I spent in England, I truly felt the gap. I had never experienced such bleak winter seasons in my hometown in North Carolina or my college town in California.

This book is about how to be mindful of that gap that presents itself in various transitions in life: when you go away to college, travel to a foreign country, move to a new city, or start a new job. The basic principle is that we should be mindful of the gap—the difference—between our former environment and our new one. When you are in a transition, it can be easy to lose your bearing, as you're essentially unmoored. You are in a state of "betwixt and between," which can be very disorienting and disconcerting. Until you start to feel at home in your new environment, you have to negotiate these feelings of discomfort.

Mindful of the gap, you draw your attention toward those feelings. Mindfulness involves cultivating an embodied presence, receptivity, and awareness of whatever arises in yourself and your surroundings, without judging or rejecting those experiences. All too often, when we feel uncomfortable or unsettled, we immediately want to alleviate our feelings of discomfort. This leads us to seek comfort, or perhaps to seek out distraction. The problem is, when we do this, we rob ourselves of the opportunity to grow and develop in new ways. We never leave the platform. We never experience the thrill of riding a train to new destinations.

You can teach yourself to be mindful, so that instead of immediately reacting to discomfort or unpleasant sensations, you can observe them, accept them, and respond to them intentionally rather than reacting automatically. This is especially important when you are experiencing a transition or undergoing difficult times in your life. Having the capacity to hold in awareness whatever arises in your life gives you the freedom to determine how you want to move forward.

The entire world experienced a gap in March 2020 with the stay-at-home orders issued in response to COVID-19. It was—and arguably still is—a time of great uncertainty and ambiguity. Although some found comfort in working and learning remotely at home, others missed the social interaction, community, and normalcy of their former lives. Many sought out digital distractions, doomscrolling news and social media outlets or binge-watching streaming videos, to alleviate their feelings of anxiety.

This book shows how attending to change, ambiguity, and discomfort can help you manage these and other changes that you will inevitably face in your life, including the loss of relationships, the death of loved ones, and transitions between jobs. You will learn how to be mindful of your breath, body, feelings, emotions, and thoughts, as well as how you might cultivate kindness, compassion, joy, and spaciousness in your life and relationships with others. By developing the core ability to attend to what you do, what you think, and what you say, you can enhance your own well-being as well as your relationships with others.

CHAPTER ONE

Allowing for Ambiguity, Uncertainty, and Discomfort

My experience is what I agree to attend to. Only those items which I *notice* shape my mind—without selective interest, experience is an utter chaos.
—William James[1]

My college send-off consisted of saying goodbye to my parents at the Raleigh-Durham airport. I had shipped my bike, twin sheets, and clothes in a trunk weeks before. On the shuttle ride from the San Francisco airport to Palo Alto, I saw densely populated outskirts of the city followed by barren, golden foothills. Nothing was familiar. Even the trees on campus—huge palm trees lining the drive to the Main Quad—differed from the pine trees of the forests where I grew up. Not only was the landscape different, but I found myself among culturally, racially, and ethnically diverse students, some of whom were from elite prep schools who tossed around words like "epistemology" and "ontology." I soon became accustomed to writing down such words and looking them up later in my *Oxford American Dictionary*:

> epistemology *n.* a philosophic theory of the method or basis of human knowledge.
> ontology *n.* the branch of metaphysics dealing with the nature of existence.
> metaphysics *n.* a branch of philosophy that deals with the nature of existence and of truth and knowledge.[2]

I felt like a fraud. "Surely," I thought, "they must have made a mistake in admitting me!" I later found out this experience of "imposter's syndrome" is all too common: an estimated 70 percent of people tend to doubt their abilities or distrust their accomplishments.[3] Being in new environments and new situations can precipitate such feelings of anxiety and discomfort, leading many people to second-guess themselves. But what if we were able to sit with those feelings of anxiety and discomfort, accepting them as a natural response to being in a new environment or situation, rather than jumping to judgment and self-criticism?

You have probably heard the process of transformation compared to a caterpillar morphing into a butterfly: after eating copious amounts of leaves and undergoing a series of molts, the caterpillar hangs upside down from a branch or leaf, spins itself a cocoon, and later emerges as a butterfly. But what does it look like in the cocoon? What does the process of transformation involve? As Ferris Jabr writes, "First, the caterpillar digests itself, releasing enzymes to dissolve all of its tissues. If you were to cut open a cocoon or chrysalis at just the right time, caterpillar soup would ooze out."[4] However, amid such ooze, one finds "imaginal discs," which are disc-shaped groups of cells that eventually turn into the eyes, head, wings, and other parts of the butterfly. As Jabr notes, "Those discs use the protein-rich soup all around them to fuel the rapid cell division required to form the wings, antenna, legs, eyes, genitals and all the other features of an adult butterfly or moth."[5]

In other words, change is messy, like caterpillar soup, but the soup is what supports and promotes the development of the butterfly. This book will help you survive the digestive process. It explores the imaginal discs that you will need to become a mature butterfly—a college graduate, an expatriate living overseas, a resident of a new city, or an employee starting a new job. Yet it also assumes that you, as caterpillars, must digest yourself. You must shed some thoughts and habits that may have served you well as caterpillars but will stall or interrupt the process of becoming a butterfly.

Ambiguity, Uncertainty, and Discomfort

This chapter explores how attending to ambiguity, uncertainty, and discomfort—allowing and willingly residing in that suspended state—can enable you to address all kinds of messy, complex situations. In our world today, we face many "wicked problems"—interpersonal, societal, and global issues that defy easy solutions. They are not black-and-white issues, but various shades of gray. In order to see those shades of gray, you need to have cognitive flexibility, moving from binary thoughts of right and wrong, or authentic and inauthentic, to admitting the possibility of contradictions, paradoxes, and puzzles. You need to allow yourself to be confused and uncomfortable, entertaining open-ended questions and reflecting on things that may perplex you.

Niels Bohr—the Danish physicist who received the Nobel Prize in Physics in 1922 for his contributions to understanding atomic structure and quantum theory—made incredible discoveries by holding space for contradiction. John Heilbron describes Bohr's method as follows:

He would collect instances of failure, examine each minutely and retain those that seemed to him to embody the same flaw. He then invented a hypothesis to correct the flaw, keeping, however, the flawed theory to cover not only parts of experience where it worked, but also parts where neither it nor the new hypothesis, with which it was in contradiction, could account for the phenomena. This juggling made for creative ambiguity as well as for confusion: Pushing the contradiction might disclose additional anomalies, and perhaps a better, more inclusive hypothesis. A coherent theory might emerge that would remove the need for cooperation with the flawed theory, and the latter would be restricted to a domain for which it fully sufficed. To work in this way one needs not only creative genius, but also a strong stomach for ambiguity, uncertainty, and contradiction.[6]

Instead of discarding the flawed hypothesis, Bohr kept it alongside new hypotheses—even those that contradicted it—which enabled him to generate more coherent theories. When we can hold contradictory ideas or theories simultaneously, that tension can potentially yield further insight or reveal additional inconsistencies. Instead of thinking about contradiction as an "either/or" scenario, we can work through "both/and" and perhaps discover unforeseen insights.

We can play with this idea on a perceptual level. Look at the image below.[7] What do you see?

As the Austrian philosopher Ludwig Wittgenstein observes, it can be seen in two ways: as either a duck or a rabbit. The image remains the same, but we have a new perception of it depending on what aspect we see. Interestingly, we see aspects all the time, but we are often unaware we are doing so. For example, we see a table as a table, but when my son was a toddler, he saw it as something to hide under or climb on. He had not yet adopted the conventional way of seeing a table.

Although our systems of perception can create useful models of reality that often serve us well, those same systems can give rise to perceptual illusions—perceiving things in a way that does not map onto reality. If we look at the image below, we might perceive the line segment on the right to be longer than that on the left.[8]

Do You See a Duck or a Rabbit?. Wikimedia Commons. Public Domain.

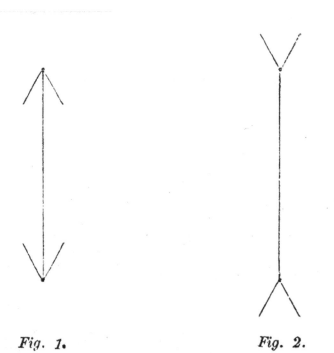

Fig. 1.   *Fig. 2.*

The Müller-Lyer Illusion. "Müller-Lyer Illusion" by Franz Bertano. Wikimedia Commons. Public Domain.

In fact, the left and right line segments are of equal length, but the orientation of the arrowheads creates an optical illusion of the right line segment looking longer than the other. These types of illusions should caution us against assuming our perception captures reality as fully or accurately as we might think.

In premodern China, early Daoist philosophers excelled at drawing conventional views of reality and perception into question. Zhuangzi, who is said to have lived in the fourth century before the Common Era (B C E), famously dreamt he was a butterfly flying about, only to wake up and wonder whether he was then a butterfly dreaming he was Zhuangzi. He calls this "the transformation of things."[9] Many of us have had such thoughts about the difference between our dream state and waking state. Zhuangzi allowed himself to entertain the possibility of such paradox. What would it look like in your own life if you were to go beyond your entrenched thoughts, even about what constitutes reality and fantasy? How might you explore alternate possibilities and cultivate more flexible thinking?

Daoists show how we might overcome the trap of conventional thinking: they know how to digest themselves. They advocate a return to a more natural state, which they call "uncarved wood": our state of being before we were cut, shaped, and molded by outside forces and social conventions. One way to do that, according to a fourth century B C E text attributed to Zhuangzi, entitled the *Zhuangzi*, is to "fast the mind":

Unify your will. Instead of listening with the ear, listen with your mind. Rather than listening with your mind, listen with your energies. The ear stops with what it hears. The mind stops at what it labels. But the vital energy—it is an emptiness which awaits the guest of beings. Only the Way gathers this emptiness. And it is this emptiness which is the fasting of the mind.[10]

To "fast the mind" means to starve it of conventional thoughts of right and wrong, or good and bad. Our mind tends to get caught up in concepts, categories, and labels. Instead, the *Zhuangzi* recommends, we should cultivate a more receptive state toward other beings. Specifically, we should develop our capacities of awareness and responsiveness. Elsewhere, the *Zhuangzi* states:

Within yourself, no fixed positions:
Things as they take shape disclose themselves.
Moving, be like water,

Still, be like a mirror,
Respond like an echo.[11]

The water follows a particular movement of a river or stream; the mirror reflects whatever appears before it. We must first be aware of what is before us, be it a place, a person, or a situation. As Jung Lee writes, early Daoists envisioned "a much finer responsiveness to the particular and concrete, a response-ability grounded in the natural patterns and processes of the cosmos."[12] Daoists espouse an ethics of attunement: by attuning ourselves to the people and places around us, we can better respond to them.

Another way of encouraging greater flexibility of thought and tolerance for ambiguity is how we tend to view objects. The Daodejing, an early Daoist text attributed to Laozi, points to the hub of wheels, insides of pots, and emptiness of rooms to suggest, "What is present is used for profit. But it is in absence that there is usefulness."[13] Although we tend to focus on the wheel, pot, or walls of a room, it is the emptiness that allows the wheel to turn, the pot to hold tea, and the room to hold people. The *Zhuangzi* makes an additional point about the "usefulness of uselessness" by sharing the story of a huge, gnarled oak tree that a carpenter dismisses as "worthless" because it cannot provide him with timber. The oak tree appears to the carpenter in a dream saying it had long tried to "be of no use": "This is of great use to me. If I had been of some use, would I ever have grown this large? Moreover you and I are both of us things. What's the point of this—things condemning things? You, a worthless man about to die—how do you know that I'm a worthless tree?"[14] To the carpenter, the tree is useless; to the tree, being useless has enabled its survival and longevity. What do you see when you look at a huge oak tree, like the one below?

Perhaps you are like my students; they say it looks like a great climbing tree, or they would enjoy sitting under its shade. When we consider the perspectives of others—including that of trees—we can appreciate the limitations and biases of our own views. In his book *The Overstory*, which won the 2019 Pulitzer Prize in fiction, Richard Powers says that the use of trees is to show that the world is not made for our utility. "Overstory" refers both to the layer of foliage in a forest canopy and to the trees that provide it. Below, you can see an overstory from a redwood forest in Sequoia National Forest.

Powers depicts the veiled, interconnected world of trees, including their underground fungal network that allows them to share water and nutrients and warn other trees in the event of drought, disease, or insect attacks.[15] He gives

The Oak Tree: Charleston, South Carolina. Photo by Andrew Shelly on Unsplash.

a vivid sense of the vastness of time when it comes to the lifespan of trees—at least, those not subject to deforestation:

> When he looks up, it's into the branches of the sentinel tree, lone, huge, fractal and bare against the drifts, lifting its lower limbs and shrugging its ample globe. All its profligate twigs click in the breeze as if this moment, too, so insignificant, so transitory, will be written into its rings and prayed over by branches that wave their semaphores against the blues of midwestern winter skies.[16]

Rings of trees form over hundreds of years—or thousands, in the case of redwood trees. They mark the passage of time on a scale that vastly exceeds our own lives. How often have you felt small when looking up at a night sky, scanning the expanse from a mountaintop, or gazing out at the ocean? When we open ourselves to others, including the natural environment, we gain a new perspective on our own sense of time and place.

The Overstory: Sequoia National Forest. Photo by Victoria Palacios on Unsplash.

The *Zhuangzi* tells the story of the Yellow River becoming flooded and flowing east to the North Sea. The North Sea says, "You can't discuss the ocean with a well frog—he's limited by the space he lives in. You can't discuss ice with a summer insect—he's bound to a single season. . . . Now you have come out beyond your banks and borders and have seen the great sea—so you know your own pettiness."[17] All too often we are like frogs in a well. Our worldview narrows to fit our particular circumstances. When we find ourselves in unfamiliar terrain, not unlike the river when it meets the sea, we can become anxious or feel overwhelmed. But by mindfully attending to what we are experiencing, we can open ourselves to new possibilities and perspectives.

Introduction to Mindfulness

Mindfulness is cultivating an embodied presence, receptivity, and awareness of whatever arises in oneself and one's surroundings. Like any practice, mindfulness is developed over time. It takes patience to change deep-rooted habits of being distracted or mindless, especially when we live at a time when digital devices constantly vie for our attention. We can fill all of our time —down time, waiting time, even dinnertime—with texts, emails, games, social media, and streamed videos. We reach for our phones instinctively when we experience any inkling of boredom in meetings, classrooms, and restaurants. We avoid uncomfortable encounters with strangers or acquaintances by looking at our phones instead of other people. We can become so engrossed by our phones that we forget where we are, or what we are doing, which can lead to collisions on sidewalks or accidents on roads.

These habitual tendencies feed what Buddhists call the "monkey mind": our natural state of mind, which tends to swing like a monkey from one thought to the next. Without any sense of goal or direction, the mind will reach for whatever calls out most forcefully: a grumbling stomach may prompt one to think about food, or an unsettling conversation may lead one to ruminate on relationships, or an upcoming deadline may lead one to stressfully strategize about how to get things done. We may not even think we have the capacity to control our mind or direct our focus, as it sometimes seems like an elephant trampling about haphazardly. However, mindfulness offers a means of fastening one's attention, which can alleviate the feelings of discomfort and anxiety that feed our mental chatter.

But we must first remember to do so. The original Sanskrit term for mindfulness—sati—meant "remembrance." We must recall that we are able to monitor our minds. The challenge is that we tend toward distraction and our habits have become so engrained that we easily fall into them. We aren't attentive. We need to train ourselves in this skill. In our society we often emphasize the importance of diet and exercise—nourishing our bodies and strengthening our muscles—but we tend to overlook the mind or downplay the importance of mental health. Until the relatively recent arrival of positive psychology, people only associated psychology with mental disorders and illnesses. Little attention was paid to how we might cultivate our minds, or the role that it plays in human flourishing.

However, Buddhists have a long history of analyzing the mind, discussing the way it contributes to well-being or suffering, and exploring various types of mental training. They believe that the mind precedes and creates our reality: we can experience the world as stressful or relaxing, as stifling or freeing, simply due to the state of our minds. Humans have the capacity to use our minds in skillful or unskillful ways, but without practice, we tend to use them unskillfully. We let them run rampant, which has emotional, psychological, and spiritual repercussions. Buddhists sought to develop their attention and concentration, starting with the body as the first field for cultivating mindfulness.

We too can attend to our bodies as we sit, stand, walk, or lie down. We begin our practice of mindfulness by noticing our posture. Although we may associate "posturing" with being fake or artificial, here it simply refers to the way that we position our body or carry ourselves. Are our feet touching the ground? Are we slumped over? Are we clenching our teeth or gripping our jaw? What we cultivate is both an awareness of our body and a conditioning where we position our bodies in the most stable and supportive way whether we are seated, standing, walking, or lying down. Because of the interconnection between our bodies and minds, we cannot cultivate our minds without also attending to our bodies. Buddhist monastics are encouraged to sit like a bell, stand like a tree, walk like the wind, and lie like a bow. During seated meditation, the practice is best supported by stability. For some, that is sitting on the ground with their feet, legs, and buttocks all resting on the floor. For others, that is sitting in a chair with the feet firmly touching the ground, the legs at a 90-degree angle, and the sitting bones ("sitz bones") resting on the front part of the chair.

Initially this may feel unnatural. Many of us are unaccustomed to paying such attention to how we hold ourselves, or we may associate it with strictness or formality. As a child, I was constantly reminded to sit up straight and stand tall. I was very self-conscious about my body: I was tall and lanky, and I tended to tower over most of my classmates. I would stoop over as much as possible in an effort not to stand out. When I first engaged in seated meditation and was told to imagine a string pulling up on the crown of my head so my spine would be erect, I drew to mind the image of a puppet. It felt very artificial. But soon afterwards I felt another sensation…of openness and freedom. I was allowing my body to be grounded, upright, open, and relaxed. By adopting a stable, upright, open, and relaxed posture, we can foster a steady, bright, receptive, and gentle awareness.

Mindfulness encourages us to be receptive to our bodily sensations, feelings, and thoughts. Because of its natural rhythm, effortlessness, and availability, the breath can serve as a useful tool for cultivating mindfulness. You can focus on the physical sensations of the in-breath and out-breath: the air moving in and out of the nostrils, the rise and fall of the chest, or the expansion and contraction of the abdomen. You can also attend to the feelings that arise, which can be pleasant, unpleasant, or indifferent. Mindfulness encourages us to be with our direct experience from moment to moment, simply acknowledging our feelings of pain, pleasure, or apathy, without feeling the need to react to them. Instead of resisting unpleasant sensations, clinging to pleasant ones, or becoming bored with neutral ones, we remain present with our feelings. We acknowledge them, instead of resisting them, or seeking to evade them, or trying to remove them. Over time, this can strengthen our resilience and build a capacity to abide with unpleasant sensations.

We start with our own bodies, feelings, and thoughts because they are readily accessible to our direct experience. When we simply receive our feelings, we can create space between what we sense and how we respond. We can change our habits. As Nyanaponika Thera writes, "Owing to a rash or habitual limiting, labeling, misjudging and mishandling of things, important sources of knowledge often remain closed."[18] Receptivity opens our perception to what we might otherwise overlook, negate, or marginalize because of our prejudices and biases. We pause, slow down, and observe instead of immediately jumping to judgments or opinions. Over time, the receptivity of the mind grows as reactions don't occur as frequently or automatically. We move from habitual reactivity to reflective response.

This not only makes us more resilient but also better people. The way that we react to our feelings and sensations contributes to our state of mind and thoughts. Instead of allowing our mind to be fixated by desire, overwhelmed by hatred, or caught up in ignorance, we cultivate a mind filled with generosity, kindness, and wisdom. We do this by simply noticing what we are sensing in our body, what feelings those sensations evoke, what mental states they contribute to, and what thoughts they give rise to.

In our practice of mindfulness, we can widen or narrow the scope of our attention. We can direct it toward a particular focal point—such as our breath, and a pleasant or unpleasant feeling—or we can broaden it to what we sense, feel, or think as we hear sounds, feel breezes, see clouds, or smell and taste foods. In experiences of more open awareness, we become more attuned to what arises inside of ourselves and from the surrounding environment. We can experience being permeated by smells, penetrated by sights, or enveloped by sounds. Natural environments can be conducive for open awareness, but we can also actively receive someone else in all of their complexity and particularity. When you widen the scope of your attention, you take what comes— painful and pleasant sensations, embarrassing or upsetting memories, jarring and soothing sounds—as they are. You cultivate a "beginner's mind" to your experience, approaching it as a novice or a child would encounter it.[19] Even in fraught relationships with long histories and deep-seated emotions, you are present with whatever arises.

Mindfulness of Breath

Mindfulness develops your capacity to tolerate ambiguity, uncertainty, and discomfort. When you first engage in mindfulness practice, you will find that your mind wanders, and that is completely normal. The moment when you notice that you're distracted is a moment of mindfulness! Try to be patient, try not to judge yourself, and just be willing to start over again . . . and again . . . and again. Mindfulness is a practice. Just as you might play scales on a piano to improve finger dexterity, you can practice mindfulness to train your attention and focus.

Sitting on a cushion or chair in a relatively quiet space, first consider your posture. There are five principles to keep in mind:

Grounded: feel your feet making contact with the floor, and feel the weight of your body in your chair

Alert: imagine a string pulling on the crown of your head, lifting your spine, so you are upright and alert

Open: roll your shoulders a few times and allow them to fall down your back, and place your hands in your lap or on your legs

Easeful: try to soften any areas of tension, such as your forehead, jaw, or belly

Still: try to cultivate stillness in your practice, and if you do move, move slowly, intentionally, and mindfully

As you can see, these principles are not only useful for your practice of mindfulness, but also for cultivating a sense of stability and resilience in the face of ambiguity, uncertainty, and discomfort. We start by tapping into these feelings of being grounded, alert, open, at ease, and still. This can support us as we encounter circumstances that may be unsettling or unfamiliar. Even the simple act of feeling into your feet can center you: observe what you are feeling in your feet. It may be feelings of weight, warmth, numbness, tingling, or other sensations. Just observe without judging or trying to change those sensations.

Mindfulness of breath involves paying attention to your direct experience of your body breathing. You use the breath as the anchor for your attention. If the breath is not a helpful anchor for your attention, due to physical or emotional circumstances, such as asthma or trauma, feel free to focus on your hands or feet. When attending to your breath, you might focus on where you notice your breath most clearly: the area just below your nostrils, your chest, or your belly. Notice any sensations that you feel in those areas, such as the coolness of the in-breath and warmth of the out-breath, or the rise and fall of your chest, or the expansion and contraction of your stomach. Allow breath to breathe itself: try not to control or change your breath. Simply observe the natural flow of breath in and out of your body, feeling into the physical sensations of your body expanding to meet the in-breath and letting go to allow the out-breath. If you notice that your mind has wandered—which is normal—gently invite your attention back to your breath. Try to bring a beginner's mind to your breath, simply observing it with curiosity and care.

Afterward, you might reflect on your experience of practicing mindfulness of breath. What did you notice? What was the quality of your breath? When your mind wandered, what was it distracted by? How did your body feel at the end of your practice?

As you establish a home practice of mindfulness, experiment with practicing mindfulness in different places and different times of the day to discover what works best for you. Think of your space as another support for your practice and try to minimize the number of distractions in that area. Start out by practicing five minutes of mindfulness, using a timer on your phone or a free app like Insight Timer to alert you to the end of practice.[20] Try to build your practice into your day and practice every day: frequent practice for shorter durations is preferable to infrequent longer practices. Also try to incorporate mindfulness informally into your everyday life. When you brush your teeth, take a shower, make your coffee, wash your dishes, or exercise: try to pay attention to how your body feels, any feelings or thoughts that arise, what you see, hear, feel, or smell. If your mind wanders, just gently return your attention to your present experience of the activity.

Know Your Window of Tolerance

Everyone can benefit from incorporating mindfulness into their everyday life, but it is important to note that not all people benefit from formal practices of mindfulness and meditation. In fact, some can experience adverse effects. If you have experienced trauma, paying close attention to your inner world may bring thoughts, images, memories, or physical sensations tied to a traumatic event, intensifying symptoms of trauma. For those reasons, you should never feel forced to engage in formal meditation, and you should always feel free to modify your practice so that you feel safe and supported throughout. For example, you might choose to keep your eyes open during meditation, take breaks to walk or stretch, take a few deep breaths, or engage in shorter periods of practice.[21] If you find yourself distressed or intensely fixated on traumatic pain during your practice, you might look around the room and name the objects that you see around you. In this way, you can orient yourself to your surroundings and return to the present moment. This type of dual awareness—of your experiencing self and your observing self—can help you learn how to witness your experience without becoming identified with it.[22]

We only benefit from mindfulness when we stay within our "window of tolerance," a term Dan Siegel, a clinical professor of psychiatry, developed to describe our optimal state of functioning and thriving, when we feel grounded, present, curious, and able to emotionally regulate ourselves. If we move outside this window, we may experience "hyper-arousal," in which we feel anxious, angry, overwhelmed, hypervigilant, or experience flight-or-fight reactions, or "hypo-arousal," in which we feel numb, passive, shutdown, frozen, or withdrawn. We can learn to identify signals that we are either inside or outside this window of tolerance.[23] This can help you track yourself so you can make an informed choice about whether you would like to stop or adjust your practice so you can stay within your window of tolerance. Sometimes the breath can help you return to your window—taking slower, deeper breaths if you feel hyper-aroused, or taking faster, shallower breaths if you feel hypo-aroused—so long as you try to avoid hyperventilating or exacerbating medical conditions such as asthma.

We can learn to shift our attention so that it supports our window of tolerance. We can establish anchors for our attention—neutral reference points like our hands in our lap or our feet on the floor—where we feel grounded and stable.[24] We can reorient our attention to our surrounding environment, opening our eyes, labeling things around the room, listening to sounds, or even touching objects.[25] We can build our resilience—"our inherent capacity to see beauty, find connection, commune with something larger than ourselves, and create—even in or after horrendous experiences"[26]—by imagining a place, activity, or memory that connects us to a sense of well-being.

Mindfulness practice can support us during times of transition. When we feel overwhelmed, we can find stability by feeling the ground beneath us, focusing on our breath, or attending to our surroundings. We can acknowledge that gaps may be dizzying and disorienting, but they also allow for change and transformation.

Notes

1. James, *Principles of Psychology*, 402.

2. Ehrlich et al., *Oxford American Dictionary*, 289, 624, and 558.

3. Abrams, "Yes, Imposter Syndrome is Real."

4. Jabr, "How Does a Caterpillar Turn into a Butterfly?"

5. Jabr, "How Does a Caterpillar Turn into a Butterfly?"

6. Heilbron, "Bohr's First Theory of the Atom."

7. The image was reprinted from *Harper's Weekly* in Jastrow, *Fact and Fable in Psychology*, 295. A simpler version was reprinted and discussed in Wittgenstein, *Philosophical Investigations*, 194.

8. The image is originally from Brentano, "Über ein optisches Paradoxon," 349.

9. Zhuangzi, *Zhuangzi: Basic Writings*, 44.

10. Zhuangzi, *Zhuangzi: Basic Writings*, 53.

11. Quoted in Jung Lee, "Finely Aware and Richly Responsible: The Daoist Imperative" *Journal of the American Academy of Religion* 68, no. 3 (September 2000), 531.

12. Lee, "Finely Aware and Richly Responsible," 512.

13. Muller, "Daode jing."

14. Zhuangzi, *Zhuangzi: Basic Writings*, 60.

15. Grant, "Do Trees Talk to Each Other?"

16. Powers, *Overstory*, 23.

17. Zhuangzi, *Zhuangzi: Basic Writings*, 98.

18. Thera, *Heart of Buddhist Meditation*, 24.

19. Suzuki, *Zen Mind, Beginner's Mind*, 1.

20. Insight Timer, "Insight Timer."

21. Treleaven, *Trauma-Sensitive Mindfulness*, 107.

22. Treleaven, *Trauma-Sensitive Mindfulness*, 38.

23. Treleaven, *Trauma-Sensitive Mindfulness*, 95.

24. Treleaven, *Trauma-Sensitive Mindfulness*, 121.

25. Treleaven, *Trauma-Sensitive Mindfulness*, 124.

26. Treleaven, *Trauma-Sensitive Mindfulness*, 125.

CHAPTER TWO

Being Alone

Many of us seek community solely to escape fear of being alone. Knowing
how to be solitary is central to the art of loving. When we can be alone,
we can be with others without using them as a means of escape.
—bell hooks[1]

A week after graduating from college, I flew to China, where I would live for almost two years as a volunteer English teacher in a town called "Horse Saddle Mountain" (Ma'anshan) in Anhui Province. Although I occasionally shared a meal with the other American teacher at the institute where we taught and later became close friends with a local Chinese painter, initially I spent copious amounts of time alone. I experienced a great deal of culture shock and missed my boyfriend, my family, my friends, and the familiarity of an English-speaking environment. But I had built up a tolerance for being alone and living in foreign countries during my time in college. I knew that feelings of isolation and loneliness are common in new environments. Eventually, I established a daily routine of doing tai chi with some elderly women in the morning, grabbing a bamboo sticky-rice dumpling from a local vendor for breakfast, teaching my classes during the day, and spending my free time reading literature or listening to music. I still spent much of my time alone, but I was intentionally doing things that I enjoyed. I discovered that I could savor solitude: I could be alone without feeling lonely.

Because we are social beings living in interconnected digital worlds, most of us have been conditioned to avoid being alone. We busy ourselves with activities, meetings, and to-do lists, rarely allowing ourselves the time to reflect on our own thoughts, emotions, or experiences. Although young children play alone happily when they feel loved and protected, later childhood has become more structured with extracurricular activities, preventing children from engaging in solitary, creative play. When you transition from high school, where you typically spend most of your time in school, to college, where you spend only a third of that time in class (with the expectation that you spend the other two-thirds reading, studying, and preparing for class), you become responsible for structuring your day and managing your time. Inevitably, some of that time—perhaps much of it—is spent in solitude.

Although time management can certainly help you plan your day and succeed academically, and you will find such strategies shared in the first two appendices, a more important life skill is developing the capacity to be alone. You can manage your time with the help of a scheduler. It is far more challenging to become comfortable with solitude. Sometimes we fill our days in an effort to prevent moments of solitude, but truly those moments are rare opportunities to reconnect with our senses (what we see, hear, smell, taste, or touch), ourselves, and our surroundings. When we are alone, we have the time and space to observe and reflect. As Stephen Batchelor writes in *The Art of Solitude*, "Liberated from social pressures and constraints, solitude can help you understand better what kind of person you are and what your life is for. In this way you become independent of others. You find your own path, your own voice."[2] When we separate ourselves from digital distractions and social pressures, we can explore and discover what we enjoy and value. We can hear our own voice instead of the clamor of other voices.

Contemplation

Contemplative practices like mindfulness encourage a slower, more deliberate approach to life, and they can reconnect you with your inner world. Mystics and contemplatives retreated to deserts, forests, and caves in mountains to find solitude that would support their practices of prayer, yoga, and meditation. In the Christian tradition, contemplative prayer was practiced and taught by the Desert Fathers of Egypt, Palestine, and Syria—hermits, ascetics and monks living in the desert from the beginning of the third century CE. The Desert Fathers movement was started by Anthony the Great, who around 270 CE heard a sermon that perfection could be achieved by selling all of one's possessions, giving the proceeds to the poor, and following Christ (Matt. 19:21). He moved to the desert to seek solitude, follow a life of extreme asceticism (renouncing pleasurable experiences such as rich foods or taking baths) and focus on praying, fasting, singing psalms, giving to the needy, and preserving harmony with others while keeping his thoughts on God.

Yogis in India also disentangled themselves from material things and retreated to forests to practice yoga. The ancient Indian philosopher Patañjali wrote in his *Yoga Sutra*, "This is the teaching of yoga. Yoga is the cessation of the turnings of thought. When thought ceases, the spirit stands in its true identity as observer to the world. Otherwise, the observer identifies with the turnings of thought."[3] Through sustained practice and dispassion towards material objects, yogis sought to stop thoughts fueled by craving and desire, and instead observe the world in its true reality.

In the Buddhist tradition, the Satipaṭṭhāna Sutra (the Sutra on the Foundations of Mindfulness) mentions four things that one can observe: the body (breath and bodily sensations), feelings (unpleasant, pleasant, and neutral), states of mind (desire, aversion, agitation, dullness, and doubt), or things as they arise and pass away. By fully attending to the body, feelings, states of mind, or the impermanence of things, they trained their minds to be focused and stable, rather than scattered and wandering. Śāntideva, an eighth-century Indian Buddhist, compares our ordinary mind to a wandering elephant that needs to be tethered by the rope of mindfulness. Like the Desert Fathers and Indian yogis, he emphasizes the importance of solitude:

In solitude, the mind and body
Are not troubled by distraction.
Therefore leave this worldly life
And totally abandon mental wandering.
Because of loved ones and desire for gain,
We fail to turn away from worldly things.
These, then, are the first things to renounce.
The prudent should conduct themselves like this.
Penetrative insight joined with calm abiding
Utterly eradicates afflicted states.
Knowing this, first search for calm abiding,
Found by people who are happy to be free from worldly ties.[4]

Although his world and our own are caught up with fame and fortune, Śāntideva encourages people to abandon those concerns and instead discover places where they can feel at ease. Christian, Hindu, and Buddhist contemplative traditions urge us to consider stopping our ordinary habits of mind, where we tend to identify with our thoughts. This can allow for profound transformation: for the Desert Fathers, it allows the Holy Spirit to enter and fill their entire being with joy and peace; for the yogis, it strips away illusion and reveals ultimate reality; for the Buddhists, it creates a state of calm and concentration that can generate liberating insight; for the Daoists, it fosters balance and alignment between themselves and the universe.

It is easier to practice contemplation in places that encourage silence and stillness. Over the years, I have spent time in Buddhist and Christian monasteries, as well as Hindu ashrams, and I have found the simplicity and sparseness of the environment conducive to contemplation. When I lived in a Taiwanese Buddhist monastery for six months, there were even signs in the bathroom reminding us to brush our teeth with as little noise as possible so as not to disrupt others, and we ate our meals together in complete silence. In this way, we were encouraged to engage in every action with mindfulness. While at a Benedictine monastery for a silent prayer retreat, we often engaged in contemplation in our rooms, where there was just a bed, table, and chair. At a Hindu ashram, we would wake up at 5 A.M. and go outside where we would sit and meditate for a half hour before doing yoga.

Although monastic environments support contemplation, you do not have to be religious or live in a monastery to engage in contemplative practice. You can create space for solitude in your own life, freeing yourself from distraction and ordinary pressures. You can spend time out in nature, practice mindfulness, make art, or engage in other activities where you are alone and feel at ease. Contemplative practices can support you during times of transition, but keep in mind that it may take time and practice before you are comfortable being alone with yourself. Michel de Montaigne wrote, "Retreat into yourself, but first of all make yourself ready to receive yourself there. If you do not know how to govern yourself, it would be madness to entrust yourself to yourself."[5] What you may find, when you spend time alone and apart from your digital devices, is that you initially struggle with that separation. You may reach for your phone, become lost in thought, or notice emotions surfacing. Your mind may run rampant like an elephant, or swing from thought to thought like a monkey. In *How to do Nothing*, Jenny Odell writes, "Nothing is harder than to do nothing. In a world where our value is determined by our productivity, many of us find our every last minute captured, optimized, or appropriated as a financial resource by the technologies we use daily."[6] For Odell, "doing nothing" means disengaging from digital devices that keep us anxious, envious, and distracted, and instead giving ourselves the time and space to observe, listen, and reflect. She describes how this deepened her attention to place: she started noticing all types of bioregionalism, she observed and recognized the plants, animals, and natural environments around her, and she began identifying with a sense of place. She writes,

> Seen from the point of view of forward-pressing, productive time, this behavior would appear delinquent. I'd look like a dropout. But from the point of view of the place, I'd look like someone who was finally paying it attention. And from the point of view of myself, the person actually experiencing my life, and to whom I will ultimately answer when I die—I would know that I spent that day on Earth.[7]

Her experiences in solitude allowed her to distinguish between cultural, environmental, and personal points of view. She was able to shift her perception between aspects, and she focused her attention on the overstory, rather than cultural stories about the need for productivity and progress.

When we are alone, we have the opportunity to attune ourselves to what surrounds us. We can develop deep listening, which the musician and composer Pauline Oliveros describes as "listening in every possible way to everything possible to hear, no matter what you are doing. Such intense listening includes the sounds of daily life, of nature, of one's own thoughts as well as musical sounds."[8] When we stop and listen, we interrupt our ordinary habits of mind and attune ourselves to our environment. As Odell writes, "Even if brief or momentary, these places and moments are retreats, and like longer retreats, they affect the way we see everyday life when we do come back to it."[9] When we intently focus on sounds around us, we suspend our ordinary activity and habitual thinking. The French philosopher and activist Simone Weil calls attention "the rarest and purest form of generosity."[10] She writes, "Attention consists of suspending our thought, leaving it detached, empty, and ready to be penetrated by the object. . . . Above all our thought should be empty, waiting, not seeking anything, but ready to receive in its naked truth the object that is to penetrate it."[11] Attention involves suspending our thought so that we can actively receive something or someone else in all of their complexity.

Awe

When we bring this level of openness and receptivity to our surroundings, especially when we are out in nature, we can experience a sense of awe— the feeling of being in the presence of something vast and mysterious that

The Night Sky. Photo by Ryan Hutton on Unsplash.

Sunset Over the Ocean. Photo by Sebastian Gabriel on Unsplash.

transcends our understanding of the world.[12] Natural objects that are vast in relation to oneself—such as mountains, vistas, waterfalls, redwoods, and oceans—can inspire feelings of wonder and amazement. Their vastness makes us stop to take in what we are seeing, because we cannot easily accommodate it within our ordinary frames of reference. When we feel that the world is much bigger than we are, our sense of ego shrinks while our sense of transcendence— of being part of the universe—expands. We start thinking about our place in the world and how to make our lives count. As Dacher Keltner and Jonathan Haidt observe, "Awe-inducing events may be one of the fastest and most pow- erful methods of personal change and growth."[13] Our sense of time expands, we have feelings of connectedness, we savor feelings and sensations, and we experience greater joy and contentment.

In *The Nature Fix,* Florence Williams discusses the science behind the "awe" response.[14] When we look up at the moon or gaze out at the sunset, we can ex- perience physiological responses including chills, widened eyes, and enhanced visual perception. Sounds of water and birds can calm nervous systems, and the smell of tree aerosols can reduce blood pressure.

We can cultivate an openness and curiosity about our natural environment so that we are able to experience such feelings of awe. When you are outside, try taking deep breaths and fully engaging your senses: looking, listening, and perhaps touching and smelling the leaves and plants around you. We can take walks in the morning to reset our circadian rhythms and take breaks outside to experience natural daylight. You can even experience awe indoors when looking at objects in your house, while cooking, or showering. Michael Amster and Jake Eagle refer to such accessing of awe in the ordinary as "microdosing mindfulness." They write,

A is for "Attention." When you choose to pay attention to things you appre- ciate, value, or find amazing, you focus your mind and heart on things that are likely to foster awe. We call this selective perception. . . .
W is for "Wait." After you focus your attention, your mind quiets down. If you wait—at least the length of one full inhalation—you can begin to experience a state of coherence. . . .
E is for "Exhale and Expand." When you exhale, you relax, and when you expand, you amplify whatever sensations you are experiencing. By combin- ing focused attention with a respiratory pattern in which your exhalation

is longer than your inhalation—about 2:1—you are opening the gateway to awe.[15]

They found that people who accessed awe in such "microdoses" of less than a minute reduced their levels of anxiety and depression, experienced relaxation, increased their connection with others, and experienced beauty, gratitude, and generosity.

Although we may be habituated to associate solitude with loneliness, we can instead see solitude as an opportunity to fully direct our attention to our mental, emotional, and bodily experience. Engaging with our life as a laboratory, we can explore how we habitually respond to being alone—how we relate to ourselves. I sometimes have students spend thirty minutes each day alone with themselves (without phones, books, or other distractions) for a week. Although some find it initially unsettling, most end the week with a greater appreciation for solitude. Take a moment to reflect on how you tend to spend your time alone. Do you find it enjoyable, or uncomfortable? Think back to a time when you enjoyed being alone. What were you doing? What contributed to that feeling of contentment?

In college I often walked alone in the dry, golden foothills behind campus. When I reached the top, I could see not only the Stanford campus, but the entire Bay Area. It gave me a sense of perspective. It reconnected me with the environment and made my worries feel less important. At my current institution—the University of North Carolina Wilmington—students often head to the beach to gaze out at the ocean and gain a similarly expansive perspective. Even in urban environments, you can often find an oasis or park to escape the hustle and bustle of city life.

Mindfulness of Body

You can be present and embodied through mindfulness of body. We spend most of our time unaware and unattuned to our bodies, instead living our lives from the neck up. Lost in our thoughts, we rarely check in with our physical sensations unless we experience illness or injury. Mindfulness encourages us to explore our bodily experience, focusing our attention on our physical sensations and examining them with curiosity and care. We approach our bodies not as we see them externally in mirrors or selfies, but instead as we experience them internally. Mindfulness encourages us to acknowledge and accept whatever we are experiencing in our bodies. We feel into our sensations of warmth or coolness, heaviness or lightness, pressure or tingling. We simply notice what we are feeling in our bodies, without trying to control or change those sensations. We allow for experiences of discomfort, trying to curiously investigate sensations instead of pushing them away. In this way, we cultivate a sense of presence and being grounded in our own bodies.

Mindful Eating

When we are alone, we can direct our attention to our physical senses—what we see, hear, smell, taste, or touch—while we are eating. Most mindfulness trainings include a mindful eating exercise with a raisin or orange (though some of my students have used M&Ms or Skittles instead). They invite you to

> Start by feeling the texture of the raisin in your hand, looking at it, smelling it. Notice any sensations that you feel in your mouth or stomach even before you put it in your mouth. As you place it in your mouth and chew with awareness, notice the taste, texture, and any other sensations such as wetness from saliva in your mouth. As you swallow, notice the sensations in your mouth and throat. Afterward, observe any sensations in your mouth, stomach, or other parts of your body.

When we bring this level of awareness to our bodies while we are eating, we realize how often we eat mindlessly, without even noticing the taste, much less the smell or texture, of our food.

The practice of mindful eating—eating slowly and deliberately, in moderation—has become increasingly popular in America.[16] My first exposure to mindful eating occurred when I lived in China. I traveled to Jiuhua Mountain, one of the five sacred Buddhist mountains in China, where I was struck by the sparseness and simplicity of the monastic eating hall: there were only narrow benches and tables facing the same direction, with bowls and chopsticks on top. I later discovered that this arrangement facilitates the practice of mindful eating: facing the same direction, you don't feel the social pressure to talk; instead, you are encouraged to focus on the bowl and food in front of you. Before each meal, we would thank everything and everyone that contributed to our vegan meal: the sun, water, and soil for helping the plant grow, the farmers who tended and harvested it, the truck drivers and vendors who transported and sold it, the cooks who washed and prepared it, and the servers who brought it from the kitchen. We were given one bowl of food, which we would eat in silence, slowly and mindfully. Chinese Buddhist monks and nuns observed the following "five contemplations" while they ate, instead of engaging in idle talk or absent-mindedness:

> Be aware of how precious the meals are; learn to appreciate them.
> Assess our virtues: are we deserving of others' offerings?
> Guard against faults, greed in particular.
> The meal is like medicine, it gives us strength.
> Sustaining ourselves for spiritual cultivation, we need this meal.[17]

Monks and nuns, whose entire livelihood depends on the generosity of donations from lay practitioners, were asked to contemplate all the work that went into producing and preparing the food, to consider their own virtue, to guard against shortcomings such as greed for more food, to view the food as nourishment, and to receive it as sustenance for their spiritual practice.

In their book *Savor: Mindful Eating, Mindful Life*, Thich Nhat Hanh and Lilian Cheung list seven practices of a mindful eater: honoring the food, engaging all six senses, serving in modest portions, savoring small bites and chewing thoroughly, eating slowly to avoid overeating, not skipping meals, and eating a plant-based diet for one's health and for the planet.[18] They write, "When practiced to its fullest, mindful eating turns a simple meal into a spiritual exercise, giving us a deep appreciation of all that went into the meal's creation as well as a deep understanding of the relationship between the food on our table, our own health, and our planet's health."[19] Their remarks underscore how food connects us to other people (farmers, truck drivers, and cooks) and the natural environment: it reflects the reality of our interdependent world. We see such interconnection reflected in their modern rendition of the "five contemplations":

1. This food is the gift of the whole universe: the earth, the sky, numerous living beings, and much hard, loving work.
2. May we eat with mindfulness and gratitude so as to be worthy to receive it.
3. May we recognize and transform our unwholesome mental formations, especially our greed, and learn to eat with moderation.
4. May we keep our compassion alive by eating in such a way that we reduce the suffering of living beings, preserve our planet, and reverse the process of global warming.

5. We accept this food so that we may nurture our sisterhood and brotherhood, strengthen our community, and nourish our ideal of serving all living beings.[20]

The amount and type of food we consume has ethical implications. As Jan Chozen Bays notes in *Mindful Eating*, "A country that consumes more than its share of the world's food is a country composed of people who are ignorant of the suffering that results when we are not aware of 'right amount.'"[21] If we eat mindfully, we tend to eat in moderation.

To engage in mindful eating, we simply focus on our physical sensations. Whenever you eat, you can:

Sense the sight, smell, and texture of your food.
Notice any sensations in your belly and mouth in anticipation.
Feel your fork in your hand, feel each bite as you chew.
Sense the taste and texture of the food in your mouth as you chew.
Feel the sensations of chewing and swallowing.
Notice when you get lost in thought and eat mindlessly.
Gently draw your attention back to the sensations of eating.

The underlying principle is that you can cultivate curiosity and connection to your direct experience. You can apply mindfulness to every moment of your day—you simply notice what your eyes see, your ears hear, your nose smells, your mouth tastes, and your hands feel.

Mindful Walking

In the case of mindful walking, you simply attune to your feet as they lift, step, and press down on the ground beneath you. You feel the shifting weight of your body and sensations of gravity. You notice what movement feels like in your body. It is helpful to keep your eyes cast down to maintain that sense of connection to your body, and to walk at a pace where you can maintain mindfulness. When you find that your attention has wandered, you simply bring it back to the sensations of walking. It can sometimes be helpful to walk back and forth in a straight line, to avoid becoming fixated on reaching some destination.

Out in nature, you can practice a different kind of mindful walking, oscillating your attention from your body to the sights, sounds, and smells around you. You can gaze at natural objects that inspire a sense of awe in you. You can appreciate the naturalness of transitions as you witness how environments change with the season. You can be alone but feel yourself as part of a wider universe.

Notes

1. hooks, *all about love.*
2. Batchelor, *Art of Solitude*, 150.
3. Miller. *Yoga Discipline of Freedom*, 29.
4. Shāntideva, *Way of the Bodhisattva*, 109.
5. Quoted in Batchelor, *Art of Solitude*, 22.
6. Odell, *How to Do NothinSg*, ix.
7. Odell, *How to Do Nothing*, 185.
8. Pauline Oliveros, *The Roots of the Moment* (New York: Drogue Press, 1998), 3.
9. Odell, *How to Do Nothing*, 9.
10. Pétrement, *Simone Weil*, 462.
11. Weil, *Waiting for God*, 62.
12. Keltner and Haidt, "Approaching Awe," 303-304.
13. Keltner and Haidt, "Approaching Awe," 313.
14. Williams, *Nature Fix.*
15. Amster and Eagle, "Stuck at Home?"
16. Gordinier, "Mindful Eating as Food for Thought."
17. The verses are derived from the *Regulations for Chan Monastery (Chanyuan Qinggui)*, which was compiled in 1103 and considered the oldest surviving Chinese monastic code
18. Hanh and Cheung, *Savor*, 124–27.
19. Hanh and Cheung, *Savor*, 119.
20. Hanh and Cheung, *Savor*, 124.
21. Bays, *Mindful Eating*, 103.

CHAPTER THREE

Building Relationships

One of the most vital ways we sustain ourselves is by building
communities of resistance, places where we know we are not alone.
—bell hooks[1]

We weathered together.
—Oprah Winfrey[2]

I went from a high school senior class of sixty people to a college first-year
class of almost 1,600. It was daunting, to say the least. When I received a
brochure about a residence-based academic program for first-year students
that offered a small, liberal arts college experience within the larger university,
I jumped at the opportunity. We lived together and had class in our residential
hall, which created a strong sense of community. We also connected with
professors who taught in the program, some of whom later became my college
mentors. The program created the space for learning with and from each other,
and I formed relationships with people whose background differed markedly
from my own.

In subsequent years, I found myself gravitating toward such residential
learning communities, rather than living in a dormitory or suite of apartments
on campus. During my sophomore year, I lived in Muwekma-Tah-Ruk, an
ethnic theme house celebrating the diversity of Native American, Alaska
Native, Native Hawaiian, and Pacific Islander people. Roughly a third of the
residents were Indigenous, a third Black, and a third were other students of
color or white. I was one of three white residents in the house. We volunteered
at the Stanford Powwow, an annual celebration dating back to 1971, and we
took a class together about indigenous culture, history, and current issues. I
was shocked to learn about atrocities committed by colonial Europeans, such
as giving Native Americans blankets infected with smallpox. In my senior
year I opted to live in Kairos, one of the cooperative houses (co-ops) where

students were responsible for cooking and cleaning, which also created a sense of community.

In college, you choose the communities you want to join and the relationships you want to cultivate. There is a huge gap between the relationships we formed growing up—living with families who were familiar (even if frustrating), hanging out with friends who we may have known since childhood, and learning from teachers who monitored whether we were present and how we were faring in their class—and those in college. In college, you decide the friends that you make, you negotiate things with your roommate, and you develop connections with your professors. Your learning is self-directed, not determined by others. The ability to build relationships and form community is a vital life skill. After graduation, you will face similar decisions: what friendships to form, where and with whom to live, and how to interact with supervisors and coworkers. For example, you will decide whether to live in a city, suburb, or rural area, or even whether to live overseas. Mindfulness can help you make more intentional choices about these connections and communities.

Friendships

Although you may have felt an instant connection with someone who later became a friend, more often friendships develop over time through shared experiences. Extracurricular activities provide an excellent way to connect with people who share your interests. In my case, my love of swimming, singing, and the outdoors led me to join the masters swim team, the symphonic chorus, and an outdoors program in college. Even when I studied overseas at Oxford, I sang in two choirs and joined the Ramblers and Hillwalkers Club—their equivalent of an outdoors program. These groups enabled me to meet people with similar interests, and our shared experiences became the foundation for later friendships.

Such friendships do not happen overnight. They take time to develop. In "Advice from a Formerly Lonely College Student," Emery Bergmann shares how she felt lonely and lost during her first weeks of college, frustrated by superficial conversations and her inability to form friendships, while others seemed to have bonded into tight-knit groups. Looking back as a sophomore, she writes, "Some of the high school friends I was missing had been my friends for my whole life. Expecting close relationships like the ones that had taken years to develop was unfair to myself and the people around me."[3] She offers several pieces of advice: you can't clone your high school friends; social media is not reality; give yourself time to adjust. Although you may feel pressure to form friendships in your first weeks or months in a new environment, you can recognize that they take time and space to develop. If you go on social media and see others forming fast friendships, keep in mind the gap between what people post and project to the outside world and their actual lived experience. She concludes her piece, "Understand that your loneliness is not failure, and that you are far from being alone in this feeling. Open your mind and take experiences as they come. You're going to find your people."[4] Recognizing that relationships take time, we can decide where we want to live, what activities we want to participate in, and what new things we want to learn. If we build our capacity to be alone, we can allow for connections and ties to grow slowly over time, without feeling the urgent need for instant friendships. We can adopt a more organic approach to our friendships.

Roommates

Chances are, you will live with roommate(s) at some point in your college career (or life). Harlan Cohen's *The Naked Roommate*, one of the most popular going-to-college books, acknowledges that even compatible roommates have disagreements. He suggests respecting your differences, understanding that roommates are not automatic friends, and above all, talking about any problems that make you uncomfortable before they become a habit (ideally within 24–48 hours)—including issues of noise, nakedness, and nastiness (i.e., smelliness and bad hygiene).[5] If you reach an impasse, you can talk to your resident advisor, and if your roommate needs help, you can use campus resources such as counseling centers.

My first-year roommate and I had different schedules. Although I consider myself an early riser, she woke up in the wee hours of the morning because she was a coxswain for the rowing club. Her alarm would wake me up, but she was otherwise conscientious about quietly getting ready in the morning so that I could fall back asleep. My sophomore year roommate and I shared an extremely small room, which meant we had to loft our beds and put our desks underneath. Such cramped quarters inevitably posed challenges when we were both in the room trying to work or relax. By my senior year in college, I had a much better sense of the give-and-take of being a hospitable roommate.

Developing such interpersonal and communication skills with roommates will serve you well after college—even, perhaps, with future partners and spouses. I considered myself a neat person until I met my spouse, who rarely, if ever, leaves dishes in the sink or things in disarray. Imagine his reaction when I confessed that I had become so habituated to conserving water living in California that I had come to espouse the view "If it's brown, flush it down! If it's yellow, let it mellow!" Needless to say, living with another person means negotiating with each other and making various kinds of agreements and adjustments.

Professional Relationships

College also allows you to interact with professors, advisors, staff, and community partners, honing professional skills for future relationships with colleagues, coworkers, and supervisors. Through your presence and participation in class, proofreading and prompt completion of assignments, and courteous communication (via email or in person), you demonstrate your work ethic, dependability, organization skills, attention to detail, and professionalism. Chances are, you will later ask some of these faculty and staff members for letters of recommendation for internships, study-abroad opportunities, jobs, and applications for graduate school. I explore the nuts and bolts of writing a professional email in Appendix 3, but the general principle is to treat these relationships differently from those of friends and roommates. Your instructors and advisors can become mentors for you in your college career, and they can speak to your skills and strengths when you apply for various kinds of opportunities in college and beyond.

Whereas friendships often develop from shared interests and values, and roommate relationships rely on mutual agreement and understanding, professional relationships form among members of a shared organization or institution. As outlined by the National Association of Colleges and Employers, one of the behaviors expected of professionals is the ability to "act equitably with integrity and accountability to self, others, and the organization."[6] When you interact with university faculty and staff, they expect you to uphold certain values of an institution of higher learning, such as inclusiveness, mutual respect, acceptance, and open-mindedness. At my institution—the University of North Carolina Wilmington—they articulate these expectations in our "Seahawk Respect Compact." We expect all members of the campus community to honor the following principles:

We affirm the dignity of all persons.

We promote the right of every person to participate in the free exchange of thoughts and opinions within a climate of civility and mutual respect.

We strive for openness and mutual understanding to learn from differences in people, ideas, and opinions.

We foster an environment of respect for each individual, even where differences exist, by eliminating prejudice and discrimination through education and interaction with others.[7]

In this way, colleges and universities create diverse, equitable, and inclusive environments that facilitate learning and growth for all people. They also expect that students will uphold the honor code—refraining from cheating and plagiarism, which I explore in Appendix 4.

Social Harmony

When members of an organization or group agree to abide by shared expectations, it facilitates social harmony. The Confucian tradition in China—which originated slightly before the Daoist tradition—paid special attention to interpersonal relationships and the importance of social harmony. In the first chapter of the *Analects*—a collection of sayings and aphorisms attributed to Confucius—we read, "Every day I examine myself on three counts. In what I have undertaken on another's behalf, have I failed to do my best? In my dealings with my friends have I failed to be trustworthy in what I say? Have I passed on to others anything that I have not tried out myself?"[8] Attesting to the importance of diligence, dependability, and dedication in relationships, he reflects on how he has treated other people—whether he has been a humane, good person. The Chinese character for humaneness or goodness is *ren,* which consists of two parts: a person and the number two. In other words, when two people meet, they should treat each other humanely.

Admittedly, the relationships envisioned by premodern Confucians were not equitable, but instead hierarchical and patriarchal. In *Analects* 1:6 Confucius says, "A young man should serve his parents at home and be respectful to elders outside his home. He should be earnest and truthful, loving all, but become intimate with his innate good-heartedness."[9] This relationship between parents and sons becomes the blueprint for all other relationships: husbands and wives, elder and younger siblings, teachers and students, and rulers and subjects. While we can certainly criticize the hierarchical and patriarchal way Confucianism envisioned such relationships, we can also appreciate the importance of connecting with our innate feeling of goodwill toward other people. Confucians recommend the practice of self-cultivation: developing these innate inclinations until we react in the ethical, humane ways in each situation in our lives. In *Analects* 12:2, when asked about humaneness, Confucius says, "When you are out in the world, act as if meeting an important guest. . . . What you don't want done to yourself, don't do to others."[10] He urges us to treat others with courtesy, generosity, honesty, and kindness (*Analects* 17:5). By treating others "as if" we were meeting an honored guest, we habituate ourselves to be good to those around us and cultivate harmonious relationships.

Mindfulness of Feeling

We can build healthy relationships and harmonious communities by being more intentional and reflective about our interactions with others. Through mindfulness of feeling, we can explore and reduce our reactivity to experience. Stephen Covey writes, "Between stimulus and response there is a space. In that space is our power and freedom to choose our response. In our response lies our growth and our freedom."[11] We have the space to determine how we want to respond to the actions and words of others, as well as our own thoughts, emotions, and sensations. Mindfulness encourages us to sit with that space, observing the stimulus without reacting.

Every experience has a corresponding feeling—sometimes referred to as "feeling tone"—of "I like it!" (i.e., you find it pleasant or comfortable), "I don't like it!" (i.e., you find it unpleasant or uncomfortable), or "Meh!" (i.e., you are indifferent or neutral toward it). For example, think of your most and least favorite songs or genres of music. I gravitate toward acoustic music, while my spouse prefers heavy metal. Over time, we have espoused the rule that the driver determines the music. When I find myself riding in his car, I experience all sorts of unpleasant feelings when I hear heavy metal. Whereas when he finds himself riding in my car, especially when he hears sitars and chanting, he winces and sometimes cannot refrain from voicing his objection to the music selection.

These feelings—pleasant, unpleasant, and neutral—arise in response to what we see, hear, smell, taste, and touch. Most of the time, we are unaware of our feelings, and we often react to them unconsciously. We desire or demand pleasant feelings, we dislike or defend against unpleasant feelings, and we space out or seek distractions from neutral feelings. However, these automatic reactions can cause frictions in our relationships or create intolerance for diversity in our communities. Mindfulness opens a space before the reaction. It gives us the freedom to determine how we want to respond to our feelings; it frees us from immediately reacting because of them. When we allow ourselves to recognize our feelings—naming them and bringing our attention to our physical experience of them in our bodies—we can then choose how (or even whether) we want to respond to them.

You can explore mindfulness of feeling in various ways. When you are eating, you can observe the types of feelings that arise in response to what you see, smell, and taste. What feeling arises when you taste something sweet or salty; spicy or bland; hot or cold? When you experience a pleasant taste, do you immediately want more? When you experience an unpleasant taste, do you immediately react in disgust? Can you create space between the stimulus and your response by observing how and where the pleasant or unpleasant feelings arise in your body? Might you even create space between the taste—the burning sensation when you eat a hot pepper, for example—and the feeling?

You can also practice mindfulness of feeling by attending to sounds that you hear around you. Be as receptive to sounds as an antenna receiving signals from a satellite. Focus your attention on your direct experience of whatever sounds arise in your environment. Perhaps you observe a space or silence between sounds, or the rising and falling of sounds. Then explore the feelings that arise as you hear the sounds, sensing any feelings of pleasantness, unpleasantness, or otherwise in your body. Perhaps you also observe feelings about physical sensations, thoughts, or emotions. Notice where those feelings arise and are felt in your body. If they are pleasant feelings, do you find yourself grasping to them? If they are unpleasant feelings, do you find yourself resisting or rejecting them? If they are neutral, do you find you are bored or restless? See if you can find space between the feeling and the reaction. Perhaps you notice your feelings change or shift, arise and cease. If nothing strong draws your attention, you can always return to mindfulness of breath.

Notes

1. hooks, *Yearning*, 213.
2. Perry and Winfrey, *What Happened To You?*, 193.
3. Bergmann, "Advice from a Formerly Lonely College Student."
4. Bergmann, "Advice from a Formerly Lonely College Student."
5. Cohen, *Naked Roommate*, 83–104.

6. "What Is Career Readiness?"

7. "Seahawk Respect Compact."

8. Confucius, *Analects* (*Lun yü*), trans. Lau, 59.

9. Confucius, "The Analects," trans. Muller.

10. Confucius, "The Analects," trans. Muller.

11. Covey et al., *First Things First*, 59. Covey says that he happened upon these words in a book from a university library, and elsewhere he attributes the idea to Viktor Frankl who was imprisoned in a concentration camp during World War II but insisted that they could not take away "the last of the human freedoms" – the freedom to determine how he would respond to his circumstances. Covey, *7 Habits of Highly Effective People*, 77.

CHAPTER FOUR

Valuing Diversity

It is easy to wonder about the internal life of the people closest to us. It is harder to wonder about people who seem like strangers or outsiders. But when we choose to wonder about people we don't know, when we imagine their lives and listen for their stories, we begin to expand the circle of those we see as part of *us*. We prepare ourselves to love beyond what evolution requires.
—Valarie Kaur[1]

My best friend in college, Keith Chen, differed from me in many ways. He was Chinese American, loved mathematics, and grew up on the outskirts of Chicago. During our first weeks in college, we walked around the campus sharing our life stories and talking about our cultural differences. Waiting for our clothes to dry in the laundry room of our residence hall, he showed me self-defense techniques that he learned through his study of hapkido. He later studied economics while I majored in comparative literature, and we would have endless debates over the assumptions underlying our disciplines. While he explored game theory, I wrote about self-deception: he studied mathematical models of strategic interactions among rational decision-makers, while I examined ways people were opaque to themselves and prone to biased perception. There were all sorts of gaps between our lived experience, our interests, and our worldviews. But we openly acknowledged such gaps, and they became fertile grounds for discovering more about each other, as well as ourselves.

College affords you the opportunity to reflect on meaningful questions about yourself, such as "Who am I?" Our identities are mediated by a variety of factors, including our individual characteristics, our cultural and family backgrounds, as well as our historical, political, and social contexts. Some aspects of our identity become salient—more noticeable—in different situations or at different moments in our life. Other aspects of our identity may be invisible to us because they are part of the dominant culture and taken for granted as being the norm.

We are born into a set of social identities—our race, ethnicity, gender, sexuality, class, religion, ability, and age—and socialized by our families, culture, and social institutions to uphold certain roles and rules associated with these identities. These socially constructed identities serve as the basis for social inequality and oppression, and we experience social advantages and disadvantages because of them. As sociologists—those who study human behavior, interaction, and organizations—point out, there are "intersections among our multiple, complex, fluid, and cross-cutting social identities and the ways they are heightened or diminished by different social settings."[2] We experience different types of privilege and oppression because of our intersectional identities, and some identities become more salient in specific situations.

To work for social justice, we must raise our awareness and understanding of social oppression, acknowledge our role(s) in systems of oppression, and commit to developing the skills, resources, and coalitions to effect social change.[3] As Cornel West says, "It takes courage to interrogate yourself. It takes courage to look in the mirror and see past your reflection to who you really are when you take off the mask, when you're not performing the same old routines and social roles. It takes courage to ask—how did I become so well-adjusted to injustice?"[4] Social justice aims to change society so that it upholds principles of equity and inclusion, and it seeks to eliminate injustices that result from unequally and hierarchically conferring power, social and economic advantages, and cultural validity to particular social groups.[5]

A good place to begin engaging in social justice is to make an inventory of your social identities with respect to each form of social oppression, otherwise known as a social identity profile.[6] You might also reflect on the way you were socialized to think, speak, and act on the basis of these social identities, what Bobbie Harro calls "the cycle of socialization": first, what your parents or caregivers taught you about the roles and rules of that identity, and how it shaped your self-perception, values, and expectations; second, messages you received from your culture and social institutions (school, religious organization, etc.) that enforced those understandings; third, the results of such socialization; and finally, whether you have interrupted that cycle of socialization, and if not, what has kept you within it.[7] To begin, Harro suggests choosing one of your social identities and writing at least ten examples of what you learned about being that identity.[8] Such exercises can reveal dominant norms that we were taught to accept in our society, which confer privileges on some and oppress others. As Maurianne Adams and Ximena Zúñiga write, "One of the subtlest advantages is the ability to see oneself and be seen as 'normal,' in contrast with those considered different, strange, alien, or 'other.' . . . For example, heterosexuality is an enforced norm. People who are heterosexual don't need to 'come out' because it is the assumed default."[9] This chapter invites you to consider the ways you were socialized about your race, class, religion, gender, sexual orientation, and ability. At the end of each section, you will find questions that encourage you to reflect further on your social identity.

Race

Race is a category that arose in the United States during colonial times to justify the dominance of European settlers, who defined themselves as "white," over Native Americans they conquered and Africans they brought over as slaves. "White supremacy" is the belief that white people are superior to others and should therefore have greater power, authority, or status.[10] "People of color" refers to groups historically targeted and marginalized by racism, including indigenous peoples and those of African, Asian, and Latin American descent.[11] As Ibram X. Kendi writes, "Racism is a marriage of racist policies and racist ideas that produces and normalizes racial inequities."[12] In other words, racism refers to institutional and cultural practices and policies—"written and unwritten laws, rules, procedures, processes, regulations, and guidelines that govern people"—that advantage whites and disadvantage people of color.[13] Racism is a systemic issue rooted in legal, political, and social systems, not just a matter of individual bias or prejudice.

Even though examples of systemic racism abound—including redlining (refusing to offer mortgage loans to people of color who live in poorer neighborhoods) and the school-to-prison pipeline (practices and policies that push children of color out of schools into the juvenile or adult criminal justice system)—some continue to frame racism as a personal issue. As Peggy McIntosh writes, "I was taught to recognize racism only in individual acts of meanness by members of my group, never in invisible systems conferring unsought racial dominance on my group from birth."[14] Of the systemic advantages afforded by her whiteness, McIntosh writes, "I have come to see white privilege as an invisible package of unearned assets which I can count on cashing in each day, but about which I was 'meant' to remain oblivious."[15] Because whiteness is the assumed norm or default in the United States, white people often overlook the fact that their whiteness is a racial identity that confers privilege. They tend not to think of themselves in racial terms, which can create significant blind spots, as they fail to see how their own lives are shaped by race.[16]

Beverly Daniel Tatum compares cultural racism to smog in the air—images and messages about white superiority that we breathe in—and urges us to examine our own behavior to assess whether we are perpetuating and reinforcing those messages or challenging them.[17] She offers a helpful metaphor for racism and antiracism, which resonates with my students:

> I sometimes visualize the ongoing cycle of racism as a moving walkway at the airport. Active racist behavior is equivalent to walking fast on the conveyor belt. The person engaged in active racist behavior has identified with the ideology of White supremacy and is moving with it. Passive racist behavior is equivalent to standing still on the walkway. No overt effort is being made, but the conveyor belt moves the bystanders along to the same destination as those who are actively walking. Some of the bystanders may feel the motion of the conveyor belt, see the active racists ahead of them, and choose to turn around, unwilling to go to the same destination as the White supremacists. But unless they are walking actively in the opposite direction at a speed faster than the conveyor belt—unless they are actively antiracist—they will find themselves carried along with the others.[18]

Antiracism is an active process of challenging racial inequities by changing racist systems, policies, practices, and attitudes.

Dismantling racism not only entails changing political and social structures, but also reckoning with the visceral experience of racism in our bodies. As Ta-Nehisi Coates writes, "It dislodges brains, blocks airways, rips muscle, extracts organs, cracks bones, breaks teeth."[19] He describes feeling fatigued and depleted by having to constantly remain vigilant and alter himself in order to accommodate others: *relatable*

> This need to be always on guard was an unmeasured expenditure of energy, the slow siphoning of the essence. It contributed to the fast breakdown of our bodies. So I feared not just the violence of the world but the rules designed to protect you from it, the rules that would have you contort your body to address the block, and contort again to be taken seriously by a colleague, and contort again so as not to give the police a reason.[20]

Coates gives a vivid sense of the constraints placed on him because of his race when he finds himself in specific social circumstances—his neighborhood, workplace, and encounters with the police. The social psychologist Claude Steele has studied the psychological costs of monitoring and adjusting your behavior so as not to be seen as confirming a stereotype. He writes,

> Stereotype and identity threats—these contingencies of identity—increase vigilance toward possible threat and bad consequences in the social environment, which diverts attention and mental capacity away from the task at hand, which worsens performance and general functioning, all of which further exacerbates anxiety, which further intensifies the vigilance for threat and the diversion of attention.[21]

Steele captures the mental, emotional, and physical toll of having to constantly anticipate how others might perceive or stereotype you based on your social identity, and then having to modify your demeanor to challenge such preconceptions. The title of Steele's book, *Whistling Vivaldi*, refers to a strategy adopted by Brent Staples when walking around New York City late at night. As a six-foot-two Black man, Staples describes how his mere presence evokes fear in white people, and how he takes precautions to make himself appear less threatening: he whistles melodies of Beethoven and Vivaldi. Staples writes, "Virtually everybody seems to sense that a mugger wouldn't be warbling bright, sunny selections from Vivaldi's *Four Seasons*. It is my equivalent of the cowbell that hikers wear when they know they are in bear country."[22] Staples's act of whistling classical music changes the way that white pedestrians perceive him and assuages their fear—a fear that stems from stereotypes about Black men being prone to violence.

We will discuss stereotypes in the next chapter, but here we might observe how they can elicit emotions of fear in white people and anxiety in people of color. To challenge racism, we must begin with our emotions, which are felt in our bodies. Resmaa Menakem describes the bodily knowledge of racism as follows:

> This knowledge is typically experienced as a felt sense of constriction or expansion, pain or ease, energy or numbness. Often this knowledge is stored in our bodies as wordless stories about what is safe and what is dangerous. The body is where we fear, hope, and react; where we constrict and release; and where we reflexively fight, flee, or freeze. If we are to upend the status quo of white-body supremacy, we must begin with our bodies.[23]

We can ground ourselves in our bodies and observe our physical sensations, noticing what causes the body to open and constrict, or become activated or settled.[24] Menakem, a social worker, guides his clients through practices where they begin by grounding in their bodies, drawing attention to their breath, the bottoms of their feet, and the chair beneath them, and they then think of a person or pet that makes them feel safe and secure, noticing how they feel in their bodies (relaxed or constricted, closed or open), and then they imagine an angry person standing in front of them with their arms crossed and a glare in their eyes, and then notice how they feel. In conclusion, they bring back the comforting person or pet before again grounding themselves in their body.[25] Such practices provide a way to experience how our bodies react when we perceive something as a threat, so we can move through it, "metabolize it," and settle our nervous systems.[26]

Mindfulness can be a powerful tool for working to dissolve stereotypes associated with the smog of cultural racism. As Rhonda Magee notes in *The Inner Work of Racial Justice*, you can practice "the pause" to better understand our experiences of race in America. She writes, "Mindfulness is essential to developing the capacity to *respond*, rather than simply *react* as if on auto-pilot, to what we experience. To practice The Pause, you simply stop what you are doing and intentionally bring your awareness to the experience of the present moment."[27] If we can pause to check in with ourselves, noticing our thoughts and emotions, and where we are feeling them in our body, we can minimize any trauma-based reactions in our body.[28] As Magee notes, when we cultivate this type of mindful reflection, we can develop "the embodied emotional intelligence, self-regulation, and overall resilience required to work through the challenges of examining racism in our lives."[29] These skills become especially important as we become aware of systematic racism since, as Beverly Daniel Tatum suggests, this often brings forth painful feelings as well as anger and guilt, and "these uncomfortable emotions can hinder further discussion."[30] Mindfulness of emotions can support us as these emotions surface in response to our increased understanding and recognition of racism in our society.

You can practice "the pause" after reflecting on your own experience of race in America. What were you socialized to believe about race? Were you taught certain ways of thinking about your racial identity and those of others? Can you list ten things that you were taught as a child about race? Reflecting on your race, what advantages did you receive because of it, and what limitations did you experience? Do you have any memories of when you became aware of your race, and if so, what brought that about? If you identify as white, how might you be an ally for people of color? (Allies are those who speak up or act against oppression that is not targeted against themselves.) If you identify as a person of color, how might others be your allies? After exploring these thoughts—perhaps writing them down—stop and observe any emotions that you are having and notice where they are surfacing in your body. As you will learn below, you can recognize the emotion, release it, and then return to mindfulness of your breath and body. In this way, we can learn to identify our emotions and regulate them, so that we can relate and respond to our experience in more intentional ways.

Class

Class refers to "a relative social ranking based on income, wealth, status, and/or power."[31] Income and wealth are material, quantifiable indicators of class: income refers to the money that one receives from wages, salary, investments, or government benefits; wealth is what one owns (assets such as investments, homes, land, business) minus what one owes (debt because of credit cards, school loans, home mortgages).[32] Nonmaterial markers of class are class culture, cultural and social capital, and political power: class culture refers to the norms, values, and lifestyles shared by those of a similar class; cultural capital are the knowledge, skills, and self-presentation that signals class; and social capital refers to the social networks that one has access to.

Economic inequality—the gap between rich and poor families—has continually increased in the United States since 1980, and such disparities have only accelerated following the recession of 2008. They stem from technology, globalization, and other factors: "job loss and wage decline resulting from increasing automation, outsourcing for cheaper labor overseas, and declining power of organized labor. Meanwhile, the wealthiest benefitted when corporations moved offshore and international financial mergers reduced U.S. tax obligations."[33] Incomes have increased faster for the top 5 percent, and the wealth gap between upper-income households and middle- or lower-income households has grown rapidly: whereas upper-income families built on their wealth from 2001 to 2016, adding 33 percent at the median, middle- and low-income families saw their median net worth shrink by 20 and 45 percent, respectively.[34] Not only is income inequality increasing in the United States, but it is higher than in other advanced economies.[35]

Despite such inequality, several myths about class persist in the United States, including the myth that we are a middle-class nation, that class doesn't matter, that we live in a land of upward mobility, and that everyone has an equal chance to succeed.[36] In fact, we live in a society where the richest 20 percent of Americans hold almost 90 percent of the total household wealth, and more than 15 percent of the American population live below the official poverty line.[37] Our class impacts our physical and mental health, our educational achievement, and our economic success, and privileges of the wealthy are linked to worlds of capital and finance.[38] In other words, meritocracy (the belief that hard work and talent result in economic success and upward mobility) is a myth, and capitalism (the economic system of private ownership of agriculture, industry, and technology, where owners profit from the labor of people who receive fixed wages, and economic growth largely benefits the owners) creates and contributes to economic inequality.

What were you socialized to believe about class? Were you taught certain ways of thinking about being rich or poor, or a member of a particular class? Reflecting on your own class background, what advantages did you receive because of it, and what limitations did you experience? Do you have any memories of when you had a strong sense of your class, and if so, what brought that about? What might you want others to know about your class? If you identify as low- or middle-class, how might others be your allies? If you identify as upper-class, how might you be an ally for others?[39] After exploring these thoughts—perhaps writing them down—practice "the pause" by noticing any emotions that have surfaced, and where you feel them in the body. Then, release them from your awareness and engage in a brief practice of mindfulness of breath.

Religion

America has always been a land of religious diversity, beginning with the practices of Indigenous peoples, continuing with Christian traditions brought over by European settlers as well as Muslim and tribal traditions brought over by African slaves, and later with immigrants who brought Jewish traditions from Europe; Buddhist, Daoist, and Confucian traditions from East Asia; as well as Sikh, Jain, and Hindu traditions from South Asia. Despite the history and present-day religious diversity of the United States, which has been thoroughly documented by the Pluralism Project at Harvard University, some view

America as a Christian nation.[40] Christian ideals certainly influenced those who drafted the Declaration of Independence and the Constitution, but as Diana Eck observes,

> There was as much debate over what constituted Christian principles then as now. This is one of the reasons the founding fathers wisely wrote what some have called a "godless" Constitution, one that deliberately steered away from the establishment of any sect of Christianity, even Christianity itself, as the basis of the new nation. They intentionally founded a nation in which no form of religious belief would be privileged in the public sphere.[41]

Nevertheless, because Christians are the dominant religious group in America, with 65 percent of American adults identifying as Christians in surveys conducted by the Pew Research Center in 2018 and 2019, Christian beliefs, values, and worldviews are promoted as normal and universal, while other religious traditions are marginalized.[42] For example, school calendars often cater to the needs of Christians, while others must request an excuse to observe their religious holidays, such as Jewish students who observe High Holy Days on and between Rosh Hashanah and Yom Kippur.[43] Christmas decorations are often hung in public squares of cities and towns across the United States.

More sobering examples of religious oppression include violent incidents against Muslims, Sikhs, Hindus, and Jews in the United States since September 11, 2001.[44] Sikhs, who wear turbans as part of their faith, were the most consistent and immediate targets for such hate crimes.[45] More recently, in the wake of the COVID-19 pandemic, violence against Asian Americans has increased, with one in six Asian American adults reporting that they experienced a hate crime or hate incident in 2021.[46] Hate crimes targeting people of color and religious minorities exemplify white Christian supremacy—the belief that white Christians occupy "the position of supreme authority or power" in the United States.[47] In her memoir *See No Stranger,* Valarie Kaur, a Sikh American, describes being pressured to convert to Christianity as a child, and she documents the targeted violence against Sikh Americans in the wake of 9/11, noting, "In the best of times, we were to be saved. In the worst of times, we were to be slain."[48] Kaur observes how white and Christian ideologies—ideologies being "the sets of beliefs and practices that are accepted by the majority as commonsense ways of organizing the world"[49]—can fuel a mentality of "us" versus "them." She writes,

The most powerful force shaping who we see as *us and them* is the dominant stories in our social landscape. They are produced by ideologies and theologies that divide the world into good or bad, saved or unsaved, with us or against us. Stereotypes are the most reductive kind of story: They reduce others to single, crude images. In the United States, the stereotypes are persistent: black as criminal, brown as illegal, indigenous as savage, Muslims and Sikhs as terrorists, Jews as controlling, Hindus as primitive, Asians of all kinds as perpetually foreign, queer and trans people as sinful, disabled people as pitiable, and women and girls as property. Such stereotypes are in the air, on television and film, in the news, permeating our communities, and ordering our institutions. We breathe them in, whether or not we consciously endorse them.[50]

Binary thinking and stereotypes maintain systems of oppression by praising those in power and denigrating the disenfranchised. Simplistic divisions of "us" and "them" discourage people from seeing the complexity and humanity of others; instead, they preserve the status quo, which benefits certain social groups over others. If we instead cultivate our capacity to wonder, we begin to consider the experiences, wants, and needs of others. Kaur writes, "We begin to sense that they are to themselves as vast and complex as we are to ourselves, their inner world as infinite as our own. In other words, we are seeing them as our equal. We are gaining information about how to love them. Wonder is the wellspring for love."[51] Wonder opens us to other people's experiences and worldviews, which can connect us with others.

Most religions emphasize interconnection and interdependence, but such messages often become eclipsed by distinctions and divisions made between religious traditions. Western religions tend to view religious identity as exclusive (either/or): for example, you are either Christian or Muslim. By contrast, Asian religions often adopt an inclusive approach to religiosity. For example, Chinese temples often house Buddhist, Confucian, and Daoist statues alongside local gods and goddesses, and people pray and making offerings to different ones for different purposes. Such inclusivity may stem from the fact that Asian religions emphasize orthopraxy (right practice), while Western religions value orthodoxy (right belief).

What were you socialized to believe about religion? Were you raised within a particular religious tradition, or were you religiously unaffiliated, atheist, or agnostic—a category that now represents 26 percent of the American population?[52] Reflecting on your religious background, what advantages did you receive because of it, and what limitations did you experience? Do you have any memories of when you had a strong sense of your religious identity, and if so, what brought that about? What might you want others to know about your religion? What might you want to discover about other religions? After exploring these thoughts—perhaps writing them down—practice "the pause" by noticing any emotions that have surfaced, and where you feel them in the body. Then, release them from your awareness and engage in a brief practice of mindfulness of breath.

Gender and Sexual Orientation

"Gender" refers to attitudes, feelings, and behaviors that a culture associates with a person's biological sex: those who conform to cultural expectations are referred to as gender-normative, while those who do not are gender nonconforming.[53] People can identify as male, female, or nonbinary (genderqueer, gender nonconforming, gender fluid).[54] People can identify as transgender when their gender identity and biological sex are not congruent; "cisgender" refers to people whose sex assigned at birth matches their gender identity. Gender is a social construct distinct from sex, which refers to one's biological status that is typically categorized as male, female, or intersex (those who do not have typical features that distinguish male from female). As Judith Lorber writes, "Most people find it hard to believe that gender is constantly created and re-created out of human interactions, out of social life, and is the texture and order of that social life. Yet gender, like culture, is a human production that depends on everyone constantly 'doing gender.'"[55] Gender signals are so ubiquitous that we often fail to notice them unless they are missing or ambiguous.

"Sexual orientation" refers to the sex of those to whom one is sexually and romantically attracted, be it members of one's own sex (gay men or lesbians), those of the other sex (heterosexual), or members of both sexes (bisexual). Some identify as pansexual or queer, which means they define their sexual orientation outside of the binary of male and female. Asexual refers to individuals who do not experience sexual attraction or have little interest in sexual activity. Research suggests that sexual orientation occurs on a continuum, rather than such clearly defined categories.[56]

Binary systems of gender and sexuality that strictly divide people as either man or woman, or heterosexual or queer, establish norms that privilege some and marginalize others. Sexism often occurs when cisgender men use structural and institutional power to restrict resources from cisgender and transgender women.[57] "Heterosexism" refers to the privileging of heterosexuality as the norm and the marginalization of lesbians, gay males, pansexuals, asexuals, intersex, and trans people. "Trans oppression" refers to the marginalization and exclusion of those who do not identify as male or female. As scholars have noted, "oppression directed against all women (sexism), LGB people (heterosexism), and trans* people (trans* oppression) are both distinctive and interlocking because we all have multiple identities that are salient at different times and for different reasons."[58] For those who hold a degree of privilege—for example, those who identify as gender-normative, cisgender, and/or heterosexual—how might one act as an ally against sexism or heterosexism? Devin Carbado raises interesting questions about what might count as resistance to heterosexual privilege: "With respect to marriage, for example, does resistance to heterosexual privilege require heterosexuals to refrain from getting married and/or attending weddings? ... A heterosexual who gets married and/or attends weddings but who also openly challenges the idea that marriage is a heterosexual entitlement is engaging in critical acquiescence. In the end, critical acquiescence might not go far enough. It might even be a cop out. Still, it is a useful and politically manageable place to begin."[59]

What were you socialized to believe about gender and sexual orientation? Were you taught certain ways of thinking about your gender and sexuality? Can you list ten things that you were taught as a child about gender and sexuality? Reflecting on your gender and sexual orientation, what advantages do you receive because of it, and what limitations do you experience? Do you have any memories of when you became aware of your gender and sexual orientation, and if so, what brought that about? If you identify as cisnormative, cisgender, or heterosexual, how might you be an ally for those who are gender fluid, transgender, or lesbian, gay, bisexual, or queer? If you identify as gender fluid, transgender, or LGBQ, how might others be your ally? After exploring these thoughts—perhaps writing them down—practice "the pause" by noticing any emotions that have surfaced, and where you feel them in the body. Then, release them from your awareness and engage in a brief practice of mindfulness of breath.

Ability

The American with Disabilities Act (ADA) defines disability as "a physical or mental impairment that substantially limits one or more major life activities."[60]

Over a billion people—roughly 15 percent of the world's population—are estimated to have some form of disability.[61] "Ableism" refers to the system of oppression that advantages those who are able-bodied and discriminates against and marginalizes people with disabilities. Although the ADA was enacted in 1990 and amended in 2008, people with disabilities still encounter challenges to equal access. Often the burden of ensuring access to facilities and services falls upon people with disabilities to identify the issue, initiate the demand, and ensure that accommodation has been made.

Historically, people associated disability with sin, and they sent those with disabilities to jails or asylums. Early Western medicine classified those with disabilities as genetically defective:

> The medical goal was to "cure" the disability, get rid of a deformity, fix the body, and/or numb the existing pain of the person who was described as the patient. This thinking and methodology resulted in solutions that were invasive—usually involving surgery or drugs—and which required the person with the disability to submit to the authority of the other as expert. The view that disabilities are deficiencies that require medical treatment and repair remains pervasive today.[62]

It was not until the Rehabilitation Act of 1973 that people with disabilities were considered a collective social group, and in the decades that followed such legislation, they began a grassroots movement to take more control over their lives and challenge the equating of dependency with laziness or being a burden in American society. As Willie Bryan notes, "Although public and private social welfare agencies and organizations including hospitals, clinics, and rehabilitation centers, to name a few, have been developed to assist persons who by virtue of illness, accident, or birth defects must rely on assistive services, the recipients are often viewed in a negative light and at best given sympathy instead of empathy and understanding."[63] Fighting against such perceptions, people with disabilities have promoted Independent Living Centers where they can receive support but manage their own affairs and make decisions for themselves.

What were you socialized to believe about able and disabled bodies? Were you taught certain ways of thinking about ability/disability? Can you list ten things that you were taught as a child about ability/disability? Reflecting on your ability/disability, what advantages do you receive because of it, and what limitations do you experience? Do you have any memories of when you became aware of your ability/disability, and if so, what brought that about?

If you identify as able-bodied, how might you be an ally for those who are disabled? If you identify as disabled, how might others be your allies? After exploring these thoughts—perhaps writing them down—practice "the pause" by noticing any emotions that have surfaced, and where you feel them in the body. Then, release them from your awareness and engage in a brief practice of mindfulness of breath.

The Value of Social Diversity

We have examined various types of social diversity, including race, class, religion, gender, sexuality, and ability. What is the value of being around people who are different from us? Although being in socially diverse groups can cause discomfort, less cohesion, and a greater perception of interpersonal conflict, diversity enhances creativity and leads to better decision-making and problem-solving.[64] Katherine Phillips—a business school professor at Columbia University—has found that when we encounter dissenting perspectives from those who differ from us, it provokes greater thought and consideration of alternatives. She writes,

> When members of a group notice that they are socially different from one another, they change their expectations. They anticipate differences of opinion and perspective. They assume they will need to work harder to come to a consensus. This logic helps to explain both the upside and downside of social diversity: people work harder in diverse environments both cognitively and socially. They might not like it, but the hard work can lead to better outcomes.[65]

We experience discomfort in socially diverse groups because they cognitively and socially challenge us to consider alternative information, experiences, and worldviews. Diversity encourages cognitive flexibility, which we discussed in the first chapter, and often generates more creative solutions to problems. As Phillips remarks, "We need diversity—in teams, organizations and society as a whole—if we are to change, grow, and innovate."[66] When we work in diverse groups, with people whose experiences, values, and backgrounds differ from our own, we think critically and creatively. We perform better than homogenous ones that encourage groupthink, which occurs when the desire to harmonize or conform with the group results in poor decisions and worse outcomes.

Often, when you meet new people who differ from you and you try to connect with them, you look for similarities: watching the same TV shows, attending the same schools, or growing up in the same area. Phillips encourages us to try a different approach, where instead of looking for commonalities we talk about what makes us different. She says, "Tell me about your life, your story, the experiences you went through that I can perhaps learn from. I don't want to know exactly how we're alike. In fact, if I do that, I haven't learned anything. I need to know how you're different from me."[67] When we create an environment where difference is normal, where we expect people to be different, we can broaden our perspective and improve our critical thinking. We also develop skills of equity and inclusion valued by employers: "the awareness, attitude, knowledge, and skills required to equitably engage and include people from different local and global cultures."[68]

Mindfulness of Emotions

Emotions readily surface when we reflect on our social identity and acknowledge the suffering caused by racism, classism, religious oppression, sexism, heterosexism, and ableism. Mindfulness enables us to recognize our emotions, acknowledge how they feel in our bodies, examine them with curiosity and care, and release them from our awareness so that we can respond skillfully to our present situation instead of reacting out of automaticity. You can explore your emotional landscape and develop greater emotional intelligence through this practice.

You can explore mindfulness of emotion in a formal seated practice by first drawing attention to your body and breath, and once you feel grounded and settled, noticing emotions as they arise and pass away. When emotions surface in your awareness, you can observe where you feel those emotions in your body. You might feel strong emotions, or subtle emotions such as calm or ease. Michele McDonald, an American mindfulness teacher, coined the acronym RAIN to describe the practice of Recognition, Acceptance, Interest, and Non-Identification, which you can use in your practice of mindfulness of emotions. First, you acknowledge whatever emotion you are experiencing (perhaps making a mental note of it), without getting caught up in a story about it. You accept your emotion—even if it is unpleasant—and investigate it with curiosity and kindness. Finally, you try not to identify with the thought. For example, instead of thinking "I am angry" or "I am sad," you reframe it as

"I am having a feeling of anger/sadness." You can observe how emotions, like bodily sensations, are impermanent. The psychologist Rick Hanson offers the following guidance on how to avoid identifying with your emotions or other aspects of your experience:

> Disentangle yourself from the various parts of the experience, knowing that they are small, fleeting aspects of the totality that you are. See the streaming nature of sights, sounds, thoughts, and other contents of mind, arising and passing away due mainly to causes that have nothing to do with you, that is impersonal. Feel the contraction, stress, and pain that comes from claiming any part of this stream as "I," or "me," or "mine"—and sense the spaciousness and peace that comes when experiences simply flow.[69]

When practicing mindfulness of emotion, you simply inquire "What am I feeling now?" and observe your emotions with curiosity and care. If the emotion is too strong or intense, feel free to direct your attention to somewhere neutral, such as your hands or feet. If you still feel overwhelmed by the emotion, you could stand up, move around, or stop your practice entirely.

Mindfulness encourages us to feel and sense our emotions—knowing where emotions arise in our bodies—rather than to resist, analyze, or try to change our emotions. As we work with our emotions, we start to notice how we relate to emotions. We may tend to avoid unpleasant emotions or to become attached to pleasant emotions. Mindfulness encourages us to feel and acknowledge when difficult emotions are present, developing kindness and compassion towards them. They are part of human experience: everyone experiences difficult emotions. In this way, mindfulness allows for freedom in our relationships with our emotions, and it can foster empathy and compassion for others. The Sufi poet Rumi speaks to this openness in "The Guest House":

> This being human is a guest house.
> Every morning a new arrival.
> A joy, a depression, a meanness,
> some momentary awareness comes
> as an unexpected visitor.
> Welcome and entertain them all!
> Even if they're a crowd of sorrows,
> who violently sweep your house
> empty of its furniture,
> still, treat each guest honorably.

He may be clearing you out
for some new delight.
The dark thought, the shame, the malice.
meet them at the door laughing and invite them in.
Be grateful for whatever comes.
because each has been sent
as a guide from beyond.[70]

Notes

1. Kaur, *See No Stranger*, 10–11.
2. Adams et al., *Readings for Diversity and Social Justice*, xxiv.
3. Adams and Zúñiga, "Core Concepts for Social Justice Education," 97.
4. West, "Courage," 635.
5. Bell, "Theoretical Foundations for Social Justice Education," 34.
6. Harro, "Cycle of Socialization," 27.
7. Harro, "Cycle of Socialization," 28.
8. Harro, "Cycle of Socialization," 29.
9. Adams and Zúñiga, "Core Concepts for Social Justice Education," 44.
10. "white supremacy, n.," *Oxford English Dictionary*, December 2021, accessed April 23, 2022, https://www-oed-com.liblink.uncw.edu/view/Entry /421025?redirectedFrom=white+supremacy#eid.
11. In this section we will address racial identity, rather than ethnic identity, which is a social group identity based on cultural criteria such as language, customs, and shared history.
12. Kendi, *How to Be an Antiracist*, 18.
13. Kendi, *How to Be an Antiracist*, 18.
14. McIntosh, "White Privilege," 10-12.
15. McIntosh, "White Privilege," 10-12.
16. Dalton, "Failing to See," 17.
17. Tatum, *Why Are All the Black Kids Sitting Together in the Cafeteria?*, 86.
18. Tatum, *Why Are All the Black Kids Sitting Together in the Cafeteria?*, 91.
19. Coates, *Between the World and Me*, 10.
20. Coates, *Between the World and Me*, 90.
21. Steele, *Whistling Vivaldi*, 125–26.
22. Staples, "Black Men and Public Space," 20.
23. Menakem, *My Grandmother's Hands*, 5.
24. Menakem, *My Grandmother's Hands*, 29.
25. Menakem, *My Grandmother's Hands*, 31–32.
26. Menakem, *My Grandmother's Hands*, 165.

27. Magee, *Inner Work of Racial Justice*, 17.

28. Magee, *Inner Work of Racial Justice*, 17.

29. Magee, *Inner Work of Racial Justice*, 18.

30. Tatum, *Why Are All the Black Kids Sitting Together in the Cafeteria?*, 89.

31. Yeskel and Leondar-Wright, "Classism Curriculum Design," 233.

32. Adams et al., "Introduction: Classism," 167.

33. Adams et al., "Introduction: Classism," 164.

34. Pew Research Center, "Most Americans Say There Is Too Much Economic Inequality in the U.S."

35. Pew Research Center, "Most Americans Say There Is Too Much Economic Inequality in the U.S."

36. Mantsios, "Class in America," 173–74.

37. Mantsios, "Class in America," 174.

38. Mantsios, "Class in America," 180.

39. These questions are adapted from Yeskel and Leondar-Wright, "Classism Curriculum Design," 242–43.

40. Pluralism Project of Harvard University, "What is Pluralism?"

41. Eck, *New Religious America*, 42.

42. Pew Research Center, "In U.S., Decline of Christianity Continues at Rapid Pace." As noted in this article, 65 percent was a 12 percentage point decrease from the previous decade. Although Christians comprise the majority of religious believers in the United States, worldwide they represent less than a third of the global population. Pew Research Center, "Global Religious Landscape." The 2010 demographic study by the Pew Research Center's Forum on Religion & Public Life found 2.2 billion Christians (32 percent of the world's population), 1.6 billion Muslims (23 percent), 1 billion Hindus (15 percent), nearly 500 million Buddhists (7 percent) and 14 million Jews (0.2 percent); they found 1.1 billion (16 percent) had no affiliation and 76 percent of these religiously unaffiliated people lived in the Asia-Pacific region.

43. Blumenfeld, "Christian Privilege," 199.

44. Blumenfeld, "Christian Privilege," 201.

45. Kaur, *See No Stranger*, 42.

46. Wang, "How Violence Against Asian Americans Has Grown."

47. Ehrlich et al., *Oxford American Dictionary*, 925.

48. Kaur, *See No Stranger*, 47.

49. Brookfield, *Teaching for Critical Thinking*, 9.

50. Kaur, *See No Stranger*, 17.

51. Kaur, *See No Stranger*, 97.

52. Pew Research Center, "In U.S., Decline of Christianity Continues at Rapid Pace." As noted in this article, 26 percent in 2019 was up from 17 percent in 2009.

53. These definitions derive from the American Psychological Association, "Key Terms and Concepts."

54. Queer is "an umbrella term that individuals may use to describe a sexual orientation, gender identity, or gender expression that does not conform to dominant societal norms." See American Psychological Association, "Key Terms and Concepts."

55. Lorber, *Paradoxes of Gender*, 13.

56. American Psychological Association, "Key Terms and Concepts."

57. These resources can be material (such as employment, education, housing) or non-material (safety, respect, voice, and representation), as noted in Catalano et al., "Sexism, Heterosexism, and Trans* Oppression," 344.

58. Catalano et al., "Sexism, Heterosexism, and Trans* Oppression," 342.

59. Carbado, "Privilege," 209.

60. U.S. Department of Justice. "Introduction to the Americans with Disabilities Act."

61. Ostiguy-Finneran and Peters, "Ableism," 467.

62. Ostiguy-Finneran and Peters, "Ableism," 469.

63. Bryan, "Struggle for Freedom," 478.

64. Phillips, "How Diversity Works," 43–47.

65. Phillips, "How Diversity Works," 43

66. Phillips, "How Diversity Works," 47.

67. Phillips, "Why Diversity Matters."

68. "What Is Career Readiness?" *NACE: National Association of Colleges and Employers*.

69. Hanson, "Let It R.A.I.N."

70. Rūmī, *Essential Rumi*, 109.

CHAPTER FIVE

Thinking Critically

All of these stories make me who I am. But to insist on only these
negative stories is to flatten my experience and to overlook the many
other stories that formed me. The single story creates stereotypes,
and the problem with stereotypes is not that they are untrue, but
they are incomplete. They make one story become the only story.
—Chimamanda Adichie[1]

As a child, I suffered terrifying bouts of asthma, often in the middle
of the night. My chest tight and my throat constricted, I would sit
up in bed, wondering if I would have to be rushed to the emergency
room yet again. Every time it happened, I felt trapped and frantic, unable
to think about anything except my struggle to breathe. Cold weather and
cat allergies were the main triggers for such attacks, and I would especially
dread physical education class during the winter when we had to run a mile
outside. After one lap around the track, I would be wheezing, unable to
breathe, and reduced to walking the remaining laps. I decided I would never
be a runner.

Much later in life when a friend suggested we sign up for a half-marathon,
I initially dismissed the idea as absurd. Although I had largely outgrown my
asthma, it was occasionally triggered by cold weather, so I assumed I would
still be unable to run one mile, let alone thirteen. But I decided to give it a try. I
did a Google search for a "half-marathon training schedule for beginners" and
saw that first I needed to be able to run three miles several times a week before
I could even start training.[2] I looked up articles about basic running stretches,
proper running form, and other advice for novice runners on *Runner's World*
and various medical and fitness websites. I went to my local running store to
purchase a good pair of running shoes. To my surprise, I found that I had the
stamina to run three miles—admittedly, at a slow pace—because I was physically active in other ways: I swam, cycled, and did yoga. Twelve weeks later, I
ran my first half-marathon.

This is an example of critical thinking in everyday life. Critical thinking involves identifying and responding to needs based on an understanding of the situation and an analysis of the relevant information.[3] In my case, I needed to determine whether I could run a half-marathon. Although I assumed it would be impossible, I researched relevant information about what it takes to run a half-marathon: the ability to run three miles several times a week, good running shoes to prevent blistering and other problems, stretches to prevent common injuries such as plantar fasciitis and shin splints, and twelve weeks to devote to increasingly long runs and cross-training exercises. I consulted sources that were reliable—*Runner's World* (an international magazine for runners in circulation over fifty years), the website of Hal Higdon (marathon runner, writer for *Runner's World*, and author of *Marathon: The Ultimate Training Guide*), and websites run by medical institutions such as the Cleveland Clinic and Yale School of Medicine that explained ways to avoid injuries. I first experimented to see if I met the training requirements, and I then equipped myself with good running shoes and organized my schedule so that I could follow the training regimen. When I sustained an injury, I modified my training and followed the advice given by doctors on the medical websites.

Questioning Assumptions

Critical thinking begins with questioning our own views and assumptions. Based on my previous experiences, I assumed I would be unable to run a half-marathon. But I allowed myself to see if in fact such assumptions were true, and to my surprise I discovered they were false. Stephen Brookfield, a scholar who has written extensively on critical thinking, says it begins by hunting assumptions guiding our thoughts and actions and checking to see if they are as accurate as we think they are.[4] He uses his own experience with clinical depression as an example, suggesting that the primary obstacle to dealing with his depression was his inability to think critically about it. Brookfield writes,

> I refused to consider the possibility that any of my assumptions regarding my depression were wrong. For example, I assumed that the right way to deal with depression was to think your way out of it. I assumed that depression was a sign of weakness, unless external circumstances (such as divorce, being fired, or the death of a loved one) warranted it. Because I assumed I was weak, I assumed I needed to hide my condition from peers

and colleagues. More fundamentally, I assumed that if I was a real man I would be able just to stare this condition down and force myself out of it by an act of will. I assumed it was up to me to "dig deep" (as the sports cliché has it) and dredge up the mental strength to beat it.[5]

Brookfield analyzes the various types of assumptions that he made: causal assumptions about what causes depression, prescriptive assumptions about how he should respond to depression, and paradigmatic assumptions about his identity, especially patriarchal views of "real" men as guided by logic and self-sufficient, having no need for a psychiatrist or medicine to help them with depression. He had to challenge and discard assumptions that depression was rationally caused, rather than the result of chemical imbalances in the brain, and a sign of weakness or a lack of manliness.[6] Brookfield writes, "Assumptions that spring from dominant ideologies are particularly hard to uncover, precisely because these ideologies are everywhere, so common as to be thought blindingly obvious and therefore not worthy of being the object of sustained questioning."[7] Assumptions underlying dominant ideologies in American society, such as white supremacy, capitalism, democracy, patriarchy, and heterosexism, become what some call "false fixities" that are difficult to identify and interrogate. As Lee Yearley writes,

> Contingent features of the self are mistakenly seen as part of the nature of things. Because it is believed that they cannot be other than they are, they therefore limit human deliberation because no sensible people attempt to deliberate about what cannot be changed. One thinks in terms of them, one does not think about them. Human history is, of course, littered with examples of false fixities, ideas that, in retrospect, we realize were social myths that protected particular ways of life. Our present thinking, however, is no less liable to be formed by them.[8]

In our previous chapter we explored some examples of "false fixities" that protect dominant ideologies in American society, including those tied to race, class, gender, and sexuality. Critical thinking encourages us to constantly question such dominant beliefs and practices.

Identifying Biases

Left to itself, our thinking tends to be biased, distorted, partial, and uninformed.[9] Identifying our biases can be challenging because they are often hidden, implicit, or unconscious. We have cognitive biases—shortcuts in our thinking that make our judgments irrational—such as confirmation bias (favoring things that confirm your existing beliefs), in-group bias (unfairly favoring those who belong to your group), and fundamental attribution error (judging others based on their character, but yourself based on the situation).[10] We also have biases about social groups gleaned from our cultural environment and stored in our brain, which can guide our behavior, even though we may be oblivious to their influence.[11] One way to reveal such hidden biases or "blindspots"[12] is by taking an Implicit Association Test that examines unconscious biases related to race, gender, sexuality, religion, and nation of origin.[13] When we start to recognize our hidden biases and develop greater self-awareness, we can minimize their impact and neutralize them before they translate into behavior.[14] We can use our reflective, analytic mind to override our tendency towards automatic, reflexive patterns of thought. For example, we may find that we have stereotypes about people, associating their social groups with certain attributes. If we develop relationships with diverse groups of people and encounter diverse images of that social group, we can build up associations that counter stereotypical ones.[15]

Engaging with people who differ from ourselves provides an invaluable opportunity to learn about other perspectives and viewpoints. As Chimamanda Adichie shares in her talk "The Danger of a Single Story," there is a danger in hearing only a single story about yourself or other people. Media coverage can make us buy into the single story by showing people as one thing—a stereotype—over and over. Adichie, a Nigerian, shares how her American roommate had a default stance toward her—that of patronizing, well-meaning pity: "My roommate had a single story of Africa: a single story of catastrophe. In this single story, there was no possibility of Africans being similar to her in any way; no possibility of feelings more complex than pity; no possibility of a connection as human equals."[16] Adichie emphasizes the impossibility of connecting with another person unless you engage all of their stories.

We all have stories that we tell ourselves based on our previous experiences. My story was that I would never be able to run because of my asthma. Your stories will stem from your own lives and histories. Such stories inform how we think of ourselves and our capabilities. However, if we make one story the only story, or we assume that our stories cannot change, they can limit us from new opportunities for growth and development.

Instead, we can approach our learning and life goals with a growth mindset. A growth mindset assumes we can change and grow through our own effort;

a fixed mindset assumes that our intelligence, personality, and character are fixed, which creates the urgent need to prove ourselves over and over.[17] As Carol Dweck, a psychologist from Stanford University, writes, "When you enter a mindset, you enter a new world. In one world—the world of fixed traits—success is about proving you're smart or talented. Validating yourself. In the other—the world of changing qualities—it's about stretching yourself to learn something new. Developing yourself."[18] People with a fixed mindset downplay the importance of effort, see failure as something that defines them (I am a failure), and tend not to cope well or take actions to confront their problems.[19] By contrast, those with a growth mindset view effort as crucial and experience failure as painful, but a problem that can be faced, dealt with, and learned from.[20] Dweck observes, "People in a growth mindset don't just *seek* challenge, they thrive on it. The bigger the challenge, the more they stretch."[21] A sense of freedom comes from adopting a growth mindset: failures can signal that we have challenged ourselves. Dweck writes, "In the fixed mindset, everything is about the outcome. If you fail—or if you're not the best—it's all been wasted. The growth mindset allows people to value what they're doing *regardless of the outcome*. They're tackling problems, charting new courses, working on important issues."[22]

Seeing Things from Many Points of View

Critical thinking involves unearthing assumptions and biases that influence our thoughts and behavior and assessing whether they are valid and reliable. As Brookfield notes, one way to assess the accuracy of our assumptions is trying to see them from many different points of view.[23] The ability to see things from multiple perspectives, analyze information from different sources, and understand the larger context constitutes a significant outcome of an education. As Tara Westover writes in her memoir *Educated*,

> Everything I had worked for, all my years of study, had been to purchase for myself this one privilege: to see and experience more truths than those given to me by my father, and to use those truths to construct my own mind. I had come to believe that the ability to evaluate many ideas, many histories, many points of view, was at the heart of what it means to self-create.

Westover speaks to the value of intellectual autonomy—having self-authorship over one's beliefs, values, and ways of thinking—instead of passively accepting the beliefs of others.[24] She can construct her own views and opinions after considering many different ideas, histories, and points of view.

College offers the opportunity to study different disciplines, experiment with different methods, and consider multiple points of view. Scientific disciplines, for example, use the scientific method as a means of limiting biases. Claude Steele writes,

> Our understandings and views of the world are partial and reflect the circumstances of our particular lives. This is where a discipline like science comes in. It doesn't purge us of bias. But it extends what we can see and understand, while constraining bias.... The constant back-and-forth between ideas and research results hammers away at bias and, just as important, often reveals aspects of reality that surpass our original ideas and insights.[25]

Using the scientific method, we make observations about a problem, create a prediction, collect data to test our prediction, and then draw conclusions based on our results. Our predictions are not always confirmed by our observations—as Steele notes, sometimes reality surpasses those original ideas, and we either further refine our predictions or abandon them entirely.

Analyzing Relevant Information

We engage in critical thinking to make informed decisions and act based on evidence.[26] In my case, after checking my assumptions and identifying my biases against running, I gathered and analyzed information from a diverse set of reliable internet sources, and I determined that I could run a half-marathon if I followed certain guidelines and took precautions. Undoubtedly, you have also used your critical thinking skills to evaluate information when faced with decisions in your life.

But, as you may have experienced, it can be challenging in digital environments to distinguish valid, reliable information from misleading or fraudulent information. Mike Caulfield, a research scientist who studies online digital literacy, has designed the SIFT model for quickly investigating online sources and checking claims:

STOP
Investigate the Source
Find better coverage

Trace claims, quotes, and media back to the original context[27]

Caulfield encourages us to make four moves when we encounter claims and sources on the web. First, we stop reading further and notice our reaction to the claims: have we immediately accepted the claims because we agree, or swiftly dismissed them because we disagree? In other words, has confirmation bias crept in? Second, we consider the source and try to decipher the expertise and agenda of the source (whether it is credible and trustworthy). Third, we find more trusted, in-depth, or more varied coverage to evaluate the veracity of the claim, and whether it is broadly accepted, rejected, or debated. As Caulfield notes, "You want to know if it represents a consensus viewpoint, or if it is the subject of much disagreement."[28] Finally, when evidence is presented (such as a quotation, image, or video), we try to locate the original context in which it appears. If we find ourselves led down a confusing maze of web pages—an online rabbit hole—Caulfield urges us to stop, back up, figure out what we need to know, and reapproach.

When investigating sources, we can draw insights from fact-checkers who often look up the source's page in Wikipedia as a first stop to understanding the website or organization, rather than relying on what the website or organization says about itself. We can do likewise, asking ourselves whether the site or organization was what we expected it to be, and if not, whether it is more trustworthy or less.[29] We can also search for "challenges to [insert idea]," "concerns about [insert idea]," or "controversies to [insert idea]" to work against confirmation bias. Although Wikipedia should be approached with caution, it can provide a useful introduction to a subject, and one can often find authoritative sources in the footnotes because it has strict rules about citing reliable sources for claims.[30] As Caulfield notes, "The effects on trust are of course contextual as well: a small local paper may be a great source for local news, but a lousy source for health advice or international politics."[31] Your initial findings on Wikipedia may change the way you read the source, or prompt you to do further research.

Critical thinking—checking our assumptions and biases, seeing things from many points of view, and analyzing relevant information—can help us in our everyday lives. We live in a complex world of accelerated change that requires us to be adaptable, regularly rethinking our decisions and reevaluating the way we work and live.[32] As Richard Paul and Linda Elder point out, lower-order thinking is unreflective, frequently relies on gut intuition, and is largely self-serving or self-deceived.[33] By contrast, critical thinking is reflective, enables us to persevere when confronted with complex situations or tasks, and encourages us to consider the perspective of others. In *Critical Thinking,* they define a skilled critical thinker as one who

- Raises vital questions and problems, formulating them clearly and precisely
- Gathers and assesses relevant information, and effectively interprets it
- Comes to well-reasoned conclusions and solutions, testing them against relevant criteria and standards
- Thinks open-mindedly within alternative systems of thought, recognizing and assessing, as need be, their assumptions, implications, and practical consequences
- Communicates effectively with others in figuring out solutions to complex problems[34]

When we think critically, we question our own views, empathetically reconstruct the strongest views of perspectives opposed to our own, engage in critical reasoning, and change our thinking when the evidence requires it.[35] Aware of our own biases and blind spots, we have intellectual humility: we are willing to admit that our beliefs could be wrong, and we are open to learning new information from others.[36] We also have intellectual empathy: "an awareness of the need to imaginatively put ourselves in the place of others so as to genuinely understand them. To have intellectual empathy is to be able to accurately reconstruct the viewpoints and reasoning of others and to reason from premises, assumptions, and ideas other than our own."[37] In this way, critical thinking can improve not only our own lives, but also our relationships with others.

Mindfulness of Thoughts

You can develop a skillful relationship to your thoughts and diminish self-judgment. Thoughts are natural and useful, and we need to be able to think and plan in our life. But we tend to get lost in thought at the expense of being present in the moment. We often have a negativity bias—one of the cognitive biases of the mind—and tend to fixate and ruminate on negative experiences, causing us pain and stress. As mindfulness teacher Mark Coleman writes,

Normally, our mind is like Velcro. Everything sticks. It is as if those judging thoughts come wrapped in hooks and barbs and lodge themselves in our mind each time they arise. The outcome is that our judging thoughts stay firmly entrenched, taking up residence in our mental attic and making it feel cluttered and full. In contrast, mindful awareness creates a sense of space. When we bring awareness to something, it becomes enveloped in spacious clarity, just as when we shine a light on something in the dark we see the object but also notice the space around it.[38]

Coleman describes the judging mind as our "inner critic" and encourages us to distinguish between discernment and negative judgment about one's self-worth. He shares a practice for working with the inner critic by "identifying your inner boardroom," listing all of the voices of the characters in your mind who judge or criticize: "Do you have the killjoy, persecutor, controller, underminer, fault finder, abuser? Or perhaps a coach, judge, perfectionist, taskmaster, tyrant, penny-pincher, nitpicker, or simply a critic?"[39] After naming them and their judgments, you try to discern the concern or fear underlying such judgment, and then write out a more constructive expression of such concern and steps you might take to address it.

Mindfulness can help us change our relationship with our thoughts. Instead of allowing our thoughts to stick in our minds, mindfulness encourages us to approach them as clouds passing in the sky. We avoid identifying with our thoughts, which allows us to detach from our thoughts and view them with more spaciousness. To be clear, we don't try to stop our thoughts. Instead, we develop a wiser relationship to our thoughts, being mindful of when thinking happens. Instead of being consumed by our thoughts, we note or label that we are thinking, and we watch as thoughts come and go of their own accord.

You may notice that your mind tends toward a certain type of thought or pattern of thinking. Five mental states may distract you or make it difficult to concentrate during your formal practice: daydreaming or fantasizing about the future, resistance to or pulling away from our experience, sleepiness or fatigue, restlessness or agitation, and judgment or self-criticism. You can become more aware of your habits of mind by labeling them and observing as they come and go. You can also address each state specifically: when you find yourself fantasizing, cultivate a sense of gratitude for what you already have; when you find yourself ruminating, broaden your focus of awareness; when you feel dull or sleepy, open your eyes, engage in walking meditation, or count your breaths; when you feel agitated, feel the ground beneath your feet or the chair beneath your body; when you find yourself being judgmental or self-critical, remember the intention behind your mindfulness practice.

Buddhist thought uses the metaphor of a pond to describe the way such habits of mind can prevent us from having a clear state of mind. When ponds are clean and their surface still, the water reflects our image. However, Buddhists liken desire or fantasy to looking into a dyed pond, resistance or aversion to a boiling pond, dullness to thick algae growing in the pond, agitation to wind-stirred waters, and judgment to water filled with mud. By drawing attention to such habits of mind—making them the object of our focus—we can change the way we relate to them. Rather than getting caught up in our fantasy, aversion, dullness, agitation, or judgment, we can observe ourselves having such thoughts. We invite some space between ourselves and our thoughts, which in turn brings clarity and stillness to the pond.

A formal practice of mindfulness of thoughts begins with grounding in your body and becoming aware of your bodily sensations, and then opening your awareness to include sounds, feelings, and emotions. You then draw your attention to your thoughts, observing your own patterns of thought: whether your thoughts tend toward the past, present, or future, whether you have a proliferation of thoughts, or whether you have a particular type of thought such as planning, judging, analyzing, or worrying. You can recognize the thoughts, release them, and then return to your breath or another anchor for your attention. In this way, you note when you are thinking, you let it go, and then come back to your breath or body. Over time, you may observe the transient nature of thoughts—that they come and go—and that you are not your thoughts. When we hold thoughts in our awareness, we can recognize our habits of mind and create some space between ourselves and our thoughts.

Notes

1. Adichie, "Danger of a Single Story."
2. Among the search results, I found this webpage incredibly helpful: Higdon, "Half Marathon Training: Novice 1," https://www.halhigdon.com/training-programs/half-marathon-training/novice-1-half-marathon/.
3. This definition of critical thinking is derived from "What Is Career Readiness?"
4. Brookfield, *Teaching for Critical Thinking*, 11.
5. Brookfield, *Teaching for Critical Thinking*, 3.
6. Brookfield, *Teaching for Critical Thinking*, 5.
7. Brookfield, *Teaching for Critical Thinking*, 9.
8. Yearley, "Selves, Virtues, Odd Genres, and Alien Guides," 131.
9. Paul and Elder, *Critical Thinking*, 6.

10. School of Thought, "Yourbias.is."

11. Banaji and Greenwald, *Blindspot*, xii.

12. Banaji and Greenwald, *Blindspot*.

13. "Implicit Association Test."

14. Banaji and Greenwald, *Blindspot*, 70.

15. Banaji and Greenwald, *Blindspot*, 152.

16. Adichie, "Danger of a Single Story."

17. Dweck, *Mindset*, 6–7.

18. Dweck, *Mindset*, 15.

19. Dweck, *Mindset*, 38.

20. Dweck, *Mindset*, 33.

21. Dweck, *Mindset*, 21.

22. Dweck, *Mindset*, 48.

23. Brookfield, *Teaching for Critical Thinking*, 12.

24. Paul and Elder, *Critical Thinking*, 44.

25. Steele, *Whistling Vivaldi*, 14.

26. Brookfield, *Teaching for Critical Thinking*, 13.

27. Caulfield, "Introducing SIFT, a Four Moves Acronym."

28. Caulfield, "SIFT (The Four Moves)."

29. Caulfield, "Information Literacy for Mortals."

30. Caulfield, "Just Add Wikipedia."

31. Caulfield, "Just Add Wikipedia."

32. Paul and Elder, *Critical Thinking*, 1.

33. Paul and Elder, *Critical Thinking*, 17.

34. Paul and Elder, *Critical Thinking*, 19.

35. Paul and Elder, *Critical Thinking*, 23.

36. Leary et al., "Cognitive and Interpersonal Features of Intellectual Humility."

37. Paul and Elder, *Critical Thinking*, 35.

38. Coleman, *Make Peace with Your Mind*, 125.

39. Coleman, *Make Peace with Your Mind*, 89.

CHAPTER SIX

Cultivating Habits

The thought manifests as the word;
The word manifests as the deed;
The deed develops into habit;
And habit hardens into character.
So watch the thought and its ways with care,
And let it spring from love
Born out of concern for all beings.
—The Buddha[1]

When I wrote, "Twelve weeks later, I ran my first half-marathon," I glossed over the fact that those weeks required me to establish entirely new habits tied to running. Before going to bed each night, I would put my running shoes and clothes on a chair beside my bed. Each morning, when I woke up, those shoes reminded me that I needed to do a morning run or cross-train. I would change into the clothes, have a cup of coffee, and go on my run or cross-train. When I returned, I would drink fluids, take a shower, and then eat my breakfast. This became my morning routine for those twelve weeks. I logged how many miles I ran, or how many minutes I swam or biked. I focused on changing one habit, which scholars call a "keystone habit": instead of eating breakfast immediately after drinking my coffee, I exercised.[2]

Habits form when our brains change a sequence of actions into an automatic routine. This process of "chunking"[3] involves three steps, as Charles Duhigg notes: "First, there is a *cue*, a trigger that tells your brain to go into automatic mode and which habit to use. Then there is the *routine*, which can be physical or mental or emotional. Finally, there is a *reward*, which helps your brain figure out if this particular loop is worth remembering for the future."[4] This loop or pattern of cue-routine-reward becomes automatic as it is repeated, until one develops a sense of anticipation and craving for the habit.

That craving becomes the driving force behind the habit.[5] For example, when you receive a text or notification on your phone, the cue of the sound or vibration makes the brain anticipate the pleasure of reading the text or opening the app. Only by recognizing such cues and rewards can we change our digital habits: we can turn off notifications and avoid succumbing to automatic behaviors of digital distraction.

To cultivate habits, we need to establish new routines with their own cues and rewards. I used my running shoes as my cue, and a sports drink and second cup of coffee as my reward; you may choose other cues to trigger your routines and different rewards to power your habit loops. This chapter explores a variety of habits that you can cultivate in your daily life, including sleeping, exercising, eating, and finding flow. I share some recommendations based on scientific research, but you can adapt such suggestions to fit your own circumstances and create your own habits. At the end of each section, you will find questions that encourage you to reflect on your habits and consider how you might establish new cues, routines, and rewards tied to new habits.

Sleeping

When we think of hygiene—practices that maintain our health and prevent disease—we might first draw to mind washing our hands, brushing our teeth, and taking showers. Sleep hygiene refers to behaviors that facilitate a good quality of sleep, which enables us to stay alert during the day. These include having a fixed wake-up time to establish a rhythm of consistent sleep, keeping any naps short and limited to the early afternoon, following a nightly routine, cultivating healthy daily habits, and optimizing our bedroom.[6] The National Sleep Foundation recommends that young adults (18–25) and adults (26-64) get between seven and nine hours of sleep each night.[7] They advise following a consistent nightly routine, unplugging from electronics thirty to sixty minutes before your bedtime (which is calculated based on your fixed wake-up time), using cues such as brushing your teeth or putting on your pajamas, dimming your lights, and budgeting thirty minutes for winding down from the day by stretching, listening to calming music, reading, doing relaxation exercises or engaging in mindfulness practice.[8] If you cannot get to sleep within twenty minutes of lying in bed, they suggest getting up, stretching, or reading before trying to fall asleep again.

Our daytime habits also influence the circadian rhythm of our sleep-wake cycle, as light exposure sends signals that keep us awake and alert, and night stimulates the production of melatonin, a hormone that helps us sleep.[9] Experts recommend getting exposure to sunlight during the day, being physically active and regularly exercising, avoiding nicotine, reducing alcohol consumption, cutting down on caffeine in the afternoon and evening, and avoiding eating dinner late in the night (especially big, heavy, or spicy meals). They also suggest using your bed only for sleep (with sex being the one exception).[10]

Finally, our sleep environment can also affect the quality of our sleep, and they recommend making it a calm space, free of disruptions. Specifically, they suggest choosing the best mattress, pillow, sheets, and blankets to meet your needs, setting a cooler temperature (around 65 degrees Fahrenheit), using heavy curtains or an eye mask to block out light, and trying earplugs or a white-noise machine to drown out noise.[11]

What are your typical sleep habits? When do you tend to go to sleep and wake up, and do you get between seven and nine hours of sleep each night? Do you have a nighttime routine that allows you to relax and wind down, or do you watch TV and look at electronic devices in bed? During the daytime, do you get enough exposure to sunlight and sufficient exercise? After exploring these thoughts—perhaps writing them down—practice "the pause" by noticing any emotions that have surfaced, and where you feel them in the body. Then, release them from your awareness and engage in a brief practice of mindfulness of breath. Afterward, you might write down new sleep habits that you would like to cultivate. What would be good cues for you to prepare for sleep? What routine might you follow afterwards? What reward might you anticipate in the morning?

Exercising

Regular physical activity can promote your health, boost your mood, reduce your stress, and improve your sleep.[12] The U.S. Department of Health and Human Services recommends adults engage in at least 150 minutes (2.5 hours) of moderate-intensity aerobic activity each week.[13] Aerobic activities include running, brisk walking, bicycling, playing basketball, dancing, and swimming; they make our hearts beat faster and increase our breathing rate, which strengthens our cardiorespiratory system.[14] The benefits of such aerobic activity include lower risks of mortality, coronary heart disease, hypertension, type-2 diabetes, anxiety, depression, and Alzheimer's disease.[15] People who do 300 minutes (5 hours) a week of moderate-intensity aerobic physical activity have additional health benefits, including the prevention of weight gain. Two minutes of moderate-intensity activity is equivalent to one minute of vigorous-intensity activity: 75 minutes (1.25 hours) to 150 minutes (2.5 hours) a week of vigorous-intensity aerobic activity is equivalent to 150 to 300 minutes of moderate-intensity activity.[16] One can determine whether an activity is moderate or vigorous by using the "talk test": if you can have a conversation, it's moderate; but if you can only say a few words before you have to take a breath, it's vigorous. They advise spreading out such aerobic activity throughout the week, doing it at least three days a week to reduce the risk of injury.[17]

They also recommend doing muscle-strengthening activities at least two days each week. One can lift weights, work with resistance bands, do push-ups, pull-ups, or planks, or even engage in heavy gardening activities. Such activities should be of moderate or greater intensity and involve all the major muscle groups, including the legs, hips, back, chest, abdomen, shoulders, and arms.[18] Finally, they also recommend reducing sedentary behavior—sitting, reclining, or lying down—which has become increasingly prevalent among both adults and children.[19]

An important rule of thumb is to mind the gap between your usual level of physical activity and the new level of activity, which is called the amount of overload. By increasing physical activity gradually over time—creating a small overload and building in rest days for the body to adapt and recover—you reduce the risk of injury.[20] Start with lower intensity activities and gradually increase the frequency and length of physical activities. Activities with the lowest risk of injury include walking, gardening, bicycling, dancing, and swimming; walking has 33 percent of the injury risk of running; sports such as football and soccer that involve collision or contact have a higher risk of injuries.[21] In my case, I found it helpful and motivating to follow a training schedule; those who are physically inactive might consider doing a "couch to 5K" program that starts with running one minute and walking one minute for twenty minutes, resting a day, then running two minutes and walking four minutes for forty minutes.[22]

Engaging in physical activity improves your physical fitness, so that you can perform daily tasks with alertness and have ample energy to engage in leisurely activities. Physical fitness consists of five components: cardiorespiratory fitness (ability to perform whole-body exercise at moderate-to-vigorous activities), musculoskeletal fitness (muscle strength, endurance, and power), flexibility (range of motion at joints or groups of joints), balance, and speed.[23] As the Centers for Disease Control and Prevention (CDC) and the U.S. Department of Health and Human Services point out, even brief amounts of physical activity throughout the day are helpful.

What are your exercise habits? What type of aerobic and muscle-strengthening activities do you do during the week? Do you get at least 150 minutes of moderate-intensity activity each week? How much time during the day are you seated or lying down—sedentary rather than moving around? After exploring these thoughts—perhaps writing them down—practice "the pause" by noticing any emotions or thoughts that have surfaced, and where you feel them in the body. If you find yourself having self-critical thoughts, invite some space between yourself and those thoughts. Then, release them from your awareness and engage in a brief practice of mindfulness of breath. Afterward, you might write down new exercise habits that you would like to cultivate. What would be a good cue for you to prepare for physical activity during your day? What exercise routine might you follow? What reward might you give yourself afterward?

Eating

We explored mindful eating practices in the second chapter, which included engaging the senses, eating modest portions, savoring small bites, eating slowly, and not skipping meals, especially breakfast. Such practices align with recommendations of the CDC. They discourage making sudden, radical changes to eating habits: although it may result in short-term weight loss, it rarely leads to long-term success. Instead, they advocate a more thoughtful approach in which you reflect on your eating habits, identify common triggers for unhealthy eating, replace unhealthy eating habits with healthier ones, and then reinforce those new, healthier eating habits.[24]

To start, you might create a list of your eating and drinking habits over the course of a few days, noting what you ate or drank, the time of day, and how you were feeling at the time, especially if you ate when you were not hungry. Then, highlight habits that led you to overeat, such as eating too fast, eating when you are not hungry, eating while standing up, always eating dessert, or skipping meals. Next, identify triggers that caused you to eat, such as watching TV, experiencing stress, or encountering snacks and sweets at home or work.

Finally, explore ways to avoid such triggers and establish new eating habits, such as putting down one's fork between bites, minimizing distractions such as TV and electronic devices, eating only when truly hungry (as opposed to when one experiences boredom or anxiety), and planning meals ahead of time to ensure that you can eat healthy, well-balanced meals.[25] In this way, we can make conscious, intentional choices about what and how we consume, such as opting to drink water instead of soft drinks, sticking to one serving, abstaining from alcohol or drinking alcohol in moderation—which means two drinks or less a day for men, one drink or less a day for women[26]—and eating healthy, well-balanced meals with plenty of fruits and vegetables.

What are your eating habits? What prompts you to eat? Do you tend to eat slowly or fast? Do you pay attention to each bite, or do you eat while watching the TV or looking at your phone? After exploring these thoughts—perhaps writing them down—practice "the pause" by noticing any emotions that have surfaced, and where you feel them in the body. If you find yourself having self-critical thoughts, invite some space between yourself and those thoughts. Then, release them from your awareness and engage in a brief practice of mindfulness of breath. Afterward, you might write down new eating habits that you would like to cultivate. What would be a good cue for you to prepare for a meal? What routine might you follow as you eat? What reward might await you (or is savoring the meal itself your reward)?

Studying

Learning requires memory, and deep, lasting learning takes effort. If your study habits consist of rereading notes, mass repetition, or cramming, you may be disheartened to discover that science shows that "for true mastery or durability these strategies are largely a waste of time."[27] Instead, try to recall facts, concepts, or events from your memory; such "retrieval practice" strengthens the neural pathways to memory and leads to long-term knowledge.[28] Try to space out practicing a task and alternate it with other subjects, for example, studying a little math, a little history, and a little psychology.[29] As scholars note, "Retrieval is harder and feels less productive, but the effort produces longer-lasting learning and enables more versatile application of it in later settings."[30] When you engage in these kinds of alternating and varied practices, you become adept at identifying the underlying principles behind different problems and better able to solve problems in new situations. You engage in "elaboration" instead of mechanical repetition. As Peter Brown, Henry Roediger, and Mark McDaniel observe in *Make It Stick: The Science of Successful Learning,*

> Elaboration is the process of giving new material meaning by expressing it in your own words and connecting it with what you already know. The more you can explain about the way your learning relates to your prior knowledge, the stronger your grasp of the new learning will be, and the more connections you create that will help you remember it later.[31]

When you make your learning personal and concrete, connecting it to your previous learning and experience, you strengthen that learning.

Spacing, alternating subjects, and testing are what cognitive psychologist Robert Bjork calls "desirable difficulties."[32] Spacing out your study allows you to forget—but then retrieve—information, which leads to long-term retention—as long as you allow enough time that a little forgetting has set in, but not so much forgetting that you have to relearn the material![33] Alternating between different subjects of study constantly challenges you to access motor programs (for motor skills) or retrieve strategies (for cognitive skills), which not only strengthens memory but allows you to extract general rules and transfer learned skills to other contexts.[34] Testing yourself forces you to recall information. These strategies provide opportunities for repeatedly retrieving memory.[35] As Brown, Roediger, and McDaniel note, "That repeated retrieval can so embed knowledge and skills that they become reflexive: the brain acts before the mind has time to think."[36]

You can use metacognition—critical awareness of how you think and learn—to direct, monitor, and assess your own learning. Before you begin a course, you can reflect on what you most want to learn or be able to do by the end of the course, why the course material is important, and how it might connect with your personal or professional goals. You might recall your prior knowledge by brainstorming or generating a concept map that graphically organizes and represents everything that you know about a subject, concept, or question.[37] Below, you can see a concept map that shows key features of a concept map.[38]

You can also construct concept maps to explore a particular question that you seek to answer; they can help you identify gaps in your knowledge, identify sub-questions that you might want to address, and connect concepts related to that question. They may also reveal inaccuracies in your understanding, and it can sometimes be helpful to create concept maps at the beginning

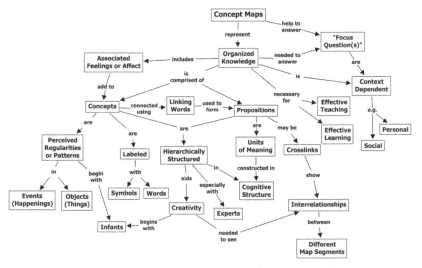

Concept Map. "Concept Map Showing Key Features of Concept Maps" by Joseph D. Novak & Alberto J. Cañas on IHMC.

and end of a course to show how your understanding has changed over time. Finally, concept maps can show how you are organizing and connecting your knowledge in a particular domain, and it can be useful to monitor how that organization of knowledge may change with time, experience, and greater expertise in an area of study.[39]

Self-reflective questions foster metacognition, allowing you to assess what you already know about a topic, to identify points of confusion that arise as you learn more about the topic, to recognize ways your thinking changes about a topic, and to consider how your learning strategies worked or did not work. Such self-reflection can enable us "to take inventory of where we currently are (thinking about what we already know), how we learn (what is working and what is not), and where we want to be (accurately gauging if we've mastered the material)."[40] For example, you can ask yourself the following questions before, during, and after class:

- Planning: What are the goals of the class session going to be? What do I already know about the topic? How could I best prepare for the class session? Where should I sit and what should I be doing (or not doing) to best support my learning during class? What questions do I already have about this topic that I want to find out more about?

- Monitoring: What insights am I having as I experience this class session? What confusions? What questions are arising for me during this class session? Am I writing them down somewhere? Do I find this interesting? Why or why not? How could I make this material personally relevant? Can I distinguish important information from details? If not, how will I figure this out?
- Evaluating: What was today's class session about? What did I hear today that is in conflict with my prior understanding? How did the ideas of today's class session relate to previous class sessions? What do I need to actively go and do to get my questions answered and my confusions clarified? What did I find most interesting about class today?[41]

These reflective questions can activate metacognition before, during, and after class. You can determine which way of taking notes works best for you, keeping in mind that taking notes by hand—rather than typing them on a computer—can allow you to process information, reframe it in your own words, and thereby improve learning.[42] You can assess which note-taking strategies work for you by taking a free online Cornell Note-Taking Strategies course.[43] The Cornell Note Taking System, developed by Walter Pauk, divides pages into three sections—notes, cue, and summary—which allows you to write down the main ideas or fact (notes), ask yourself questions about what you are learning (cue), and summarize what you learned (summary).[44] In this way, the system encourages you to actively reflect on what you are learning in class and assess what you have learned afterwards. After writing down questions in class, you can later try to answer those questions when you study.

You also raise metacognitive, reflective questions before, during, and after you engage in homework assignments or other activities for the course. You might ask:

- Planning: What is the instructor's goal in having me do this task? What are all the things I need to do to successfully accomplish this task? What resources do I need to complete the task? How will I make sure I have them? How much time do I need to complete the task? If I have done something like this before, how could I do a better job this time?
- Monitoring: What strategies am I using that are working well or not working well to help me learn? What other resources could I be using to complete this task? What action should I take to get these? What is most challenging for me about this task? Most confusing? What could I do differently mid-assignment to address these challenges and confusions?

- Assessing: To what extent did I successfully accomplish the goals of the task? To what extent did I use resources available to me? If I were the instructor, what would I identify as strengths of my work and flaws in my work? When I do an assignment or task like this again, what do I want to remember to do differently? What worked well for me that I should use next time?[45]

These types of questions encourage you to take ownership over your own learning and improve your performance in a course.

What are your study habits? How do you prefer to take notes? What learning strategies have been effective for you? Where do you see gaps in your learning strategies? After exploring these thoughts—perhaps writing them down—practice "the pause" by noticing any emotions that have surfaced, and where you feel them in the body. If you find yourself having self-critical thoughts, invite some space between yourself and those thoughts. Then, release them from your awareness and engage in a brief practice of mindfulness of breath. Afterward, you might write down new study habits that you would like to cultivate. What would be a good cue for you to study? What routine might you follow as you study? What reward might await you after your study session?

Recharging

In addition to promoting your physical and intellectual well-being through healthy sleeping, exercising, eating, and studying, you can engage in practices that support mental health, which encompasses your emotional, psychological, and social well-being. As the CDC note, "[Mental health] affects how we think, feel, and act. It also helps determine how we handle stress, relate to others, and make healthy choices."[46] Along with taking care of your body, they recommend meditation, engaging in activities you enjoy, connecting with others, connecting with community or religious organizations, and taking breaks from the news and social media. In his humorous yet heartfelt video "Why Mindfulness Is a Superpower," Dan Harris predicts that mindfulness and meditation will become the next public-health revolution, joining "the pantheon of no-brainers like brushing your teeth, eating well, and taking the meds your doctor prescribes for you."[47] Mindfulness invites us to allow and accept our experiences with curiosity and care, and it encourages openness to other people, situations, and events. Research has shown that mindfulness can especially benefit those in their first year of college by decreasing depression and anxiety,[48] improving well-being and engagement,[49] cultivating an ability to process emotions and cope with stressful circumstances.[50] Research has also shown that the mental-health benefits of mindfulness exceed those from other self-care practices such as diet and physical exercise.[51]

To prevent ourselves from becoming overly drained or stressed, we can take moments to recharge ourselves every day, or build in activities over the course of our week. If we find ourselves being sedentary and sitting for long periods, we can invite movement into our bodies through yoga, tai chi, or another practice. If we find ourselves staring at a screen or trapped behind a desk, we can go for a quick walk outside and engage in the practice of "microdosing mindfulness" described in the first chapter. If we notice we are holding tension in our bodies— often in our jaw, neck, shoulders, or back—we can stretch, do gentle yoga, or engage in progressive muscle relaxation, a technique where you contract muscle groups, hold that muscular in tension, release the tension, and invite relaxation into those areas of your body. If we find ourselves breathing shallowly, we can practice taking slow, deep breaths to calm our nervous systems. If we feel lonely, we can connect and spend time with friends and family. We can also listen to music, sketch or draw, or engage in other creative activities to take a break. These restorative practices can help us bring balance back into our lives.

How do you care for your mental health? What are your ways of recharging? What brings you relaxation, or what energizes you? After exploring these thoughts—perhaps writing them down —practice "the pause" by noticing any emotions that have surfaced, and where you feel them in the body. Then, release them from your awareness and engage in a brief practice of mindfulness of breath. Afterward, you might write down new habits that you would like to cultivate. What would be a good cue for you to recharge? What routine might you follow? What reward might await you afterward?

Finding Flow

We can also engage in activities that challenge us, completely absorb our attention, and bring us joy. Such experiences of "flow" require disciplined concentration, effort, and emotional commitment.[52] As Mihaly Csikzentmihalyi writes, "It is not enough to *know* how to do it; one must *do* it, consistently, in the same way as athletes or musicians who must keep practicing what they know in theory. And this is never easy."[53] In such states of flow, "Thoughts, intentions, feelings, and all the senses are focused on the same goal. Experience is in harmony. And when the flow episode is over, one feels more 'together' than before, not only internally but also with respect to other people and to the world in general."[54] As Czikszentmihalyi notes, flow experiences occur when we engage in tasks that challenge us to exert our skills, that have clear goals and provide immediate feedback, that require our complete attention and psychic energy, that we have a sense of control over, that rid us of self-preoccupation and facilitate greater integration, and that alter our sense of time.[55] These flow states result in a sense of deep enjoyment.

Many activities provide the opportunity to experience flow, including art, music, sports, science, and cooking. Any activity that requires you to develop your skills, that challenges you to apply those skills, and that demands your complete and utter focus can result in experiences of flow, which stimulate growth. By contrast, passive entertainment such as watching TV rarely leads to flow conditions.[56] Yoga is one example of a flow activity: the Sanskrit term *yoga* means "harnessing"—disciplining your body, senses, and mind. In his *Yoga Sutra*, Patañjali describes eight limbs or stages of yoga: moral principles (such as nonviolence and truthfulness), observances (engaging in ascetic practices and cultivating contentment), steady posture, breath control, withdrawal of the senses, concentration, meditation, and pure contemplation on a single object.[57] These moral, physical, and mental activities increase your ability to control your consciousness. For this reason, Czikszentmihalyi considers yoga to be "one of the oldest and most systematic methods of producing the flow experience."[58]

Flow experiences require passion and perseverance—two components of what Angela Duckworth calls "grit."[59] Becoming skilled at an activity requires not only talent, but also effort and endurance—establishing a goal and holding to it in a steadfast way. Duckworth writes,

> First comes *interest*. Passion begins with intrinsically enjoying what you do.... Next comes the capacity to *practice*. One form of perseverance is the daily discipline of trying to do things better than we did yesterday.... Third is purpose. What ripens passion is the conviction that your work matters. For most people, interest without purpose is nearly impossible to sustain for a lifetime.... And, finally, *hope*. Hope is a rising-to-the-occasion kind of perseverance.[60]

When you engage in an activity that aligns with your interests, it leads to greater satisfaction. This requires you to discover that passion, develop it, and deepen it over the course of your life.[61] As Duckworth writes, "The process of interest discovery can be messy, serendipitous, and inefficient. This is because you can't really predict with certainty what will capture your attention and what won't. You can't simply *will* yourself to like things, either."[62] In other words, to find flow, you must first explore activities and identify those that trigger your interests. She suggests asking questions such as, "What do I like to think about? Where does my mind wander? What do I really care about? What matters most to me? How do I enjoy spending my time? And, in contrast, what do I find absolutely unbearable?"[63] After that discovery phase, you develop your interests through deliberate practice, which involves a clearly defined stretch goal, full concentration and effort, immediate feedback, and repetition.[64] When you make such activities part of your daily life, challenges become opportunities to grow, use your skills, and experience flow.

Where do you find flow? What are your interests? How do you practice and develop those skills each week? After exploring these thoughts—perhaps writing them down—practice "the pause" by noticing any emotions that have surfaced, and where you feel them in the body. Then, release them from your awareness and engage in a brief practice of mindfulness of breath. Afterward, you might write down ways you might find flow in your day or week. If you have a clearly identified interest, how might you engage in that activity? If you have not yet identified a clear flow activity, explore what activities you find meaningful and enjoyable, and how you might make time for them. What would be a good cue for you to engage in your flow activity? What routine might you follow? What reward might await you?

Open Awareness

In previous chapters, we explored ways to cultivate mindfulness by focusing on our breath, our body, our feeling tone, our emotions, and our thoughts. With focused attention we keep returning our attention to a particular object, such as the breath, when our minds wander. This chapter invites us to open our awareness to all experience—within ourselves and our surroundings. Instead of bringing our attention back to a particular anchor, we instead rest, relax, and explore the awareness that is already present within us. This type of mindfulness meditation is sometimes called "open monitoring" or "choiceless awareness," as we do not choose to focus on a particular object but instead pay attention to what is most alive for us from one moment to the next. We simply witness things that arise and pass in our awareness. We broaden our awareness to be as spacious, open, and expansive as the sky, and we encounter thoughts, emotions, sounds, sensations, and other things as clouds passing through this sky of awareness.

You may have experienced this sense of spacious awareness out in open spaces. In a similar way, open awareness invites you to include everything within your field of awareness. Just as one might look out at the ocean, taking in its expanse as well as seagulls, pelicans, waves, and boats on the horizon, you cultivate a receptivity to whatever arises in your experience. Instead of becoming lost in thought, distracted, or spacing out, we become attuned to our inner and outer environments. We allow ourselves to be vulnerable, for the sounds, sensations, and emotions to come and go, and we accept everything that arises and passes within our awareness.

Notes

1. Quoted in Salzberg, *Lovingkindness*, 83.

2. Duhigg, *Power of Habit*, xiv.

3. Duhigg, *Power of Habit*, 17.

4. Duhigg, *Power of Habit*, 19.

5. Duhigg, *Power of Habit*, 33.

6. Suni and Vyas, "Sleep Hygiene."

7. Suni and Singh, "How Much Sleep Do We Really Need?"

8. Suni and Vyas, "Sleep Hygiene."

9. Suni and Dimitru, "Circadian Rhythm."

10. Suni and Vyas, "Sleep Hygiene."

11. Suni and Vyas, "Sleep Hygiene."

12. U.S. Dept. of Health and Human Services, *Physical Activity Guidelines for Americans*, 19.

13. U.S. Dept. of Health and Human Services, *Physical Activity Guidelines for Americans*, 8.

14. U.S. Dept. of Health and Human Services, *Physical Activity Guidelines for Americans*, 57.

15. U.S. Dept. of Health and Human Services, *Physical Activity Guidelines for Americans*, 57.

16. U.S. Dept. of Health and Human Services, *Physical Activity Guidelines for Americans*, 58.

17. U.S. Dept. of Health and Human Services, *Physical Activity Guidelines for Americans*, 58.

18. U.S. Dept. of Health and Human Services, *Physical Activity Guidelines for Americans*, 61.

19. They note that adults and children spend approximately 7.7 hours per day (55 percent of their waking time) being sedentary. U.S. Dept. of Health and Human Services, *Physical Activity Guidelines for Americans*, 21.

20. U.S. Dept. of Health and Human Services, *Physical Activity Guidelines for Americans*, 90.

21. U.S. Dept. of Health and Human Services, *Physical Activity Guidelines for Americans*, 89.

22. Runner's World, "This Plan Will Take You."

23. U.S. Dept. of Health and Human Services, *Physical Activity Guidelines for Americans*, 33.

24. Centers for Disease Control and Prevention, "Improving Your Eating Habits."

25. Centers for Disease Control and Prevention, "Improving Your Eating Habits."

26. Centers for Disease Control and Prevention, "Dietary Guidelines for Alcohol."

27. Roediger et al., *Make It Stick*, 3.

28. Roediger et al., *Make It Stick*, 3–4.

29. UCLA Block Learning and Forgetting Lab, "Research."

30. Roediger et al., *Make It Stick*, 4.

31. Roediger et al., *Make It Stick*, 5.

32. UCLA Block Learning and Forgetting Lab, "Research."

33. Roediger et al., *Make It Stick*, 63.

34. UCLA Block Learning and Forgetting Lab, "Research."

35. UCLA Block Learning and Forgetting Lab, "Research."

36. Roediger et al., *Make It Stick*, 29.

37. Ambrose et al., *How Learning Works*, 228.

38. Novak and Cañas, "Theory Underlying Concept Maps."

39. Ambrose et al., *How Learning Works*, 63–64.

40. Learning Center, "Metacognitive Study Strategies."

41. Tanner, "Promoting Student Metacognition."

42. Mueller and Oppenheimer, "Pen Is Mightier than the Keyboard."

43. Cornell University, "Note Taking Strategies."

44. Pauk and Owens, *How to Study in College*, 261–86.

45. Tanner, "Promoting Student Metacognition."

46. Centers for Disease Control and Prevention, "Mental Health."

47. Harris, "Why Mindfulness Is a Superpower."

48. Dvořáková et al., "Promoting Healthy Transition to College."

49. Wingert et al., "Mindfulness-Based Strengths Practice Improves Well-being and Retention in Undergraduates."

50. Weston, "Mindfulness in Class and Life."

51. Moses et al., "When College Students Look After Themselves."

52. Csikszentmihalyi, *Flow*, 4.

53. Csikszentmihalyi, *Flow*, 21.

54. Csikszentmihalyi, *Flow*, 41.

55. Csikszentmihalyi, *Flow*, 49.

56. Csikszentmihalyi, *Flow*, 83.

57. Miller, *Yoga Discipline of Freedom*, 52.

58. Csikszentmihalyi, *Flow*, 106.

59. Duckworth, *Grit*, 9.

60. Duckworth, *Grit*, 91.

61. Duckworth, *Grit*, 103.

62. Duckworth, *Grit*, 104.

63. Duckworth, *Grit*, 114–15.

64. Duckworth, *Grit*, 137.

CHAPTER SEVEN

Using Digital Technologies

The only meaningful questions are: *which* technologies should we
create, with what knowledge and designs, affording what, shared
with whom, for whose benefit, and *to what greater ends*?
—Shannon Vallor[1]

I am not particularly adept at digital technology. During my first week in
college when I set up my email account—admittedly, this was in 1994
when email was in its infancy, the internet was known as the World Wide
Web, and Netscape was the only public web browser—I remember seeing
"username," wondering what might make for a memorable password, and
typing in "platypus." When the next prompt appeared—"password"—I
panicked. There was no backspace, no way of undoing my choice. Resigned, I
entered a password—this time, a much more secure one. For my entire college
career, my email was platypus@stanford.edu. People did tend to remember it,
and I encountered one other person who had (intentionally) chosen "pebble"
for their email instead of their own name, but we were the outliers.

As you can imagine, when faced with taking a general education course
that fulfilled the "Technology and Applied Sciences" category, I found myself
in a conundrum. In fact, I avoided making the decision until the spring of
my senior year. Ultimately, I decided to take a course entitled "Web Design
and Development," lured by the promise that it would enable me to create
and design my own web page. The course taught me how to write HTML
(Hypertext Markup Language) code for websites, and two years later when I
needed a part-time job in graduate school, that training enabled me to work
as a webmaster's assistant at the Pluralism Project. While my first encounter
with digital technology made me feel foolish, my studies improved my digital
skills and began a lifelong exploration of digital technologies.

Digital technologies have advantages and drawbacks, and using them can
impact our thoughts, emotions, actions, and values. As Shannon Vallor writes,

"Technologies invite or afford specific patterns of thought, behavior and valu- ing; they open up new possibilities for human action and foreclose or obscure others."[2] Social media platforms, for example, may limit the number of words in a post or the amount of emoji reactions. These constraints then influence what we write and how we respond, and they may not capture our actual sentiments or emotions. Social media allows people to interact and connect online, but it can also result in less connection to people immediately around us, creating a situation where we are "alone together."[3] We can form "virtual tribes" of friends, family, and acquaintances with which we can stay connected twenty-four hours, seven days a week.[4] In turn, we become more comfortable communicating with others electronically rather than face-to-face, weakening our social and interpersonal skills, and we become dependent on our digital devices and fearful of being without them.[5]

Because digital devices allow us constant access to a wide range of media, most of us tend toward "continuous partial attention," a phrase that tech writer Linda Stone coined to describe the process of attending to multiple sources of information, but at a superficial level. Fueled by the desire to con- tinuously connect and be connected in an effort not to miss out on anything, as Stone remarks, "it is an always-on, anywhere, anytime, anyplace behavior, and it involves an artificial sense of constant crisis."[6] Although useful in certain contexts and reasonable doses, when taken to the extreme, continuous partial attention can increase stress by promoting the belief that one must always be on alert, scanning for a potential opportunity, so as not to miss anything. This creates a feeling of being overwhelmed, overstimulated, and unable to find the "off switches on our devices or ourselves."[7] Continuous partial attention also impedes our ability to perform tasks that require our undivided attention.[8]

In addition to its psychological effects, continuous partial attention has ethical implications, as it makes us less attentive to people surrounding us and to our environment. As Martha Nussbaum has emphasized, moral attention requires that one be "finely aware and richly responsible." She writes, "We live amid bewildering complexities. Obtuseness and refusal of vision are our besetting vices. Responsible lucidity can be wrestled from that darkness only by painful vigilant effort, the intense scrutiny of particulars. Our highest and hardest task is to make ourselves people 'on whom nothing is lost.'"[9] Moral attention requires considerable effort and concentration on the particularity of people and situations, which continuous partial attention undermines.

This chapter invites you to reflect on the ways that you use digital technol- ogies and the effects that they have on you. Are you among the 79 percent of smartphone owners who check their device within fifteen minutes of waking each morning?[10] Do you find yourself pulled to social media and still scrolling hours later? As Nir Eyal notes, technologists use cycles of hooks, beginning with external triggers like push notifications and emails, to form habits until users eventually engage with their products without being prompted.[11] Once users form positive associations with the technology, feelings of boredom or fear of missing out elicit negative sensations that automatically prompt them to turn to the technology to alleviate their discomfort.[12] At that point, they are hooked. As Eyal writes, "With every post, tweet, or pin, users anticipate social validation. Rewards of the tribe keep users coming back, wanting more. . . . The uncertainty of what users will find each time they visit the site creates the intrigue needed to pull them back again."[13] The automaticity of such habits and the addictive potential of digital technologies warrant further consideration and caution. As Jenny Odell writes,

> We need to be able to think across different time scales when the medias-cape would have us think in twenty-four-hour (or shorter) cycles, to pause for consideration when clickbait would have us click, to risk unpopular-ity by searching for context when our Facebook feed is an outpouring of unchecked outrage and scapegoating, to closely study the way media and advertising play upon our emotions, to understand the algorithmic versions of ourselves that such forces have learned to manipulate, and to know when we are being guilted, threatened, and gaslighted into reactions that come not from will and reflection but from fear and anxiety.[14]

Digital technologies, by design, play on our emotions: they depend on our feelings of boredom and anxiety, they entice us with endless distractions, and they enflame us into states of righteous indignation. If I were to interrupt you while you were scrolling through social media or clicking through websites, and I asked you how you felt physically, mentally, and emotionally, chances are you would be sitting in an uncomfortable position, distracted, and emo-tionally charged. We rarely feel attentive, relaxed, or emotionally balanced when we're online.[15] But unless we are resigned to being pawns in our digital world, we need to interrupt the cycle of hooks, invite space for reflection, and develop new digital habits. Mindfulness can provide us with "mental antibod-ies" to resist succumbing to the manipulation of habit-forming technologies.[16] We can practice "the pause" before immediately clicking, sharing, or posting. This chapter explores ways of approaching multitasking, web searching, and social media with greater intention and awareness. At the end of each section, you will find questions that encourage you to reflect further on your digital habits.

In addition to engaging more mindfully with digital technologies, we can develop our digital literacy skills so that we find, create, and share digital content ethically and responsibly. "Digital literacy" refers to the ability to find, evaluate, create, and communicate or share digital content.[17] Unlike printed media, digital media can contain hyperlinks, videos, audio clips, images, graphics, share buttons, and comments sections, and you choose how to navigate through those features, whether to click on a link to another text, and whether to share information with other people. You can create and share various types of digital content, including emails, blogs, social media posts, videos, and podcasts. Digital sharing can be a powerful tool for collaboration and civic engagement, but it can also have repercussions for safety and privacy.[18]

Multitasking

We have all done it. In fact, my six-year-old during remote learning quickly discovered ways of remaining undetected as he read comic books while on Zoom. Zoom has become an efficient and convenient way to meet with others, either one-on-one, in small groups, or even large webinars. But Zoom fatigue is real, and you likely experienced it at some point during the COVID-19 pandemic. Jeremy Bailenson, the founding director of the Stanford Virtual Human Interaction Lab, argues that this is because Zoom requires excessive amounts of close-up gaze (in face-to-face situations, we would not be interacting as close), increases our cognitive load (for example, in gallery view, we constantly jump from face to face), heightens our self-evaluation (unless we "hide self view"), and constrains our physical mobility, which contributes to a more sedentary lifestyle.[19] Zoom also affects our sense of social connection: millisecond audio delays in responses negatively impact our perception of interactions, and Zoom does not allow us to align our gaze with those on the screen: in order for the viewer to feel seen, the other person has to stare at the camera instead of their face.[20]

There are several strategies for mitigating against screen fatigue and enabling you to stay more alert and engaged online. You can take breaks, stepping away from the screen, moving around, and stretching your body. To avoid eye strain, which can cause blurred vision, dry eyes, and headaches, you can follow the "20-20-20" rule recommended by ophthalmologists: for every 20 minutes you spend looking at a screen, spend 20 full seconds looking at an object 20 feet away from you.[21] You can also engage in mindfulness or other contemplative practices, grounding yourself in your body and taking slow deep breaths. These techniques can help us take a respite from the screen and center ourselves.

We make moment-to-moment decisions of what we pay attention to— online and offline. As David Levy, author of *Mindful Tech*, points out, "The challenge we now face boils down to this: our devices have vastly extended our attentional choices, but the human attentional capacity remains unchanged."[22] When we are multitasking, we are constantly shifting our attention back and forth between tasks, and this rapid task-switching diverts time from paying attention to either task. Moreover, we are simultaneously maintaining a degree of "open attention, which will allow us to notice other interesting attentional opportunities as they arise."[23] As a result, most studies have found multitasking less efficient than working on a single task and that it results in lower performance.[24] Nevertheless, many of us continue to multitask, our attention diverted by distractions.

But, by training our attention, we can strengthen our ability to decide whether to switch tasks. Levy's research shows that people given eight weeks of attention training were less stressed, less fragmented in their work, switched tasks less frequently, and spent more time on their primary task.[25] To cultivate skillful digital behavior, Levy recommends we learn to engage and strengthen two forms of attention: task focus (the ability to remain focused on what you are doing in a particular moment) and self-awareness (the ability to notice how you are feeling when you are doing whatever you are doing).[26] We may even benefit from periods of being unplugged entirely—either not using our digital devices (laptop, phone, tablet), or deciding not to use a particular application such as email or social media. Levy's research has shown three main benefits of unplugging: increased productivity and focus, better use of time, and greater relaxation and stress reduction.[27]

Here, I invite you to reflect on your own experience of multitasking. What makes you multitask? When do you decide to switch from one task to another, and why? When do you refrain from switching tasks, and why? Do you notice any emotions that prompt you to multitask? After exploring these thoughts—perhaps writing them down—practice "the pause" by noticing any emotions that have surfaced, and where you feel them in the body. If you find yourself having self-critical thoughts, invite some space between yourself and those thoughts. Then, release them from your awareness and engage in a brief practice of mindfulness of breath. Afterward, you might write down ways you might want to approach your multitasking behavior. What would be a good cue for you to stay on task? What routine might you follow? What reward might you give yourself for staying on task?

Web Searching

"Google it." Often when we have a question, we turn to web search engines like Google to find answers. However, their results are not always reliable or credible. Google uses an algorithm to search its own index of the web and locate relevant results based on keywords, links, location, and fresh content.[28] Search results vary from person to person, location to location, computer to computer, and day to day. Moreover, Safiya Umoja Noble has shown that search algorithms can yield racist and sexist results: one such instance of "algorithmic oppression" was finding that searches for Black, Latinx, and Asian girls typically resulted in pornographic websites.[29] In this way, search engines amplify certain voices and silence others.[30] Top search results are not necessarily more reliable or relevant, so try to resist the temptation to consider ease of access as determining the quality of information, an unfortunately widespread view among college students.[31] As others have pointed out, "A typical Google results page these days is packed with advertisements, recommended results, and websites that are the best at search engine optimization rather than the most reliable, accurate answers to your questions."[32]

You can improve your search results by using targeted search strategies. You can put search terms in quotation marks, use a minus sign (-) immediately before a keyword to exclude it, or a plus sign (+) immediately before a keyword to ensure it is included. To search particular websites, you can include "site:" followed by the main URL after our search terms (e.g., site:wikipedia.org). You can use Google's Advanced Search page to restrict results to a particular language, region, or to search for particular file types (PDFs, Word documents, Excel spreadsheets, GIFs, etc.). Finally, you can use search operators, such as OR between keywords to search for several terms at once, parentheses to group search terms (e.g., (McGuire (Beverley OR Bev))), or an asterisk (*) as a sort of wildcard for Google to return the most popular hits (e.g., how to learn * on YouTube).[33] You can also use Google's specialized sites in your web search: on Google Image you can search for images, or even do a reverse image search to fact-check an image's source; on Google Trends you can see trends in Google searches; on Google Scholar you can find scholarly articles and citations within them.

After identifying relevant sources from your search, evaluate and fact-check them. Use the SIFT model—Stop, Investigate the source, Find better coverage, Trace claims, quotes, and media back to the original context—to determine if the source is significant and trustworthy, to evaluate whether their claims are broadly accepted, rejected, or debated, and to locate the origin of the source. In *Web Literacy for Student Fact-Checkers*, a freely accessible online resource for developing digital literacy, Mike Caulfield writes, "When you feel strong emotion—happiness, anger, pride, vindication—and all that emotion pushes you to share a 'fact' with others, STOP. Above all, these are the claims that you must fact check."[34] Research has shown that digital content that elicits strong emotions—anger, but also awe—goes viral quicker.[35] As a result, Caulfield suggests using strong emotions as a cue: "a trigger for your new fact-checking habit."[36] You can fact-check a claim, quote, or article by searching reputable fact-checking sites using the "site:URL" function on Google. Caulfield recommends Politifact, Factcheck.org, Washington Post Fact Checker, Snopes, Truth Be Told, NPR Fact-Check, and Hoax Slayer, though he also mentions more specialized sites such as SciCheck and Quote Investigator.[37]

The second move—investigating the source—means examining the source of the digital content. Identify sponsored content, such as ads made to look like news stories, and notice when articles have a "sponsored" indicator above or below them.[38] On news sites, be careful to distinguish their news articles from syndicated content from the *Associated Press, Reuters*, or another site. For viral content that tends to hide or not link its source, Caulfield recommends right-clicking your mouse (or control-clicking on a Mac) to search Google for the highlighted source and adding a term or bit of text from the article, then scanning the URLs of the results to determine which source looks best.[39] For viral images, he suggests using textual information from the image for a Google search to determine the earliest post, or doing a reverse image search on Google to locate the earliest image by clicking on the "Tools" button, using the "Time" dropdown to select "custom range," and then selecting 2009 or 2010 as a starting point, and either increasing the date if it does not yield results, or decreasing the date if it yields too many.[40]

The third move—finding better coverage—encourages you to "read laterally" about a source instead of vertically. In lieu of staying within a website to evaluate its reliability, leave the site after quickly scanning it, open up new browser tabs, and see what other authoritative sources say about the site to judge its credibility.[41] As Sam Wineburg and Sarah McGrew emphasize, "Any organization with a competent web designer and a modicum of digital savvy can design a site that aces these questions [of whether they update their site and provide their author's credentials], whether the organization is a trusted purveyor of information or not."[42] As a result, they emphasize the importance of taking bearings and lateral reading. They write,

> Before diving deeply into unfamiliar content, chart a plan for moving forward. Taking bearings is what sailors, aviators, and hikers do to plot their course toward a desired destination. Landing in unfamiliar territory, fact checkers set out for their destination—making a judgment of credibility— only after gaining a sense of where they had landed.[43]

On the internet, this often entails reading laterally: drawing on other internet resources to learn more about the website and its claims, rather than examining the appearance or content of the original website. Lateral reading differs significantly from close reading, in which you carefully analyze a text, attend to an author's syntax or word choice, and consider how such choices impact the meaning of the text. You cannot determine the credibility of a website by focusing on whether the URL is an .org or .com, the page is free of typos, or it includes advertisements.[44] As Wineburg and McGrew write, "At a time when the Internet is characterized by polished web design, search engine optimization, and organizations vying to appear trustworthy, such guidelines create a false sense of security."[45] Instead, they recommend following the habits of fact-checkers who carefully reviewed search results (the URL and sentence fragments) before clicking on a result, demonstrating "click restraint."[46] By scanning the search-engine results—not only the first, but also the second and third pages—they "gain an overall picture of the digital territory into which they had landed."[47] As Mike Caulfield writes, "Only when they've got their bearings from the rest of the network do they re-engage with the content."[48]

As you evaluate a website or publication to determine its authority and reliability, you could follow guidelines followed by Wikipedia and espoused by the Digital Polarization Initiative, which define reliable sources according to their process, expertise, and aim.[49] As Mike Caulfield writes,

> A reliable source for facts should have a process in place for encouraging accuracy, verifying facts, and correcting mistakes. Note that reputation and

process might be apart from issues of bias: the *New York Times* is thought by many to have a center-left bias, the *Wall Street Journal,* a center-right bias, and *USA Today* a centrist bias. Yet fact-checkers of all political stripes are happy to be able to track a fact down to one of these publications since they have reputations for a high degree of accuracy and issue corrections when they get the facts wrong.[50]

Similarly, the process of peer review seeks to ensure reliability by having experts in the field review submissions without knowing the name of the author (which is called "blind peer review"), so they can identify any flaws or inaccuracies of data or analysis. In addition to process, you can consider the expertise of the author: researchers in a particular area of study, professionals in an area specialization, and reporters who communicate views of experts and professionals. Finally, you can judge the aim of the source: "what the publication, author, or media source is attempting to accomplish."[51] As Caulfield notes, "Aims are complex. Respected scientific journals, for example, aim for prestige within the scientific community, but must also have a business model. A site like the *New York Times* relies on ad revenue but is also dependent on maintaining a reputation for accuracy."[52] For this reason, he suggests thinking about the incentives of an article or author to get things right: if they have strong incentives, which you can see in the intent of the author, business model, and reputation and history of the publication, they are more reliable. To identify these three elements (process, expertise, and aim) of an unfamiliar site, Caulfield recommends searching the site on Google, or for smaller sites, using WHOIS to determine the administrator of the site domain.

The final move—tracing a source to its original context—involves locating the original source of a claim, quote, or image. For example, you might trace data from a research study back to the original scholarly article and journal in which it was published. Then you can determine whether the source has been altered or accurately represents the way it appears in its original context.

Here, I invite you to reflect on how you engage in web searches. When and how do you usually search for information on the internet? When you share content on social media, what motivates you to do so? Are you driven by emotion? Do you fact-check content before you share it? After exploring these thoughts—perhaps writing them down—practice "the pause" by noticing any emotions that have surfaced, and where you feel them in the body. If you find yourself having self-critical thoughts, invite some space between yourself and those thoughts. Then, release them from your awareness and engage in a brief practice of mindfulness of breath. Afterward, you might write down ways you might encourage "click restraint" and lateral reading in the future. What would be a good cue for you to fact-check? What routine might you follow? What reward might you give yourself for ensuring the accuracy and reliability of what you share?

Social Media

Social media, such as social networking sites, video sharing sites, as well as blogging and microblogging platforms, enable people to participate in and create what danah boyd calls "networked publics."[53] These have four characteristics that distinguish them from traditional physical public spaces:

Persistence: the durability of online expression and content
Visibility: the potential audience who can bear witness
Spreadability: the ease with which content can be shared
Searchability: the ability to find content[54]

As a result of the endurance, visibility, and accessibility of social media posts, you are "often 'on the record' to an unprecedented degree . . . in networked publics, interactions are often public by default, private through effort."[55] Social media also encourages you to easily share and spread content by clicking on simple buttons for reposting, which can be used for different purposes: as boyd notes, "Spreadability can be leveraged to rally people for a political cause or to spread rumors."[56] Finally, search engines make it possible for others to access social media posts and potentially take them out of context.

When navigating social media, it becomes important to pay attention to context, audience, and identity. Social media tends to collapse contexts that we can more easily keep separate offline. As boyd notes, "A context collapse occurs when people are forced to grapple simultaneously with otherwise unrelated social contexts that are rooted in different norms and seemingly demand different social responses."[57] Second, when we are on social media, our audiences may not be visible or known to us.[58] Finally, social media can influence our sense of identity and self-worth as we engage in self-presentation and social comparison. When we feel pressured to present ourselves only in a positive light, it can prevent us from expressing and exploring other aspects of ourselves, which in turn may hinder our growth and personal development.[59]

Teenagers and young adults tend to be less skeptical of social media compared to adults. As boyd explains, social media enables teens' entry into public life and meets their desire for social connection, whereas adults already have access to public environments and tend to compare networked public spaces to those other spaces. Unlike previous generations of teenagers who could roam about their neighborhood or congregate in malls, teenagers now have limited geographic freedom and less time. boyd writes,

> Teens simply have far fewer places to be together in public than they once did. And the success of social media must be understood partly in relation to this shrinking social landscape. Facebook, Twitter, and MySpace are not only new public spaces: they are in many cases the only "public" spaces in which teens can easily congregate with large groups of their peers. More significantly, teens can gather in them while still physically stuck at home.[60]

This affordance of social media—the ability to connect online with others while at home—was especially important under stay-at-home orders and remote learning during the pandemic.

Social media can be used as a tool for connection, but it can also fuel rumination and isolation. One research study suggests that social media can decrease experiences of loneliness if used to communicate directly with others through personalized messages or semi-public conversations, but it correlates with feelings of disconnection and depression if passively consumed through scanning friends' updates or broadcasting one's own activities.[61] As Stephen Marche writes, "It's a lonely business, wandering the labyrinths of our friends' and pseudo-friends' projected identities, trying to figure out what part of ourselves we ought to project, who will listen, and what they will hear."[62] Social media compels us to constantly consider how we present and package ourselves; it demands that we continually assert and maintain the appearance of being happy and upbeat. As Howard Gardner and Katie Davis observe, "This packaging has the consequence of minimizing a focus on an inner life, on personal conflicts and struggles, on quiet reflection and personal planning."[63] Ultimately, they have found, it can discourage taking risks. Moreover, when we compare ourselves with others on social media—especially when we make upward social comparisons with those whom we consider superior or better to ourselves—it can result in negative views of the self, negative emotions, and depressive symptoms.[64] It can also lead to rumination or brooding, where we become trapped in repetitive and anxious thoughts about ourselves or our experiences, which contributes to depression.

We can engage with social media actively or passively, in enjoyable or depleting ways.[65] As Howard Gardner and Katie Davis observe, "Technology is neither inherently benign nor inherently evil. Instead, it is the *uses* to which we put various technologies that shape the outcomes. . . . It is the interaction between technology and individual and social values, practices, and norms that determine whether the outcomes are positive or problematic."[66] They distinguish between what they call "app mentality," "app-enablement," and "app-dependence." "App mentality" refers to the fast, on-demand nature of apps, that "any question or desire one has should be satisfied immediately and definitively."[67] Apps can be enabling if used "as springboards to new experiences and areas of knowledge, meaningful relationships, and creative expression,"[68] but they can foster dependence if we allow them to restrict or even determine our values and goals, or if we turn to them before looking within ourselves or reaching out to friends.[69] As Gardner and Davis emphasize, "Apps can make you lazy, discourage the development of new skills, limit you to mimicry or tiny trivial tweaks or tweets—or they can open up whole new worlds for imagining, creating, producing, remixing, even forging new identities and enabling rich forms of intimacy."[70]

For these reasons, we should pay attention to our social media habits and the impact they have on us. When you feel the urge to use social media, Catherine Price, author of *How to Break Up with Your Phone*, encourages you to ask the questions: What for? Why now? What else?[71] What is it for—what is your purpose for going on social media? Why now—did you need to do something, or was it boredom, anxiety, or some other craving? What else could you be doing? Here, I invite you to reflect on your use of social media. What makes you use it? Do you tend to compare yourselves to others on social media? When you post, what motivates you to do so? How do you usually feel afterward—physically, mentally, and emotionally? After exploring these thoughts—perhaps writing them down—practice "the pause" by noticing any emotions that have surfaced, and where you feel them in the body. If you find yourself having self-critical thoughts, invite some space between yourself and those thoughts. Then, release them from your awareness and engage in a brief practice of mindfulness of breath. Afterward, you might write down ways you might change your social media habits. What would be a good cue for you? What routine might you follow? What reward might you give yourself?

ePortfolios

We have explored ways that social media encourages a presentation and performance of a polished, packaged self, which can discourage you from entertaining ambiguity, sitting with uncertainty, or exploring alternative identities. Moreover, the constant need to project and track oneself online leaves little time for contemplation or personal development. As Gardner and Davis write,

> Researchers have identified a number of benefits that accrue when a brain is at rest (relatively speaking) and focused inward. The downtime appears to play a restorative role, promoting feelings of well-being and, ultimately, helping individuals to focus their attention more efficiently when it's needed. Daydreaming, wandering, and wondering have positive facets. Introspection may be particularly important for young people who are figuring out who and what they want to be. Without time and space to ponder alternative ways of being in the world—without breaking away from an app-determined life path—young persons risk prematurely foreclosing their identities, making it less likely that they will achieve a fully realized and personally fulfilling sense of self.[72]

When we turn to our digital devices to seek outside assurance, instead of looking within ourselves, we lose opportunities for self-exploration and developing a sense of autonomy.

ePortfolios can provide space for this kind of reflection, enabling you to consider what you are learning and discovering personally and professionally through your classes and extracurricular experiences. An ePortfolio is an electronic collection of materials—such as papers, creative work, presentations, leadership activities, and other projects—that shows your learning over time. It allows you to store these artifacts and reflect on what you learned from them, which heightens your metacognitive awareness. ePortfolios also encourage you to integrate what you have learned across disciplines and experiences, so that you can apply your learning to new contexts and situations. You can create multiple ePortfolios and explore various avenues of self-exploration and self-expression. ePortfolios can also allow you to take ownership of your learning: you can select work that you consider significant and meaningful, and you determine the insights you had and skills you gained from your experiences. You can tailor ePortfolios to showcase your achievements for professional purposes, but you can also keep them private and use them to reflect and deepen your learning. For the former, you could consider ways that your experiences helped you develop career competencies, such as self-development, communication, critical thinking, equity and inclusion, leadership, professionalism, teamwork, and technology.[73] For the latter, you could reflect on your development and synthesize your learning across multiple contexts.

When using an ePortfolio platform—as when using any digital technology—you should consider how your content will be viewed or used. Some companies and institutions collect personal information from ePortfolios, and if they do, you have the right to know what data is collected, by whom, and for what purpose. Most ePortfolio platforms allow you to determine the privacy settings for your ePortfolio, so you can decide with whom you share it, or whether you make it public. However, whenever you work in digital environments, it raises ethical questions and uncertainty about ownership of data, privacy, and disclosure in online contexts.[74] As Jen Ross remarks, "Every time we act online, something is left behind that is us, but not us—a trace. Database structures, the technical underpinnings of online services and applications, including blogs and e-portfolios, produce and work with traces through categorization, identification, sorting, storage, and reconfigurability."[75] Because you lack control over your digital traces, and you may associate online writing with performance, you might consider reflecting on your work and experiences offline—even by hand. This can also encourage a slower process of reflection. If you do choose to make your ePortfolio public, it will become part of your digital presence and digital footprint. Consider how you are presenting yourself online to ensure that it aligns with the values, skills, and identity that you hope to convey.[76] You can learn about your online presence by Googling yourself, listing the top five sites from the search result, and considering what someone might say about you from the sites (first, without looking at the content, and then, after looking at the content on the sites).[77] This can help you identify your "digital shadow" or passive digital footprint; ePortfolios, by contrast, can allow you to shape and manage your online presence. A final consideration pertains to the work you share publicly in your ePortfolios: be sure to follow copyright laws, including references and citing sources for images used, and be aware that your work may then be used and repurposed by others.

Kindness

To counterbalance social comparisons and negative views of self that are often fueled by social media, we can engage in practices of kindness toward ourselves and others. Kindness, sometimes called loving-kindness, refers to a quality of goodwill, human warmth, and friendliness towards others. We have this potential to meet ourselves and others with care and tenderness—what some have called "a boundless heart."[78] Kindness does not refer to an emotion or fleeting state, but instead an attitude and way of being in the world where we befriend all people and circumstances, even those that may be challenging or difficult. We meet them with care and gentleness. As Sharon Salzberg notes, "[Kindness]—the sense of love that is not bound to desire, that does not have to pretend that things are other than the way they are—overcomes the illusion of separateness, of not being part of a whole."[79] Buddhist traditions liken kindness to gentle rain that falls on everything without discrimination, or true friends who remain constant during times of happiness or sadness.[80] Jon Kabat-Zinn, the pioneer of mindfulness-based stress reduction, refers to kindness as "the affirmation and honoring of a core goodness in others and in oneself."[81]

The foundation of kindness is befriending oneself—knowing how to be our own friend. It draws from our own innate wish to be happy, healthy, free from harm, and live with ease. A simple practice of kindness meditation involves repeating four phrases of kindness, first for ourselves and then for others. I use, "May I be happy, may I be healthy, may I be free from harm, and may I live with ease," but you can experiment and alter the phrases. Salzberg encourages you to "discover personally in your own heartfelt investigation what is truly significant for you."[82] You can begin a formal practice of cultivating kindness by sitting comfortably and reflecting on your wish to be happy, or the good within you. Without trying to force any feelings of kindness within yourself, you simply gently repeat the phrases. As Salzberg notes, "There are times when feelings of unworthiness come up strongly, and you clearly see the conditions that limit your love for yourself. Breathe gently, accept these feelings to have arisen, remember the beauty of your wish to be happy, and return to the [kindness] phrases."[83]

Next, you can reflect on what you value most in a friend, or what you would like to offer others as their friend, and you direct kindness toward a friend. Calling to mind someone that you easily feel warmth and friendliness for—it may be a friend, a loved one, or a pet—take a moment to visualize them. Recall their good-heartedness, their good qualities, and their own wish to be happy, and feel any natural warmth and friendliness that arises toward them. You can then direct your phrases to them: "May they be happy, may they be healthy, may they be free from harm, and may they live with ease."

Third, you can draw to mind a stranger—someone you may encounter occasionally at a food store, gas station, or restaurant, but toward whom you have no strong feelings of like or dislike. Calling them to mind and sensing their own wish to be happy, you can then direct the phrases to that person.

Fourth, you can call to mind someone with whom you have some minor tension, frustration, or difficulty—not someone who has deeply hurt or harmed you. After directing kindness toward yourself, a friend, and a neutral person, you then draw this person to mind. Recognizing that all beings deserve care, well-being, and happiness, as Salzberg notes, "we put aside the unpleasant traits of such a being and try instead to get in touch with the part of them that deserves to be loved."[84] You then direct the phrases toward that person. If feelings of anger or sadness arise, you allow them to pass through; if they become overwhelming, you can return to directing kindness toward a friend. Be patient with yourself and, Salzberg writes, "remember that whatever anger, fear, or sorrow arises will pass away, and we can always return to the intention to care for ourselves and for all beings."[85]

Finally, we can repeat the phrases and direct kindness to all beings—"to all beings everywhere, without division, without exclusion, and without end."[86] In this way, kindness practice begins with yourself and then extends outward to friends, neutral people, those with whom we may have slight difficulties, and all beings everywhere.

Afterward, you might reflect on your experience of practicing kindness. What did it feel like to direct kindness to yourself, and to others? What supports this attitude of kindness, and what are the challenges to opening your heart in this way? How might you cultivate an attitude of kindness in your everyday life? For example, when you are waiting in line, instead of viewing the people in front of you as obstacles and fueling a sense of impatience, can you connect to them as fellow human beings wishing to be happy and instead direct kindness towards them? We have many opportunities to cultivate this attitude of care and concern for others. When we encounter resistance to cultivating kindness, we can direct our attention to those obstacles, cultivating care and kindness toward them as well.

In addition to honing our ability to attend to our physical sensations, emotions, and thoughts, we can cultivate this quality of kindness within ourselves that can improve our relationship with ourselves and with others. Kindness shares many qualities with mindfulness, including presence and acceptance, and we can bring an attitude of kindness to each moment and every person we encounter. To be clear, kindness practice is not about manufacturing feelings of niceness, or liking people that you dislike. Instead, kindness involves acknowledging that all people wish to be happy and deserve kindness, and it extends feelings of goodwill and friendliness to others.

Notes

1. Vallor, *Technology and the Virtues*, 13.
2. Vallor, *Technology and the Virtues*, 2.
3. Turkle, *Alone Together*.
4. Levine and Dean, *Generation on a Tightrope*, 53.
5. Levine and Dean, *Generation on a Tightrope*, 75.
6. Stone, "Continuous Partial Attention."
7. Stone, "Continuous Partial Attention."
8. McHaney, *New Digital Shoreline*, 34–36.
9. Nussbaum, "'Finely Aware and Richly Responsible,'" 516.
10. Eyal, *Hooked*, 1.
11. Eyal, *Hooked*, 5.
12. Eyal, *Hooked*, 48–49.
13. Eyal, *Hooked*, 101.
14. Odell, *How to Do Nothing*, 93.
15. Levy, *Mindful Tech*, 3.
16. Eyal, *Hooked*, 176.
17. Loewus, "What Is Digital Literacy?"
18. Loewus, "What Is Digital Literacy?"
19. Bailenson, "Nonverbal Overload."
20. Hudson, "Why Video Conferencing Is So Tiring"; Lee, "Neuropsychological Exploration of Zoom Fatigue."
21. Boyd, "Computers, Digital Devices and Eye Strain."
22. Levy, *Mindful Tech*, 3.
23. Levy, *Mindful Tech*, 32.
24. Levy, *Mindful Tech*, 86.
25. Levy, *Mindful Tech*, 113.
26. Levy, *Mindful Tech*, 4.
27. Levy, *Mindful Tech*, 142.
28. Google, "How Google Search Works."
29. Noble, *Algorithms of Oppression*, 4.
30. USC Annenberg, "Algorithms of Oppression: Safiya Umoja Noble."
31. Burton and Chadwick, "Investigating the Practices of Student Researchers."

32. Nield, "How to Get Google Search Results That Are Actually Useful."

33. Nield, "How to Get Google Search Results That Are Actually Useful."

34. Caulfield, "Building a Fact-Checking Habit By Checking Your Emotions."

35. Shaer, "What Emotion Goes Viral the Fastest?"

36. Caulfield, "Building a Fact-Checking Habit By Checking Your Emotions."

37. Caulfield, "Fact-Checking Sites."

38. Caulfield, "Identifying Sponsored Content."

39. Caulfield, "Tracking the Source of Viral Content."

40. Caulfield, "Filtering by Time and Place to Find the Original."

41. Wineburg and McGrew, "Lateral Reading and the Nature of Expertise."

42. Wineburg and McGrew, "Lateral Reading and the Nature of Expertise," 2.

43. Wineburg and McGrew, "Lateral Reading and the Nature of Expertise," 30.

44. Wineburg and McGrew, "Lateral Reading and the Nature of Expertise," 31.

45. Wineburg and McGrew, "Lateral Reading and the Nature of Expertise," 31.

46. Wineburg and McGrew, "Lateral Reading and the Nature of Expertise," 32.

47. Wineburg and McGrew, "Lateral Reading and the Nature of Expertise," 33.

48. Caulfield, "What 'Reading Laterally' Means."

49. Caulfield, "Evaluating a Website or Publication's Authority."

50. Caulfield, "Evaluating a Website or Publication's Authority."

51. Caulfield, "Evaluating a Website or Publication's Authority."

52. Caulfield, "Evaluating a Website or Publication's Authority."

53. boyd, *It's Complicated*, 6.

54. boyd, *It's Complicated*, 11.

55. boyd, *It's Complicated*, 11.

56. boyd, *It's Complicated*, 12.

57. boyd, *It's Complicated*, 31.

58. Betton and Woolard, *Teen Mental Health in an Online World*, 29–30.

59. Yang et al., "Social Media Social Comparison."

60. boyd, *It's Complicated*, 21.

61. Marche, "Is Facebook Making Us Lonely?"

62. Marche, "Is Facebook Making Us Lonely?"

63. Gardner and Davis, *App Generation*, 61.

64. Yang et al., "Social Media Social Comparison."

65. Betton and Woolard, *Teen Mental Health in an Online World*, 31.

66. Gardner and Davis, *App Generation*, xiii.

67. Gardner and Davis, *App Generation*, xi.

68. Gardner and Davis, *App Generation*, xiii.

69. Gardner and Davis, *App Generation*, 10.

70. Gardner and Davis, *App Generation*, 33.

71. Price, *How to Break Up with Your Phone*, 92–93.
72. Gardner and Davis, *App Generation*, 74.
73. "What Is Career Readiness?"
74. Ross, "Engaging with 'Webness.'"
75. Ross, "Engaging with 'Webness,'" 103.
76. Reynolds and Patton, *Leveraging the ePortfolio*, 102.
77. Reynolds and Patton, *Leveraging the ePortfolio*, 107.
78. Feldman, *Boundless Heart*.
79. Salzberg, *Loving-Kindness*, 21.
80. Salzberg, *Loving-Kindness*, 24.
81. Jon Kabat-Zinn, foreword to *Loving-Kindness* by Sharon Salzberg, ix.
82. Salzberg, *Loving-Kindness*, 30.
83. Salzberg, *Loving-Kindness*, 32.
84. Salzberg, *Loving-Kindness*, 79.
85. Salzberg, *Loving-Kindness*, 82.
86. Salzberg, *Loving-Kindness*, 98.

CHAPTER EIGHT

Engaging in Difficult Conversations

On the turning away
From the pale and downtrodden
And the words they say
Which we won't understand.
Don't accept that what's happening
Is just a case of others' suffering,
Or you'll find that you're joining in
The turning away.
—Pink Floyd, "On The Turning Away"

Living in the Native American theme house Muwekma-Tah-Ruk and studying the history of Indigenous peoples in the United States made my social identity as a white American very salient, especially when I engaged in difficult conversations about systems of oppression with my housemates of color. Sometimes, I would accompany them to political rallies where student activists would protest what was being done by white people, and I experienced considerable dissonance because I was white. Despite my discomfort—or perhaps, because of it—engaging in dialogue across difference profoundly transformed my worldview and opened my eyes to entirely new life experiences and perspectives. Sharon Holland, a professor from the English department, would facilitate our conversations, never shirking away from controversial and troubling topics. She held space for all voices to be heard and respected, and I learned the value of listening for understanding. Our residential learning community provided a model and foundation for later conversations I would have with people from different countries, cultures, and religious traditions. It taught me the value of situating yourself (where you come from and where you are), sharing a context (attending to where we stand together), and acknowledging such situatedness when entering conversations, since our relationships to shared contexts differ.

As we explored in the previous chapter, digital technologies have impacted the degree to which we engage in conversations with other people. As Sherry Turkle writes in *Alone Together*,

> People will readily say that in face-to-face conversation they learn how to get on with other people and gather important understandings about their children, spouses, parents, and partners. And yet they will also say that they are happy to use technology to flee these conversations. Why? Because face-to-face conversations are difficult. Awkward. Spontaneous. Unscripted. Messy. One young man tells me he will do anything to avoid a conversation. "Conversation? I'll tell you what's wrong with conversation. It takes place in real time, and you can't control what you're going to say."[1]

While text messages and emails may not fully capture or convey our meaning, they give us a sense of control. Conversations, by contrast, challenge us because of their unpredictability. In the wake of the COVID-19 pandemic, face-to-face communication may seem even more daunting. Although we may have newfound appreciation for conversation, our skills are rusty. This chapter explores how to create conditions for meaningful conversations and relationships with others by maintaining awareness of oneself while cultivating openness to others. Oren Jay Sofer, author of *Say What You Mean: A Mindful Approach to Nonviolent Communication*, recommends three steps for effective conversation: lead with presence, come from curiosity and care, and focus on what matters. He writes,

> To show up and be fully in the moment rests on training ourselves in the first foundation of mindful communication: *presence*. Coming from curiosity and care is the foundation of our *intention*. Focusing on what matters is about honing our *attention*, training our mind's capacity to discern what's essential and shift its focus in a nimble and responsive manner.[2]

Presence entails an embodied awareness we have explored in mindfulness practice—one that attends to our physical sensations, emotions, and thoughts. We anchor our attention on our bodies, our breath, hands, or feet to invite a state in which we feel grounded, settled, and relaxed. During our conversation, we try to maintain that awareness as we choose whether to listen or speak, and we practice "the pause" to notice if we are experiencing any physical tension, emotional activation, or proliferating thoughts.[3]

Our motivation or intention should be that of understanding the other person, so that we come from a place of curiosity and care, rather than judgment, blame, or criticism. If we enter conversations with the aim of criticizing others, they naturally become anxious, defensive, or shut down. In such circumstances, Sofer notes, "we easily lose touch with our deeper values, the importance of a relationship, or our capacity to see things from multiple perspectives."[4] Instead of getting caught up in habitual patterns of inciting or avoiding conflict, we can draw insights from nonviolent communication (NVC) that encourages us to observe behaviors or conditions that affect us, articulate our feelings about those situations, identify the deeper needs from which those feelings arise, and then make a request of how to move forward together. As Marshall Rosenberg writes in *Nonviolent Communication,*

> First, we observe what is actually happening in a situation: what we are observing others saying or doing that is either enriching or not enriching our life? The trick is to be able to articulate this observation without introducing any judgment or evaluation—to simply say what people are doing that we either like or don't like. Next, we state how we feel when we observe this action: are we hurt, scared, joyful, amused, irritated? And thirdly, we say what needs of ours are connected to the feelings we have identified. . . . [The] fourth component addresses what we are wanting from the other person that would enrich our lives or make life more wonderful for us.[5]

In our conversations with others, we focus on meeting our needs and those of others. The principle underlying nonviolent and mindful communication is, "Everything we do, we do to meet a need."[6] All humans have needs tied to subsistence and security, freedom, connection, and meaning, including

Physical Sustenance: air, food, health, movement, shelter, touch, water
Security: consistency, peace of mind, protection, safety, stability, trusting
Autonomy: choice, independence, power, self-responsibility
Leisure/Relaxation: humor, joy, play, pleasure, rejuvenation
Affection: appreciation, attention, companionship, intimacy, love, support, warmth
To Matter: acceptance, care, consideration, empathy, kindness, respect, to be heard and seen
Community: belonging, cooperation, equality, inclusion, participation, self-expression, sharing

Sense of self: authenticity, competence, dignity, growth, honesty, integrity, self-acceptance, self-care, self-knowledge

Understanding: awareness, discovery, learning, making sense of life

Meaning: aliveness, challenge, creativity, exploration, integration, purpose

Transcendence: beauty, communion, flow, hope, inspiration, mourning, presence[7]

Listening to others and sensing their feelings, we try to identify and discern these underlying needs. As Sofer writes, "When we understand each other at the level of our needs, our similarities outweigh our differences. This, in turn, creates a generative, positive cycle of views, intentions, and experiences."[8] For example, in the practice of kindness we acknowledge that everyone wants to be happy: even if their visions of happiness or strategies for achieving happiness may differ, the underlying need is the same. Strategies address how we meet our needs, and they are tied to certain people, places, objects, and actions; by contrast, "needs are what matter beneath our strategies. They are fundamental values that drive our actions."[9] In mindful communication, we try to identify our own needs—why we want what we want—as well as the needs of others. We seek to understand experience instead of trying to control it.

Deep Listening

Most of us are uncomfortable with silence. When we encounter lengthy pauses in a conversation, we have the urge to fill them by speaking. But, as Thich Nhat Hanh observes, silence allows for deep listening and mindful response. Turning inward and listening to ourselves, we can discern our own needs and values, which prepares us to listen to others. Hanh writes,

> When you've been able to still all the noise inside you, when you've been able to establish silence, a thundering silence, in you, you begin to hear the deepest kind of calling from within yourself. Your heart is calling out to you. Your heart is trying to tell you something, but you haven't yet been able to hear it, because your mind has been full of noise. You've been pulled away all the time, day and night. You've been full of thoughts, especially negative thought. . . . The deepest concern in you, as in many of us, is one you may not have perceived, one you may not have heard. Every one of us has an

ultimate concern that has nothing to do with material or affective concerns. What do you want to do with your life? That is the question. We are here, but *why* are we here? Who are we, each of us individually? What do we want to do with our life? These are questions that we don't typically have (or make) time to answer.[10]

When we allow for silence—a spacious silence—we can better discern our own hopes and aspirations. When we hold space for silence in conversation, we invite others to do the same, and we create openness and receptivity to hear what they say.

Deep listening means we suspend our own thoughts, feelings, or views so that we can actively receive and understand what others say. Often, when others speak, we find ourselves internally commenting on their remarks or planning what we will say in response. By contrast, deep listening encourages us to fully attend to the other person. We stay connected to them through our nonverbal communication, such as nodding our head and looking them in the eyes. We can ensure we have understood correctly by verbally restating or inquiring about what they have said: "We listen, then get confirmation at key moments that what one person *hears* matches what the other person *meant*, that message sent equals message received."[11] We ask questions to check and see if we have understood them correctly. We might say, "Let me see if I'm hearing you right. Are you saying . . . ?" This type of listening builds empathy— our capacity to feel into their experience from their point of view.[12]

Instead of focusing solely on our own needs, we widen our perspective and appreciate that all humans have these fundamental needs. To be clear, deep listening does not mean we abandon our needs or values, but that we shift the way we relate to them. We expand our awareness and commit to meeting both our needs and those of others. As Sofer emphasizes,

> When we understand what matters most, we can de-escalate tension, nurture empathy, and support collaboration. The more we know our own needs and trust our ability to meet them, the more space we have to hear others. At the same time, identifying others' needs allows us to make heartfelt connections across differences. We gain the ability to sense the deeper values behind positions quite different from our own. Views that may seem incomprehensible on the surface become expressions of our shared humanity.[13]

When you find yourself moving toward blaming another person, nonviolent communication invites you to trace your emotions back to the needs from which they arise. Marshall Rosenberg suggests connecting a feeling with a particular need: I feel [*x emotion*] because I need or value [*y need*].[14] He encourages us to make an observation about what happened, how it made us feel, and why it matters (in other words, what underlying need was or was not met). For example, if your roommate leaves their dishes in the sink without washing them, you might say to them, "When I see dishes piling up in the sink, I feel anxious because I value cleanliness." Then, we can make requests asking if another person might be willing to do something to meet our needs. Sofer explains, "It's best to formulate requests with three qualities: (1) Positive: requests state what we *do* want rather than what we *don't* want; (2) Specific: requests are concrete and doable rather than vague or abstract; (3) Flexible: requests are distinct from demands; they offer a suggestion for how to move forward, with openness to other ideas."[15] Before engaging in problem-solving, however, we must first ensure there is a foundation for mutual understanding.

To experience the power of deep listening, you can engage in a mindful communication exercise with a partner. Decide who will speak first and set a timer for three minutes. The speaker will speak, uninterrupted, for three minutes about an experience (or you could both respond to a shared question). As a listener, give your full attention to your partner and what they are saying. Notice if you have the tendency to tune out, or the urge to jump into the conversation. You can demonstrate you are present, engaged, and listening by your eye contact, nodding your head, or other body language, but try to avoid asking questions or redirecting the conversation. Simply listen without talking or interrupting. After three minutes, you can switch roles. Following the exercise, you might reflect on the questions: how was it to talk without being interrupted? How did that allow you to inquire into a topic? How was it to listen without interrupting or giving advice?

Speaking to be Understood

When we become comfortable with silence, and we learn how to identify our emotions and trace them to underlying needs, we become better equipped to make conscious choices in our conversations with others. We create space for reflection, and we can choose when to speak and when to listen, rather than speaking to fill the silence or to avoid feelings of discomfort. Oren Jay Sofer describes these as "choice points": "During a conversation, notice when you choose to speak. If you find yourself talking without having consciously chosen to do so, try stopping and leaving space for the other person to continue. Notice what it's like to actively choose to say something rather than doing so automatically."[16] In particular, he suggests paying attention to when we feel an urgent need or reluctance to speak, or we feel a sense of inner pressure to speak. By being mindful of such signals, we can prevent them from automatically triggering us to speak. He also suggests pausing or slowing down the pace of your speech as a means of gathering your thoughts and making more intentional choices about speaking.

When we speak to be understood, we seek to maintain connection with the other person, ensuring that they are understanding what we are saying. We look out for nonverbal clues that they are paying attention, and we invite them to reflect or inquire about what they have heard. We do not seek to persuade them or convince them of anything. Instead, our aim is mutual understanding: we speak to be understood, and we listen to understand. This is especially important when we engage in dialogue across differences—where we do not share the same cultural, social, or religious worldviews.

In these situations, ground rules or guidelines for discussion can help create a space where people feel safe enough to give voice to their experiences. Safe spaces are places where marginalized individuals can come together without the fear of violence, harassment, or hate speech. Dialogue across difference may not be entirely safe, as it can elicit strong emotions and feelings of discomfort, but ground rules ensure that it does not cause harm. Some have proposed using the term "brave space," as it avoids conflating safety with comfort, and it captures the types of risks, difficulties, and controversies that accompany such dialogues.[17] For example, dialogues focused on race and racism should encourage taking risks and invite "courageous conversations about race."[18] Glenn Singleton and Cyndie Hays outline four agreements of brave conversations: stay engaged, expect to experience discomfort, speak your truth, and expect and accept a lack of closure.[19] They stress the importance of being honest about your thoughts, feelings, and opinions: "Too often participants are afraid of offending, appearing angry, or sounding ignorant in conversations about race and fall silent, allowing their beliefs and opinions to be misinterpreted or misunderstood."[20] We can draw attention to such moments of silence, reflecting on the feelings that result in silence, such as white people feeling their comments will be misconstrued as racist, or people of color feeling it is unsafe or futile to share their thoughts.[21]

Ground rules can be generated by the group or determined in advance, and participants commit to adhere to these rules for the duration of the discussion.

Such rules may include expecting and honoring diverse viewpoints, seeking to understand sources of disagreement, using "I" statements that speak from your own experience, owning your intentions and impact, choosing the degree to which you participate and challenge yourself in dialogues, avoiding attacking, shaming, or belittling others, and respecting confidentiality by sharing lessons learned without using names or identifiers.

It can be helpful to have a facilitator oversee the dialogue process, manage group dynamics, and appropriately challenge and support participants. Facilitators play an especially important role when groups examine issues of social justice, as they can manage emotions that surface in the room and navigate defense mechanisms than can arise when dominant group members learn about their privilege—such as denial, deflection, rationalization, intellectualization, and minimization—and resistance that can come from target group members who do not want to be spokespeople for their social identities.[22] They can also check in with participants, making sure that they are taking care of themselves and seeing if they need to take a break.

Compassion

Mindful communication and dialogue ask the question "What are you going through?"[23] Often people share difficulties they have experienced, and when we listen deeply to them and turn towards their suffering, our hearts naturally respond with compassion. Compassion has three components: you emotionally feel the pain of another person, you mentally put yourself in their shoes, and you want to respond to and alleviate their distress. Compassion relies on the ability to recognize, open to, and acknowledge the pain and suffering of others. In this way, it requires that we be receptive and attuned to others as well as our surroundings. Simone Weil writes, "This way of looking is first of all attentive. The soul empties itself of all its own contents in order to receive into itself the being it is looking at, just as he is, in all his truth. Only he who is capable of attention can do this."[24] We turn toward another person, and we sense and feel their sorrow and distress. As Christina Feldman observes,

> To turn away from pain and suffering is to embed ourselves in a life of denial, avoidance, and agitation—a life disconnected from the universal story of all beings. To turn toward the reality of distress and pain is to open the door to the immeasurable compassion possible for each of us and to take our seat in the family of all beings. Compassion dignifies our life, widening the circle of concern to include and to care for all.[25]

Compassion connects us to humankind, as we all experience suffering and difficulty in our lives. We experience the pain of separation, loss, and death; we witness social injustice, human cruelty, mistreatment of other species, and destruction of the natural world. We instinctively feel pain in response to such suffering: it speaks to our love of justice, equity, respect for all species, and care for our natural world. The practice of compassion calls us to fully meet and freely allow space for such suffering.[26] Instead of becoming overwhelmed and feeling hopeless in the face of suffering or shutting down and numbing ourselves to the reality of suffering, we open our hearts and allow ourselves to feel pain. Through the practice of compassion, we become less fearful of pain and more capable of taking care of each other. We sense each other's pain and feel impelled to act in response.

When we engage in practices that nurture compassion, we orient our attention to the suffering of others. We can use phrases such as "May you be free of pain and sorrow" and "May you hold your suffering with kindness and ease." The former phrase hopes for the elimination of suffering, while the latter phrase acknowledges that a person's pain and suffering may not go away. As Sharon Salzberg notes, "You should experiment with different phrases, seeing which ones support a compassionate opening to pain and which ones seem to lead you more in the direction of aversion or grief."[27] We focus our attention on someone in our lives who is experiencing suffering, directing the compassion phrases to that person, keeping their struggles and difficulties in our awareness. We can then follow the same sequence as the kindness practice, directing compassion to ourselves, friends and loved ones, strangers, difficult people, and ultimately all beings.

An alternate compassion practice begins by orienting our attention toward a loved one experiencing happiness and wellness, wishing them kindness and freedom from suffering, and then attends to a loved one who is suffering, wishing them freedom from suffering. It invites you to attend to a friend who is flourishing and a friend who is suffering, and then yourself and any difficulty you may be experiencing: "May I be free of pain and struggle, and may I hold my difficulties with kindness, ease, and love." You then radiate compassion to encompass suffering in your community and the world at large—those who are sick, homeless, imprisoned, dying, and mourning. For each of these practices, notice when your mind drifts from the quality of compassion and gently guide it back to hold experiences of suffering with tenderness.

Self-Compassion

We can also bring compassion to ourselves, holding our own pain and suffering with a tender heart. Self-compassion means that instead of judging ourselves for mistakes or failures, we treat ourselves with care and concern. We let go of unrealistic expectations of perfection. Kristin Neff, a specialist in self-compassion, writes, "By giving ourselves unconditional kindness and comfort while embracing the human experience, difficult as it is, we avoid destructive patterns of fear, negativity, and isolation."[28] Neff outlines three core components of self-compassion:

> First, it requires *self-kindness*, that we be gentle and understanding with ourselves rather than harshly critical and judgmental. Second, it requires recognition of our *common humanity*, feeling connected with others in the experience of life rather than feeling isolated and alienated by our suffering. Third, it requires *mindfulness*—that we hold our experience in balanced awareness, rather than ignoring our pain or exaggerating it.[29]

Instead of disparaging ourselves for mistakes, we actively comfort ourselves and recognize that everyone experiences failure at some point. In this way, we realize our interconnectedness rather than isolating ourselves.[30]

Several practices can encourage self-compassion. You can think of ways that you responded to close friends who were suffering, write them down on a sticky note, and then say those words to yourself when you have difficult experiences. Or you can think of a difficult situation in your life, feeling the stress and discomfort in your body, and then say to yourself,

1. This is a moment of suffering (or: this hurts, ouch, this is stress)
2. Suffering is a part of life (or: other people feel this way, I'm not alone)
   Now, put your hands over your heart, feel the warmth of your hands and the gentle touch of your hands on your chest. Or adopt a soothing touch that feels right for you. Say to yourself,
3. May I be kind to myself (You can also ask yourself, "What do I need to hear right now to express kindness to myself?")[31]

You can also keep a self-compassion journal, writing down difficult experiences, regrets, or judgments about yourself. You then bring mindfulness to the painful emotions that arise, write ways that they connects you to common humanity, and offer kind, understanding words of comfort to yourself.[32]

Tara Brach, a mindfulness teacher, adapts the practice of RAIN (Recognize, Allow, Investigate, Nurture) to combine mindfulness with heartfulness, encouraging what she calls "radical compassion."[33] The practice begins by taking a "U-turn" in attention: "We are taking a U-turn whenever we shift our attention from an outward fixation—another person, our thoughts, or our emotionally driven stories about what's going on—to the real, living experience in our body."[34] In this practice, you begin by connecting with your body, understanding that your body holds emotions that create stress and pain, or "issues in your tissues."[35] Instead of getting caught up in stories or fixating on other people, you go under the storylines to ask "How am I experiencing this?" You then proceed to

Recognize What Is Happening
Allow Life to Be Just as It Is
Investigate with a Gentle, Curious Attention
Nurture with Loving Presence.[36]

In this way, you reorient to presence—wakefulness, openness, and tenderness[37]—by connecting with your felt sensations in your body, sensing into places of pain or vulnerability, and naturally responding to what you need, whether it is a loving message, a hand placed on your heart, a visualization of being surrounded by soft, luminous light, or imagining someone you trust holding you with love.[38] As Brach notes, RAIN creates a clearing when "we all get lost in the dense forest of our lives, entangled in incessant worry and planning, in judgments of others, and in our busy striving to meet demands and solve problems. When we're caught in that thicket, it's easy to lose sight of what matters most. We forget how much we long to be kind and openhearted."[39] Instead of getting caught up in reactivity, self-judgment and blaming others, the practice encourages you to move from a sense of separateness to one of belonging, shifting from the sense of "I" (illness) to "we" (wellness).[40]

Notes

1. Turkle, *Alone Together*, xxii.
2. Sofer, *Say What You Mean*, 5.
3. Sofer, *Say What You Mean*, 45.
4. Sofer, *Say What You Mean*, 70.
5. Rosenberg, *Nonviolent Communication*, 6.

6. Sofer, *Say What You Mean*, 77.

7. Inbal and Kashtan, "Universal Human Needs." Their list builds on Rosenberg, *Nonviolent Communication*, 54–55.

8. Sofer, *Say What You Mean*, 77.

9. Sofer, *Say What You Mean*, 112.

10. Hanh, *Silence*, 12–14.

11. Sofer, *Say What You Mean*, 95.

12. Sofer, *Say What You Mean*, 99.

13. Sofer, *Say What You Mean*, 126.

14. Rosenberg, *Nonviolent Communication*, 52; Sofer, *Say What You Mean*, 149.

15. Sofer, *Say What You Mean*, 194.

16. Sofer, *Say What You Mean*, 44.

17. Arao and Clemens, "From Safe Spaces to Brave Spaces," 141.

18. Singleton and Hays, "Beginning Courageous Conversations about Race," 18–23.

19. Singleton and Hays, "Beginning Courageous Conversations about Race," 18–23.

20. Singleton and Hays, "Beginning Courageous Conversations about Race," 21.

21. Singleton and Hays, "Beginning Courageous Conversations about Race," 19-20.

22. Vaccaro, "Building a Framework for Social Justice Education," 23–44.

23. Noddings, *Educating Moral People*, 17.

24. Weil, *Waiting for God*, 64–65.

25. Feldman, *Boundless Heart*, 57–58.

26. Aylward, *Awake Where You Are*, 160–62.

27. Salzberg, *Loving-Kindness*, 116.

28. Neff, *Self-Compassion*, 12.

29. Neff, *Self-Compassion*, 41.

30. Neff, *Self-Compassion*, 65.

31. Kristin Neff, "Self-Compassion Guided Practices and Exercises."

32. Neff, *Self-Compassion*, 103–4.

33. Brach, *Radical Compassion*.

34. Brach, *Radical Compassion*, 8.

35. LaBarre, *Issues in Your Tissues*.

36. Brach, *Radical Compassion*, 33-35.

37. Brach, *Radical Compassion*, 9.

38. Brach, *Radical Compassion*, 45.

39. Brach, *Radical Compassion*, 3.

40. Brach, "Radical Compassion—Loving Ourselves and Our World Into Healing."

CHAPTER NINE

Collaborating with Others

If you are a poet, you will see clearly that there is a cloud floating in
this sheet of paper. Without a cloud, there will be no rain; without
rain, the trees cannot grow; and without trees, we cannot make
paper. The cloud is essential for the paper to exist. If the cloud is
not here, the sheet of paper cannot be here either... We cannot
just *be* by ourselves alone. We have to inter-be with every other
thing. This sheet of paper is, because everything else is.
—Thich Nhat Hanh[1]

During my senior year in college, I lived in a cooperative house (co-op)
where students cooked and cleaned for one another. Although I felt
comfortable cleaning bathrooms, I felt anxious when it came time to
cook my first meal for the house. My mom was an amazing cook, and while
my sister inherited her culinary skills—later completing a degree in culinary
arts and teaching at the Culinary Institute of America—I felt ill-equipped to
cook a meal for thirty-five people. When Pete, the kitchen manager, asked me
what ingredients he should buy at the store the weekend before, I stared at
him blankly. I showed him a recipe for tuna casserole that my mom had sent,
unsure of how many servings it yielded. He patiently scanned the card and
estimated how many times I should multiply the recipe to accommodate for all
the co-op residents. When the day arrived, he and another housemate served
as sous-chefs in the kitchen, helping me cut vegetables and prepare the food.
Over time, I looked forward to the days when I cooked or helped others with
their meals: we would play music as we prepped the food, and I found myself
enjoying the conversation, camaraderie, and community of the kitchen.

Collaboration entails working together with others to accomplish common goals, and it involves sharing responsibilities and drawing on diverse
viewpoints. As Lynn Wilson observes, collaboration requires technical,
disciplinary, and process skills: "Collaborative partners must obtain factual

knowledge on the topic to participate. Then they rely on procedural knowledge for group decision-making and collaborative leadership. Self-knowledge is also important because collaborative partners need to recognize their own abilities and limits when it comes to how they work with others."[2] In my case, I realized my limited experience cooking, relied on Pete's expertise and knowledge as kitchen manager to determine how to multiply the recipe for a different yield, and followed co-op procedures for preparing, cooking, and serving the meal together with my housemates. Collaboration often involves working across disciplinary, organizational, and cultural boundaries, as well as accommodating different worldviews, communication styles, and technological abilities.[3] Common complaints of collaboration include unbalanced group work and social loafing, where some people pull all the weight of others who stand by idly and produce nothing.[4] But clearly defined responsibilities and accountability—for example, through agreements and evaluation of individuals as well as groups—can mitigate against such concerns.[5]

Collaborative partners must agree about what they intend to produce together. In the business world, this is referred to as a "deliverable"—a tangible or intangible good or service produced from a project that is meant to be delivered to a customer. Collaborative partners must also determine the process they will use to integrate their efforts into one outcome, which requires planning, communication, conflict resolution, and project management.[6] They might adopt a parallel structure where they allocate tasks among participants, a sequential structure where they complete a project in multiple steps over time, or a synergistic structure where they synthesize ideas and work together through all stages from planning to completion.[7]

Collaboration has benefits and drawbacks, which scholars refer to as collaborative advantage and collaborative inertia, respectively. On the one hand, collaboration can produce synergistic outcomes that would be unachievable by an individual working alone. On the other hand, there can be barriers to collaboration, including "unwillingness to seek input and learn from others; inability to seek and find expertise; unwillingness to help, also called hoarding expertise; and inability to work together and transfer knowledge."[8] Collaboration requires trust: confidence in our partners' abilities, integrity, and commitment to accomplishing our shared goal. This includes personal trust, for example, "I trust that others will be honest; value my point of view; honor our agreements; respect confidentiality; and provide fair, constructive comments to me."[9] To establish trust, in addition to clearly defining your task, goal, and purpose, you must make collaborative decisions about the operation of the group, assign responsibilities to accomplish the task, ensure active and constructive participation, and assess the collaborative effort.

Collaborative Work Design

After determining your outcome or goal, strategize about how you want to organize work: do you want to divide it into discrete tasks for individuals or small groups, or work together throughout the project? If you decide to divide tasks, determine whether they can be completed at the same time (parallel), or whether tasks depend on each other and steps need to build progressively (sequential). Decide what platform or shared folder you are using for your work, what formatting and citation style you are using (for written work) or what file type you are creating (for audiovisual media). Also, decide what criteria you will use to determine whether you are on track with tasks: what are your expectations about quality of work and timing for completion of each task?[10] How frequently will you communicate with each other about your progress, or come together as a team? If you are combining parts into one deliverable, you will need to review, refine, and revise one another's work so that it fits together. At that stage, working together synergistically, in dialogue with one another, can help you create a coherent, cohesive result.

Agreements set clear group expectations about goals, roles, group processes, and climate, which can ensure transparency, equal participation, and accountability. You can create an agreement together through dialogue where you actively listen, mutually exchange ideas, clearly define roles and expectations, and design the work process. You can discuss the following questions to determine how you will organize the group, distribute work, communicate with each other, review and revise work, deliver the product, and assess each other's contributions:

> What skills and knowledge do people bring to the group? What do people hope to gain from the collaboration?
> Will you have a leader? If so, who will this be, and will this role be rotated? What are the group's expectations of this person?
> How will work be distributed? Who does what, when and how? Which parts of the work will be completed individually, and which parts completed together?

What are the steps or tasks that need to be completed, and what is their timeline for completing these milestones?

Do you know of any problems or problematic dates or times that need to be factored in?

When and how will you meet and communicate with each other? How often? What are the group's ground rules for those meetings?

How will iteration and version-control get handled?

Who will post the team deliverables?

How will you provide constructive feedback to one another?

How will you handle work that is subpar, incomplete, or not done?[11]

By thoroughly discussing and clearly establishing roles and expectations, you create a climate of trust and accountability. You attend to important elements of collaboration, including group structure (its goals, roles, and leadership plan), group process (strategies for solving problems, making decisions, communicating, and managing conflict), and group norms (acceptable and unacceptable behaviors).[12] You can determine how the group will make decisions: by majority vote, negative minority (where you eliminate the most unpopular ideas until you get to the single idea remaining), consensus, or using criteria.[13] You can establish group ground rules about committing to participate and contribute, coming prepared, listening actively to others, and supporting the efforts of others. You can also discuss how group members might compensate if they fail to attend a meeting, or if they are unable to prepare in advance. Group roles can vary depending on whether you are engaging in face-to-face or online collaboration, but they might include the roles of facilitator (who moderates discussions), recorder (who keeps notes and records), reporter (who is the group spokesperson), timekeeper, and materials manager (who organizes, stores, and distributes any group materials).[14] Online collaboration could include data gatherers, multimedia specialists, data managers, project managers to oversee the timeline and completion of tasks, technology specialist, and editor of the final product.[15]

You can evaluate yourself, your individual collaborative partners, and your group to mitigate against unequal participation and social loafing. You might reflect on what you learned from the collaboration that you wouldn't have learned working alone, how you might apply what you learned to new situations, your greatest contribution to the group, the most challenging thing that happened, and what you might do differently next time. You might evaluate individual team members on the extent to which they stayed on task, did a fair share of the work, responded to communications, actively participated, shared ideas with the group, maintained a positive attitude, and made an effort to include all group members in activities; you might also list a strength they brought to the group and a constructive "tip" that might help them improve or grow. Finally, you can assess the extent to which your group worked together effectively, and one change that might enable the group to improve its performance.[16]

Design Thinking

People bring different backgrounds and skills to the collaborative process, and design thinking can enable you to draw on that diversity of experience. Design thinking is an iterative process of generating ideas, testing them out, and seeing if they work. Individually, you can engage in mind mapping—freely associating words, one after another—to create space for ideation.[17] This involves three steps: picking a topic, making the mind map, and making secondary connections and creating concepts.[18] As Bill Burnett and Dave Evans recommend, the free association of words should be done fast: "Just write down the first words that come to mind. If you censor yourself, you limit your potential for generating new and novel ideas."[19]

Collectively, you can engage in brainstorming: in groups of four to six people, you can spend twenty minutes generating as many ideas as possible to solve an open-ended question. The question should not assume a particular solution or come across as vague. Burnett and Evans suggest the phrasing, "How many ways can we think of to . . . ?"[20] Before posing the question, you want to warm up the group to help people "move from their analytical/critical brain to a synthesizing/nonjudgmental brain."[21] You then provide each person with a pen and sticky notes to write their ideas, and encourage them to follow the following rules:

1. Go for quantity, not quality.
2. Defer judgment and do not censor ideas.
3. Build off the ideas of others.
4. Encourage wild ideas.[22]

You can conclude by grouping the ideas together by subject or category, voting on them, discussing the results, and then deciding what to prototype first.[23]

In this way, design thinking entertains multiple ideas simultaneously before prototyping: "If your mind starts with multiple ideas in parallel, it is not prematurely committed to one path and stays more open and able to receive and conceive more novel innovations."[24]

After generating ideas, you test them out. When prototyping, designers "create prototype after prototype, failing often, until they find what works and what solves the problem. Sometimes they find the problem is entirely different from what they first thought it was. Designers embrace change."[25] When prototypes fail, or their understanding of a problem changes, designers reframe: "We take new information about the problem, restate our point of view, and start thinking and prototyping again."[26] Reframing allows them to explore possibilities and think of small prototypes that might creatively address the problem.[27]

Appreciative Inquiry

Appreciative inquiry can help improve communication, trust, and relationships between collaborative partners; it encourages questions and dialogues about strengths, successes, values, hopes, and dreams.[28] "Appreciative Inquiry suggests that human organizing and change at its best is a relational process of inquiry, grounded in affirmation and appreciation."[29] Shifting attention from identifying problems toward envisioning future possibilities, it focuses on appreciation—recognizing, valuing, and expressing gratitude for strengths, successes, assets and potential—and inquiry, in which one cultivates curiosity and openness to new possibilities, directions, and understandings.[30] In Appreciative Inquiry, one first defines the focus of inquiry on an affirmative topic valued by participants and central to the success of the group.[31] The group then engages in a "4-D cycle," pictured below, in which one first discovers the "best of what is"[32] by sharing stories of best practices and exemplary actions, then dreams about "what might be"[33] by envisioning possibilities for their relationships, communities, and the world, then designs provocative statements about positive ideals or "what should be,"[34] and finally invites actions to support innovation and change, or "what will be."[35]

Unlike deficit-based approaches that focus on failure, gaps, barriers, threats, or resistance to change, Appreciative Inquiry focuses on future possibilities and building the capacity for positive change.

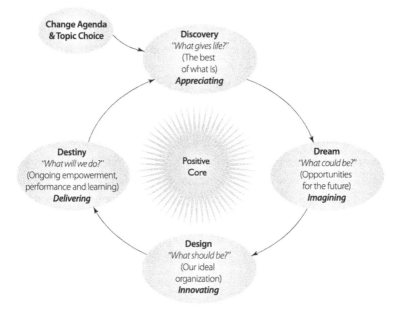

4-D Cycle. "The Appreciative Inquiry 4-D Cycle" by Diana D. Whitney & Amanda Trosten-Bloom. Used with permission.

Interdependence and Joy

Just as we can move from a deficit-based to a strengths-based approach to change, we can free ourselves from feeling that we are separate, in competition with others, or deficient. Our brains have a "negativity bias" that Rick Hanson likens to "Velcro for negative experiences, but Teflon for positive ones."[36] It orients us toward fault-finding and nit-picking, and it makes painful experiences more memorable than pleasurable ones. However, as Hanson notes, we can tilt toward the good: notice good experiences, take thirty seconds to savor the feeling of goodness, and feel it sinking into us: "the longer that something is held in awareness, and the more emotionally stimulating it is, the more neurons that fire and thus wire together, and the stronger the trace in memory."[37]

We can also cultivate joy by shifting our perspective from an isolated fixation on "me" to an interdependent acknowledgement of "we." As we have seen, collaboration involves interdependence, interaction, and teamwork. Many religious traditions espouse the idea of interdependence—that we are dependent on others as a necessary condition for our own existence. In Buddhism, interdependence means "ultimately, there is nothing and no one with whom we are not connected."[38] In Christianity, as Archbishop Desmond Tutu writes, "We depend on the other in order for us to be fully who we are."[39] He connects it to the southern African concept of Ubuntu, which says, "A person is a person through other persons."[40] In *The Book of Joy* the Dalai Lama describes how self-centered attitudes distance a person from others, leading to feelings of insecurity, anxiety, frustration, and even anger. By contrast, the more we turn toward others, the more joy we experience, and the more we can bring joy to others.[41] As he observes,

> The paradox is that although the drive behind excessive self-focus is to seek greater happiness for yourself, it ends up doing exactly the opposite. When you focus too much on yourself, you become disconnected and alienated from others. In the end, you also become alienated from yourself, since the need for connection with others is such a fundamental part of who we are as human beings.[42]

Similarly, when we hear of another person's success, we may find that our mind tends toward envy and jealousy, as we judge or compare our own accomplishments with theirs. Buddhists view envy as particularly corrosive to joy, and they identify joy as the antidote to envy. Archbishop Desmond Tutu explains that "in African villages, one would ask in greeting, 'How are we?' This understanding sees that someone else's achievements or happiness is in a very real way our own."[43]

We can cultivate this sense of joy and delight in our lives, in each other, and in the happiness of others. Just as we can turn toward the suffering of others and feel compassion, we can turn toward the happiness of others and feel delight and joy in our hearts. Think about a time when someone that you love—a friend or family member—was happy, or a time when you were out in nature. You might recall feelings of warmth, lightness, or delight that you felt from that interconnection. We can savor the happiness of others, and we can delight in and feel grateful for things in our lives that we may otherwise take for granted, such as the breath, our bodies being alive, sunshine, air, or sounds of birds. In *The Book of Joy*, the Dalai Lama and Desmond Tutu write, "Gratitude is the recognition of all that holds us in the web of life and all that has made it possible to have the life that we have and the moment that we are experiencing. . . . It moves us away from the narrow-minded focus on fault and lack and to a wider perspective of benefit and abundance."[44] We can shift from a sense of lack and deficiency toward a stance of gratitude and appreciation.

You might direct phrases toward those experiencing happiness and success in their life, wishing for it to continue and flourish. Drawing to mind that person, you might direct phrases towards them, such as "I delight in your happiness" and "May your joy and success continue to flourish." The Dalai Lama shares the following practice for rejoicing in others' good fortune:

1. Imagine the person who has something that you envy.
2. Recognize your shared humanity. Focus on the hopes, dreams, fears, disappointments, and suffering of the person you envy. Recognize that, just like you, the person you envy wishes to achieve happiness and to avoid even the slightest suffering.
3. Imagine how happy what they have must make them. Think about what it must mean to them and to their family that they have what you envy. The car, the house, or the position may be a source of great satisfaction. Try to expand your heart to include them and their good fortune. Rejoice in their good fortune.[45]

In this way, you can delight in another person's happiness, overcoming the tendency toward jealousy, comparison, or competitiveness. We can cultivate appreciation for the happiness of others, gratitude for good fortune in our own lives, and wonder in our interdependence and interconnection.

Notes

1. Hanh, *Peace Is Every Step*, 95–96.
2. Lynn Wilson, foreword to *Learning to Collaborate, Collaborating to Learn*, by Janet Salmons, xiv.
3. Salmons, *Learning to Collaborate*, xvii.
4. Barkley et al., *Collaborative Learning Techniques*, 32.
5. Salmons, *Learning to Collaborate*, xviii.
6. Salmons, *Learning to Collaborate*, 4–5.
7. Salmons, *Learning to Collaborate*, 16–18.
8. Salmons, *Learning to Collaborate*, 31.
9. Salmons, *Learning to Collaborate*, 45.
10. Salmons, *Learning to Collaborate*, 62.
11. Adapted from Barkley et al., *Collaborative Learning Techniques*, 70; and Salmons, *Learning to Collaborate*, 92–94.

12. Salmons, *Learning to Collaborate*, 90.

13. Barkley et al., *Collaborative Learning Techniques*, 94.

14. Barkley et al., *Collaborative Learning Techniques*, 86.

15. Barkley et al., *Collaborative Learning Techniques*, 89.

16. Barkley et al., *Collaborative Learning Techniques*, 111.

17. Burnett and Evans, *Design Your Life*, 70.

18. Burnett and Evans, *Design Your Life*, 71.

19. Burnett and Evans, *Design Your Life*, 74.

20. Burnett and Evans, *Design Your Life*, 121.

21. Burnett and Evans, *Design Your Life*, 123.

22. Burnett and Evans, *Design Your Life*, 124.

23. Burnett and Evans, *Design Your Life*, 125.

24. Burnett and Evans, *Design Your Life*, 91.

25. Burnett and Evans, *Design Your Life*, xxvi.

26. Burnett and Evans, *Design Your Life*, xx.

27. Burnett and Evans, *Design Your Life*, 81.

28. Whitney and Trosten-Bloom, *Power of Appreciative Inquiry*, 1.

29. Whitney and Trosten-Bloom, *Power of Appreciative Inquiry*, 1.

30. Whitney and Trosten-Bloom, *Power of Appreciative Inquiry*, 2, 3.

31. This has led some to argue it is a 5D cycle of definition, discovery, dream, design and destiny/delivery, but if the topic is clear, one can begin in the discovery phase. "5-D Cycle of Appreciative Inquiry," *AI Commons*, accessed March 13, 2022, https://appreciativeinquiry.champlain.edu/learn/appreciative-inquiry-introduction/5-d-cycle-appreciative-inquiry/.

32. Whitney and Trosten-Bloom, *Power of Appreciative Inquiry*, 7.

33. Whitney and Trosten-Bloom, *Power of Appreciative Inquiry*, 8.

34. Whitney and Trosten-Bloom, *Power of Appreciative Inquiry*, 8.

35. Whitney and Trosten-Bloom, *Power of Appreciative Inquiry*, 9.

36. Hanson, "Take in the Good."

37. Hanson, "Take in the Good."

38. Karmapa, "Understanding Emptiness & Interdependence."

39. Dalai Lama and Tutu, *Book of Joy*, 60.

40. Dalai Lama and Tutu, *Book of Joy*, 60.

41. Dalai Lama and Tutu, *Book of Joy*, 63.

42. Dalai Lama and Tutu, *Book of Joy*, 130.

43. Dalai Lama and Tutu, *Book of Joy*, 141.

44. Dalai Lama and Tutu, *Book of Joy*, 242.

45. Dalai Lama and Tutu, *Book of Joy*, 322–23.

CHAPTER TEN

Finding Balance

Today, like every other day, we wake up empty and frightened.
Don't open the door to the study and begin reading. Take down
a musical instrument. Let the beauty we love be what we do.
There are hundreds of ways to kneel and kiss the ground.
—Rumi[1]

During my graduate studies, I spent most of my time alone in a library, reading classical Chinese texts, consulting classical Chinese dictionaries, and writing papers that were only read (perhaps even understood) by my professors. Over time, I started to question the purpose for pursuing a PhD. What was the value of spending so much time on such a specialized area of research that only a handful of people might read and benefit from? I felt I was living from the neck up, only in my head, disconnected from my body. I longed to learn a useful skill—one that might benefit others. That is why, in the third year of my doctoral program, I enrolled in a 600-hour massage therapy program. Twice a week, I would bike from Cambridge to Somerville, Massachusetts, to learn about anatomy and physiology, and to engage in hands-on practice of various massage-therapy techniques. My friends and family were confused: "Why on earth would you start another program of study? Aren't you going to stress yourself out even further?" To their surprise, I became more relaxed—not only from receiving weekly massages, but also from seeing the tangible benefits of massage for my clients. I later volunteered as a massage therapist at the Charlotte Maxwell Clinic, a nonprofit organization that provides complementary integrative therapies (acupuncture, massage, and Chinese/Western herbs) to low-income and underserved women with cancer. I found that massage therapy, as well as yoga and meditation, helped me feel more grounded in my body, and it gave me a sense of meaning and purpose.

Oftentimes, we can sense when we are out of balance. We may feel tense, irritable, and anxious, or we may feel disengaged, numb, and tired. Perhaps you have found in your mindfulness practice that your mind habitually tends toward feeling agitated and restless, or feeling dull and sleepy. Just as you can bring balance to your mind by grounding yourself when you feel anxious, or engaging in walking meditation when you feel sleepy, you can bring balance to your life. Stewart Friedman, author of *Leading the Life You Want*, says that instead of thinking about balance in terms of trade-offs, we should think about how we integrate four domains of life: "work or school; home or family; community or society; and the private realm of mind, body, and spirit."[2] Balance entails bringing these four domains into greater alignment, being intentional about what we value and who matters to us.[3] Friedman shares the following skills for integrating these domains, which fall under three principles: being real about what matters most to you in life, being whole by acting with integrity, and being innovative by acting in ways that are good for you and the people around you:

- Skills for Being Real: know what matters, embody values consistently, align actions with values, convey values with stories, envision your legacy, and hold yourself accountable.
- Skills for Being Whole: clarify expectations, help others, build supportive networks, apply all your resources, manage boundaries intelligently, weave disparate strands of your life so that it has coherence.
- Skills for Being Innovative: focus on results, resolve conflicts among domains, challenge the status quo, see new ways of doing things, embrace change courageously, create cultures of innovation.[4]

He emphasizes the importance of making skillful choices, so you spend your time and energy in ways that align with your values.

To determine whether your life aligns with your values, you must first have a clear sense of those values. As Russ Harris notes, values describe "how you want to act on an ongoing basis, what you want to stand for in life, the principles you want to live by, the personal qualities and character strengths you want to cultivate."[5] Values are ongoing qualities and actions, as opposed to goals, which are outcomes you seek to achieve. Harris identifies many common values, including acceptance, adventure, assertiveness, authenticity, beauty, caring, challenge, compassion, connection, contribution, conformity, cooperation, courage, creativity, curiosity, equality, fairness, fitness, friendliness, forgiveness, generosity, honesty, humor, humility, independence, justice, kindness, open-mindedness, patience, persistence, pleasure, power, reciprocity, respect, responsibility, safety, self-awareness, self-care, self-development, self-control, spirituality, supportiveness, and trust.[6] He suggests identifying which values are very important, somewhat important, or not so important, and then selecting the top six values as reminders of what you want to stand for as a person.

Bill Burnett and Dave Evans make similar observations in their book *Designing Your Life: How to Build a Well-Lived, Joyful Life*. They write, "A well-designed life is supported by a healthy body, an engaged mind, and often, though not always, some form of spiritual practice."[7] They encourage you to take stock of where you are—"how it's going" in your work, play, love, and health—just as gauges on a car's dashboard tell you about the state of your car.[8] Afterward, you can reflect on any issues that you identified, consider whether you can take actions in response, and look for ways of bringing greater balance to your dashboard.[9] They also emphasize the importance of discerning your views on work—what you think work is for and what makes good work good—and clarifying your views on life by reflecting on the questions "What gives life meaning? What makes your life worthwhile or valuable? How does your life relate to others in your family, your community, and the world? What do money, fame, and personal accomplishment have to do with a satisfying life? How important are experience, growth, and fulfillment in your life?"[10] Just as Friedman highlights the importance of living in alignment with your values, Burnett and Evans stress the importance of having a coherent life that clearly connects who you are, what you believe, and what you are doing.[11]

A Healthy Body

We can understand balance in terms of our bodies, minds, and spirits. We previously explored the importance of physical activity for health, and the recommendation by health officials that we engage in at least 150 minutes (2.5 hours) of moderate-intensity aerobic activity each week and muscle-strengthening exercises twice a week. This approach to physical fitness, which emphasizes exercise and muscle-strengthening, emerged in late nineteenth-century America in response to urbanization—specifically, the unhealthy diets and lifestyles that people adopted after moving from farms to cities. Prior to this period, and in other cultural contexts, people thought differently about the body, and as a result, they experienced their bodies differently. For example, in China, prior to the modern focus on "physical culture" (*tiyu*), they emphasized "the cultivation of life" (*yangsheng*) that sought to retain and circulate *qi* (energy,

Diagram of the Supreme Ultimate. "Yin and Yang Symbol."
Wikimedia Commons. Public Domain.

vitality, life force) so that it flowed freely throughout the body. This underlies the practices of acupuncture and acupressure in traditional Chinese medicine, which seek to facilitate the flow of *qi* through pathways called "meridians" in the body by inserting needles or applying pressure to specific points along these meridians. The practice of *taiqi* (also spelled "tai chi"), which has a long history dating back to at least the second century BCE, also promotes the circulation of *qi*.

Although it could sometimes become blocked, *qi* was understood as having a natural propensity to circulate in the body and the universe, and the ability to manifest as *yin* or *yang* energy. *Yin* represents coolness, darkness, stillness, and receptivity, while *yang* connotes heat, light, movement, and activity. The goal was to bring them into balance, as illustrated in the Diagram of the Supreme Ultimate above. As Randall Nadeau writes, "These forces are not seen to be in conflict with one another, but rather exist in a complementary relationship; that is to say, one cannot exist without the other. Humans should strive to preserve the two forces in equal measure in their social interactions, in the natural environment, and in their physical selves."[12] People sought to circulate their *qi* and harmonize energies of *yin* and *yang* in their bodies, and they similarly sought to preserve this flow and balance in the natural world when they built homes, villages, and cities. The practice of *fengshui*—which means "wind and water"—traditionally focused on the best sites for the living to live and the dead to be buried without disrupting the flow of *qi*. Internally, they understood their bodies as having five *zang* (liver, heart, spleen, lung, and kidneys) and six *fu* (gall bladder, small intestines, stomach, large intestines, and bladder), but they did not view them as we do internal organs. Instead, as Shigehisa Kuriyama notes, they were repositories for storing *qi*: "To the extent that the *zang* storehouses kept vital breaths secure within the body, a person could deflect the perils of chaotic change. Empty winds could inflict no harm, for the fullness within left them no room to enter."[13] Insofar as the focus was on preserving *qi* and preventing it from escaping the body, it differed significantly from the emphasis on strengthening muscles that one finds in Greek traditions. Kuriyama writes, "The fullness of yogic figures in China portrayed selves preserving their integrity by resisting the depleting outflow of life, the loss of vital energies and of time. Whereas the autonomy of the muscleman lay in the capacity for genuine action, for change due neither to nature nor chance, but dependent solely on the will."[14] Modern-day America focuses primarily on the latter view of the body, namely muscles and voluntary motion, but the former view invites us "to reassess our own habits of perceiving and feeling, and to imagine alternative possibilities of being—to experience the world afresh."[15] Similarly, when we practice mindfulness of body, we invite ourselves not to conceive of our body or think about it, but instead to feel and sense into it. Mindfulness of body can allow us to observe and allow whatever we are experiencing physically, so that we can then respond in skillful ways to what we have discerned. Many of us may find that our bodies need sleep, rest, or relaxation; others may discover the need for movement, activity, and exertion. Although we may not share traditional Chinese views of the body, we can seek harmony and balance within our bodies.

Here, I invite you to reflect on your body. What do you consider a healthy body? Does your body need more sleep, more exercise, or something else? What habits might you cultivate to promote your body's health? After exploring these thoughts—perhaps writing them down—practice "the pause" by noticing any emotions that have surfaced, and where you feel them in the body. If you find yourself having self-critical thoughts, invite some space between yourself and those thoughts. Then, release them from your awareness and engage in a brief practice of mindfulness of breath. Afterward, you might write down ways of supporting your bodily health.

An Engaged Mind

Mindfulness similarly encourages us to observe our minds, allowing our thoughts to arise and pass without identifying with them. We can discern our habits of mind, such as our tendency to desire or fantasize about the future, or to resist and push away past and present experiences. We can also engage our minds by enhancing our curiosity and experiences of flow. Emily Grossnickle writes, "At its core, curiosity is the desire for new knowledge, information, experiences, or stimulation to resolve gaps or experience the unknown."[16] We become curious when we notice something that intrigues, puzzles, or surprises us, which prompts us to raise questions and want to better understand it.

We can also allow our minds to engage in unguided attention, wandering from one thought to the next. Zachary Irving explains that in this state, our thoughts often uncover our goals: "Mind-wandering is purposeless in one way—it is unguided—but purposeful in another—it is frequently caused, and thus motivated, by our goals."[17] Unlike absorption, when we are engrossed by an idea, or rumination, when we fixate on our distress, mind-wandering allows our minds to relax instead of maintaining focus. Irving explains, "Having a free-association thought process that randomly generates memories and imaginative experiences can lead you to new ideas and insights."[18] If, instead of busying or distracting our minds, we let them idle and free associate, we allow for originality and creativity.[19] I often have spontaneous, original thoughts while swimming laps in the pool. With my body occupied by the physical motions of strokes and flip turns, my mind freely wanders and makes novel connections. You may find that you have insights doing other activities, such as driving a familiar route or taking a shower.

However, we may find it challenging to engage in mindfulness or mind-wandering if we are experiencing depression, anxiety, or other mental health conditions. I have experienced situational depression at several points in my life: as a teenager when my mother was hospitalized due to illness, in my twenties after a relationship ended, and in my thirties following the sudden death of my boyfriend. Such experiences of illness, loss, and death can make us feel vulnerable and fragile. They disrupt our "assumptive world"[20]—everything that we assume to be true based on our previous experiences. As Robert Neimeyer and Diana Sands observe, "At such moments, we can feel cast into a world that is alien, unimaginable, and uninhabitable, one that radically shakes or severs those taken-for-granted 'realities' in which we are rooted, and on which we rely for a sense of secure purpose and connection."[21] We can feel lost and disoriented, and the world can seem suddenly unreal. In each instance of situational depression, I not only reached out to family and friends for support, but I also sought the help of therapists, who used various techniques to treat my depression, including Eye Movement Desensitization and Reprocessing (EMDR), Cognitive-Based Behavioral Therapy (CBT), and Grief Counseling. When we experience trauma—which Pat Ogden defines as "any experience that is stressful enough to leave us feeling helpless, frightened, overwhelmed, or profoundly unsafe,"[22] such as witnessing or experiencing violence, losing a loved one, or being targeted by oppression—relationships with other people can help us regulate our emotions and give us a sense of perspective.[23]

The novelist William Styron shares the story of his struggles with severe depression in *Darkness Visible,* comparing the suffering of depression with Dante's journey through hell in the *Inferno.* Alluding to the opening lines of Dante's *Inferno*—"In the middle of the journey of our life I found myself in a dark wood, for I had lost the right path"[24]—Styron writes,

> For those who have dwelt in depression's dark wood, and known its inexplicable agony, their return from the abyss is not unlike the ascent of the poet, trudging upward and upward out of hell's black depths and at last emerging into what he saw as "the shining world." There, whoever has been restored to health has almost always been restored to the capacity for serenity and joy, and this may be indemnity enough for having endured the despair beyond despair.
>
> *And so we came forth, and once again beheld the stars.*[25]

Feelings of despair and desolation can narrow our worldview and prevent us from seeing beyond the dark woods. We forget "the shining world" and the possibility of feeling awe or transcendence as we look at a starry night sky. However, Styron's concluding words evoke a sense of hope, pointing to an alternate trajectory that leads to mental health and well-being.

Here, I invite you to reflect on your mind. When do you find your mind engaged? When do you experience flow or find your curiosity enhanced? What activities facilitate mind-wandering for you, and what insights have you had as a result? Have you experienced—or are you currently experiencing—depression? If so, what types of treatment and support have you found helpful in your recovery? After exploring these thoughts—perhaps writing them down—practice "the pause" by noticing any emotions that have surfaced, and where you feel them in the body. If you find yourself having self-critical thoughts, invite some space between yourself and those thoughts. Then, release them from your awareness and engage in a brief practice of mindfulness of breath. Afterward, you might write down ways to you might engage your mind.

Spiritual Practice

If I were to ask you how you were feeling in mind and body, you would likely draw attention to your thoughts and physical sensations. But what if I were to ask you how you were doing spiritually? Where might you look to check in with your spirit? A Jew, Christian, or Muslim might identify it as their soul; a Confucian or Daoist might equate it with *qi*; a Hindu might point to a soul (*atman*) that is a part of ultimate reality (*Brahman*); a Jain might equate spirit with the life substance (*jiva*) or soul. A Buddhist might explain that there is no inherent self-nature because our physical form, sensations, perceptions, formations, and consciousness constantly change, or they might say that it refers to our potential to become enlightened. Someone unaffiliated with a religion—which now accounts for a fifth of the American public and a third of adults under thirty—may or may not believe in a spirit: 68 percent of them say they believe in God, 58 percent feel a deep connection with nature and the earth, and 37 percent identify as "spiritual but not religious."[26] Those who identify as "spiritual but not religious" often describe themselves as "seekers"[27] searching for what they believe in, rather than accepting something familiar that "doesn't feel quite right."[28] In our digital age, spiritual seekers often use the internet as a means of spiritual exploration.[29]

We typically distinguish spirit from body or matter, or spiritual from physical or material. For example, the *Oxford English Dictionary* defines spirit as "the animating or vital principle in humans and animals; that which gives life to the body, in contrast to its purely material being; the life force, the breath of life."[30] The latter understandings derive from the Greek notion of *pneuma*, which was initially understood as air drawn into the body from the outside. As Shigehisa Kuriyama notes, "Once inside the body this air had to be substantially altered—become subtler, lighter—before it flowed through the brain and nerves and made possible thought, sensation, and movement. For Christians like Origen and Augustine, *spiritus* would constitute nothing less than a divine essence, a person's inner core."[31] Discovering this essence required turning inward, and today many contemplative practitioners locate the spirit within the heart and describe spiritual practice as an inward journey to the heart.

Those who believe in God might engage in prayer, which some describe as "to descend with the mind into the heart."[32] The Catholic priest Henri Nouwen writes, "Prayer is standing in the presence of God with the mind in the heart—that is, in the point of our being where there are no divisions or distinctions and where we are totally one within ourselves, with God, and with others and the whole of creation. In the heart of God the Spirit dwells, and there the great encounter takes place."[33] He describes the heart as a place of spiritual communion. Centering prayer is a form of practice that involves quietly repeating a single word. As Henri Nouwen writes,

> A word or sentence repeated frequently can help us to concentrate, to move to the center, to create an inner stillness and thus to listen to the voice of God. When we simply try to sit silently and wait for God to speak to us, we find ourselves bombarded with endless conflicting thoughts and ideas. But when we use a very simple sentence such as "O God, come to my assistance," . . . such a simple, easily repeated prayer can slowly empty out our crowded inner life and create the quiet space where we can dwell with God.[34]

Repeated words or phrases can help one remain centered and quiet minds otherwise busy with thoughts.

Those who feel deeply connected with the natural world can engage in spiritual practices tied to nature. John Muir, the naturalist whose writings contributed to the establishment of Yosemite National Park and Grand Canyon National Park, wrote, "Climb the mountains and get their good tidings. Nature's peace will flow into you as sunshine flows into trees. The winds will blow their own freshness into you, and the storms their energy, while cares will drop off like autumn leaves."[35] Arthur Zajonc suggests that such encounters with nature can lead us to experience wonder, reverence, a blurring of boundaries, and self-surrender.[36] He notes how nature evokes a sense of the sublime—awe, terror, and astonishment in us—saying, "In it we sense the infinite in the finite and are drawn out and beyond our smaller selves to sample that unending expanse. Time slows or even stops as we settle into the sky, sea, or mountain."[37] We connect with something much larger than ourselves, and we experience reality in a way that differs from our ordinary, everyday life.

Many observe that the active life and the contemplative life engender different experiences of time. Whereas the former uses up time, Byung-Chul Han notes, "contemplative lingering *gives* time. It widens that being that is more than being-active. When life regains its capacity for contemplation, it gains in time and space, in duration and vastness."[38] Contemplation opens us to experience time in ways other than our eight-hour workdays and forty-hour workweeks. Henri Nouwen suggests that spiritual practice can transform all moments of time, moving them from being experienced as *chronos* (a series of events) to *kairos* (right time or opportune moment).[39] Nowadays, we associate time with money: both are spent, saved, wasted, or invested. We have a quantified, linear understanding of time, where we want to make efficient use of our time, and time never seems enough. This creates stress in our lives, as we feel pressured to always be productive. By contrast, spiritual practices invite space for reflection and openness to our experience, which can lead to personal growth and making meaning in our lives.[40]

Here, I invite you to reflect on your spiritual practice (if you have one). What spiritual practices have you engaged in? What impact have they had on yourself and your relationships with others? Are there any spiritual practices that you would like to explore further? After exploring these thoughts—perhaps writing them down—practice "the pause" by noticing any emotions that have surfaced, and where you feel them in the body. If you find yourself having self-critical thoughts, invite some space between yourself and those thoughts. Then, release them from your awareness and engage in a brief practice of mindfulness of breath. Afterward, you might write down ways you might make space for spiritual practice in your life.

Living Intentionally

By taking time to gauge how we feel in body, mind, and spirit, to reflect on what we value, and to align our lives with our values, we can live with greater intention and purpose. As the poet Rumi writes, "When water gets caught in habitual whirlpools, dig a way out through the bottom to the ocean."[41] Often we are unaware that we are caught up in whirlpools, and we live our lives on autopilot. To dig a way out, we must first identify our priorities in life—those things that truly matter, that give you a sense of purpose—and say no to everything else. As Greg McKeown observes in his book *Essentialism: The Disciplined Pursuit of Less*, "If you don't prioritize your life, someone else will."[42] He recommends first identifying what you feel deeply inspired by, or what you consider truly meaningful, and then eliminating the nonessentials: "If it isn't a clear *yes*, then it's a clear *no*."[43] McKeown writes, "To discern what is truly essential we need space to think, time to look and listen, permission to play, wisdom to sleep, and the discipline to apply highly selective criteria to the choices we make."[44] He suggests keeping a journal and looking for the essentials in your life that surface there, or engaging in activities that you enjoy for their own sake, and then designing a routine that safeguards them. McKeown emphasizes, "If you have correctly identified what really matters, if you invest your time and energy in it, then it is difficult to regret the choices you make."[45] When we give precedence to what we consider significant or meaningful in our lives, we create the conditions for flourishing and fulfilling our potential.

We can set intentions for our day and check in with our intentions throughout the day, especially before we engage in important tasks. As the Dalai Lama and Desmond Tutu share in the *Book of Joy*, we can engage in "morning intention setting." After finding a comfortable seated position and taking several deep breaths, we can ask ourselves what we wish for ourselves, our loved ones, and the world. Then, we can state our intention for the day, such as "Today may I greet everyone with kindness":

> It can be specific or general. If you do not know your intention, you can repeat the following four lines adapted from the traditional Tibetan prayer of the Four Immeasurables, which has guided many on their journey to more compassion and greater happiness:
> *May all beings attain happiness.*
> *May all beings be free from suffering.*
> *May all beings never be separated from joy.*
> *May all beings abide in equanimity.*[46]

Setting intentions allows us to choose how we approach our daily lives: what we choose to do and how we choose to be. When we feel imbalanced or constrained, we can reflect on and set intentions about what we might do for our lives to be the way we want them to be.

Psychological research has shown that about 40 percent of our happiness is determined by the choices we make. Sonja Lyubomirsky refers to this as the "40 percent solution": whereas 50 percent of our happiness is determined by genetically determined set points and 10 percent by our circumstances (rich or poor, healthy or unhealthy, etc.), 40 percent depends on our daily, intentional activities—"what we *do* in our lives and how we *think*."[47] Her research found that the happiest study participants nurtured and enjoyed relationships with their family and friends, felt comfortable expressing gratitude for what they had, helped others, thought optimistically about their future, savored life's pleasures, sought to live in the present moment, and were deeply committed to lifelong goals and ambitions.[48]

Scholars typically distinguish between two types of happiness: hedonism, which entails the pursuit of pleasure such as food and sex, and eudaemonia, a Greek word that refers to a sense of meaning and fulfillment, which Aristotle equated with "the flourishing life," Socrates viewed as "the examined life," and Marcus Aurelius saw as "the practical-contemplative life." Hedonic happiness tends to be short-lived: we soon adapt to its effects and return to our baseline level of happiness determined by our genetics and circumstances, which scholars call the "hedonic treadmill" or "hedonic adaptation."[49] By contrast, eudaemonic happiness tends to last longer.[50]

Relationships are the most important factor for happiness—having a partner, friends, and close family members.[51] Experiences bring people more happiness than possessions. When we wait for experiences, it elicits more happiness and excitement than waiting for material things, which typically fuels impatience.[52] In addition, we continue to enjoy the experience through our memories and conversations about it afterward.[53] We can also increase our happiness by recognizing when "good enough" will do: being what Barry Schwartz calls a "satisficer" rather than a "maximizer" who broods over decisions and experiences a greater amount of regrets and thoughts of "if only," which diminishes their satisfaction with choices they have made.[54]

Sonja Lyubomirsky shares a variety of activities that enhance happiness in her book *The How of Happiness*. You can express gratitude and thankfulness by keeping a gratitude journal outlining what you are grateful for each day or week. You can cultivate optimism by keeping a diary of your "Best Possible Selves," where you imagine yourself in the future, after you have realized your life dreams and potential.[55] You can avoid overthinking by asking yourself, "Will this matter in a year?" Lyubomirsky writes, "Your answer will afford you a big picture view of your troubles and diminish your worries. It's remarkable how quickly things that seem so momentous and pressing this very moment emerge as fairly trivial and insignificant."[56] You can savor positive experiences in your life by taking pleasure in everyday activities such as eating and showering, or by reminiscing about positive memories with family members and friends. You can take care of your body through meditation, physical activity, or even "acting like a happy person": she shares the remarkable finding that if we smile and mimic enthusiasm, those acts can make you feel happy.[57]

Equanimity

Equanimity means finding balance amid the ups and downs of our life. Our hearts make room for all experiences, encountering the vicissitudes of life with steadiness. We still experience joy and sorrow, but instead of grasping after the former and rejecting the latter, we open ourselves to both. We allow joyful and sorrowful states to arise and pass by freely. Just as the earth makes space for plants to blossom and wilt, and creatures to live and die, in its vastness and steadiness, we open ourselves to whatever we are experiencing in our bodies, minds, and hearts in this moment. We accept that "right now, it's like this."[58] As Martin Aylward explains, this does not mean we are passive or fatalistic; we can still do something, but our response is not driven by reactivity, fear, or our need to control the situation.[59] Instead, it is motivated by a spacious heart—one willing to lean into whatever is happening in our lives.

Equanimity can support and sustain many of the practices that we previously explored, not only mindfulness but also cultivating kindness, compassion, and joy. Richard Davidson outlines four skills that we can cultivate to promote well-being: attention, resilience, outlook, and generosity.[60] Attention and resilience—the ability to recover from adverse events—can be strengthened through mindfulness. Outlook—the "ability to see the positive in others, the ability to savor positive experiences, the ability to see another human being as a human being who has innate goodness"[61]—and generosity can be improved through kindness and compassion practices.

Here, I invite you to reflect on how you might find balance in your life. How do the gauges of your body, mind, and spirit look? Where do you find meaning and fulfillment in your life? What relationships and experiences have made you happy? After exploring these thoughts—perhaps writing them down—practice "the pause" by noticing any emotions that have surfaced, and where you feel them in the body. If you find yourself having self-critical thoughts, invite some space between yourself and those thoughts. Then, release them from your awareness and engage in a brief practice of mindfulness of breath. Afterward, you might write down ways you might find balance in your life.

Notes

1. Rūmī, *Essential Rumi*, 36.
2. Friedman, *Leading the Life You Want*, 4.
3. Friedman, *Leading the Life You Want*, 4.
4. Friedman, *Leading the Life You Want*, 10–15.
5. Harris, *Confidence Gap*, 16.
6. Harris, *Confidence Gap*, 138–40.
7. Burnett and Evans, *Design Your Life*, 18.
8. Burnett and Evans, *Design Your Life*, 16–17.
9. Burnett and Evans, *Design Your Life*, 26.
10. Burnett and Evans, *Design Your Life*, 31.
11. Burnett and Evans, *Design Your Life*, 32.
12. Nadeau, *Asian Religions*, 66.
13. Kuriyama, *Expressiveness of the Body*, 268.
14. Kuriyama, *Expressiveness of the Body*, 268.
15. Kuriyama, *Expressiveness of the Body*, 272.
16. Grossnickle, "Disentangling Curiosity," 26.
17. Irving, "Mind-Wandering Is Unguided Attention."
18. Escalante, "New Science."
19. Zomorodi, *Bored and Brilliant*.
20. Parkes, "Bereavement as a Psychosocial Transition," 56.
21. Neimeyer and Sands, "Meaning Reconstruction in Bereavement," 10.
22. Quoted in Treleaven, *Trauma-Sensitive Mindfulness*, 66.
23. Treleaven, *Trauma-Sensitive Mindfulness*, 159.
24. Cited in Styron, *Darkness Visible*, 83.
25. Styron, *Darkness Visible*, 84.
26. Pew Research Center, "'Nones' on the Rise."
27. Clarke-Roof, *Generation of Seekers*.
28. Kitchener, "What It Means to Be Spiritual But Not Religious."
29. Hoover, *Religion in the Media Age*, 81, 177–91.
30. "Spirit, n.," *Oxford English Dictionary*, December 2021, accessed March 6, 2022, https://www-oed-com.liblink.uncw.edu/view/Entry/186867?rskey=yZCWbi&result=1.
31. Kuriyama, *Expressiveness of the Body*, 261–62.

32. Nouwen, *Way of the Heart*, 73.

33. Nouwen, *Spiritual Formation*, xvi.

34. Nouwen, *Way of the Heart*, 81.

35. Muir, *Our National Parks*, 56.

36. Zajonc, *Meditation as Contemplative Inquiry*, 56–57.

37. Zajonc, *Meditation as Contemplative Inquiry*, 54.

38. Han, *Scent of Time*, 113.

39. Nouwen, *Spiritual Formation*, 9.

40. Yang et al., "Social Media Social Comparison."

41. Rūmī, *Essential Rumi*, 52.

42. McKeown, *Essentialism*, 10.

43. McKeown, *Essentialism*, 109.

44. McKeown, *Essentialism*, 60.

45. McKeown, *Essentialism*, 237.

46. Dalai Lama and Tutu, *Book of Joy*, 312.

47. Lyubomirsky, *How of Happiness*, 22.

48. Lyubomirsky, *How of Happiness*, 22–23.

49. "Hedonic Treadmill" *Psychology Today*, accessed March 5, 2022, https://www.psychologytoday.com/us/basics/hedonic-treadmill.

50. McMahan and Estes, "Hedonic versus Eudaimonic Conceptions."

51. Schwartz, *Paradox of Choice*, 107.

52. Hamblin, "Buy Experiences, Not Things."

53. Ben-Shahar, *Choose the Life You Want*.

54. Schwartz, *Paradox of Choice*, 86.

55. Lyubomirsky, *How of Happiness*, 103–6.

56. Lyubomirsky, *How of Happiness*, 123.

57. Lyubomirsky, *How of Happiness*, 250–51.

58. Sperry, "'Right Now, It's Like This.'"

59. Aylward, *Awake Where You Are*, 128–29.

60. Davidson, "Four Keys to Well-Being."

61. Davidson, "Four Keys to Well-Being."

CHAPTER ELEVEN

Reading

The kiss of his memory made pictures of love and light against the wall.
Here was peace. She pulled in her horizon like a great fish-net. Pulled
it from around the waist of the world and draped it over her shoulder.
So much of life in its meshes! She called in her soul to come and see.
—Zora Neale Hurston, *Their Eyes Were Watching God*[1]

"Thimk!" This sign hung on the wall in the classroom of my high school history teacher, Mr. Dave Gould. Strategically placed under the clock, so that we would see it every time we found ourselves looking at the time, it reminded us about the importance of reading, and how it was tied to critical thinking. Mr. Gould would always start class with a quotation written on the board. We would pay close attention to who said it, what cultural, historical, and social context they were speaking from, whom they were addressing, and its overall significance. He taught me the importance of critical reading, a skill which I continued to develop as a comparative literature major in college. In my first year of college, I wrote a paper about how conversion narratives of slaves emphasized the importance of culture and community, while those of slave owners spoke in more individualistic terms, analyzing how these divergent understandings stemmed from their different cultural backgrounds. I continued my research by reading books about Black, womanist, and liberation theologies, as well as Afrocentrism, which led me to African literature. I eventually wrote an honors thesis on African literature written in French, focusing on the work of Henri Lopes and Sony Lab'ou Tansi.

Reading, writing, and speaking are forms of communication—not only means of exchanging information or ideas, but also ways of connecting, inter-acting, and engaging with people. We write or speak to a particular audience, and we have a particular purpose that motivates our writing or speech. That message influences the medium we choose for our communication, be it a blog, an infographic, an essay, an elevator pitch, or TED talk. When we read or listen, we try to understand that message and discern the author or speaker's purpose. We may not be successful in that endeavor. We may have difficulty understanding what they have said, or our interpretations may not align with their intentions. While we can check for understanding in our conversations with others to ensure that the message sent was the message received, when we read printed texts or look at works of art, we rarely have access to their creators to ask them about their vision or motivations. Instead, we try to make meaning of what we read, hear, or see. We connect it with our previous knowledge and experience, we attend to what we are reading, hearing, or seeing, and we consider the cultural, historical, social, and political contexts in which it was created. We read generously, trying to capture the author's original meaning or argument as best we can, and representing it in our own words. We can also read critically, weighing what we have read and evaluating it.

This sort of active reading may seem unfamiliar or even feel uncomfortable at first. It may go against your ordinary reading habits of consuming information by scrolling through news or social media. Such digital reading is more akin to "downloading, main-point gleaning, bullet-point grabbing, gist getting, plot summarizing."[2] We skim for ideas or survey for main points. We read and react, driven by strong emotions, in our post-truth culture which values opinions more than facts and has multiple outlets for spreading those opinions.[3] You previously learned lateral reading strategies that you can use to determine whether a source is trustworthy. In this chapter you will learn different ways of reading, including rhetorical reading, close reading, and critical reading. You will also explore mindful reading—how you can become deliberate and reflective about how you read, and the demands that different contexts place on your reading.[4] For example, when you read a textbook or encyclopedia article, you read for information or main points, but when you read poetry, you attend to the poet's choice of words or phrasing. Different genres of writing call for different ways of reading, just as disciplines have their own conventions and expectations for writing. Literary genres stem from the four literary forms of nonfiction prose, fiction prose, poetry, and drama, and you are likely familiar with fictional prose genres, such as mystery, historical fiction, fantasy, science fiction, horror, adventure, and romance novels. This chapter explores other genres of writing, including academic articles, book reviews and literature reviews. It discusses ways you might read such texts, and how you might apply such strategies to visual and material artifacts.

Rhetorical Reading

Rhetoric refers to the art of effective or persuasive writing or speech, and rhetorical reading considers various factors that contribute to the production and interpretation of texts. It attends to the writer and their frames of reference, the intended audience, the genre of text they produce, the purpose of the text, the exigence or perceived need for the text, as well as cultural, historical, social, and political factors that influence the writer and readers of the text. Together, these elements constitute the "rhetorical situation" pictured below: how writers engage with their audience, what they seek to accomplish, and their goals or motivations. As Justin Jory notes, "Because writing is highly situated and responds to specific human needs in a particular time and place, texts should be produced and interpreted with those needs and contexts in mind."[5] This way of reading draws attention to the writer, their imagined audience, and the

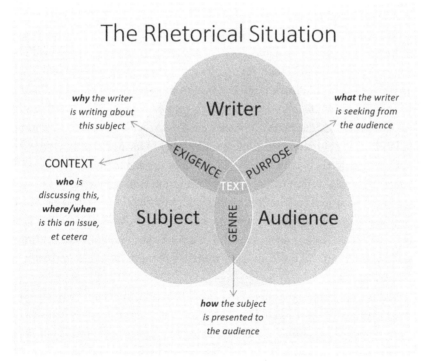

The Rhetorical Situation. "The Rhetorical Situation" by Justin Jory on Open English @ SLCC.

ways that they appeal to their audience, anticipating the values and expectations that their target audience will bring to the text.

For example, we might attend to the rhetorical situation surrounding Zora Neale Hurston's *Their Eyes Were Watching God* (1937), quoted at the beginning of the chapter. Zora Neale Hurston (1891–1960) was an anthropologist and author whose writing was widely published during the Harlem Renaissance movement, a flourishing period for Black artists, writers, and musicians in the 1920s and 1930s. The novel centers on the character of Janie Crawford, a Black woman in her forties, who recounts her life story to her friend Pheoby. At the end Janie says, "It's uh known fact, Pheoby, you got tuh *go* there tuh *know* there. Yo' papa and yo' mama and nobody else can't tell yuh and show yuh. Two things everybody's got tuh do fuh theyselves. They got tuh go tuh God, and they got tuh find out about livin' fuh theyselves."[6] Janie's remarks capture the author's purpose: to share a story about a Black woman who develops her personal autonomy—the capacity to be her own person and live according to their own values and dreams.

Some criticized *Their Eyes Were Watching God*—especially Hurston's use of the Black southern vernacular—as denigrating Blacks to entertain whites. Author Richard Wright (1908-1960) argued that her dialogue portrayed Black characters as simple-minded, and she was promoting "the minstrel technique that makes the 'white folks' laugh."[7] Others praised her use of the Black southern vernacular and Hurston's "accurate ear for its raciness, its rich invention, and its music."[8] Hurston's work fell into obscurity in the decades following the Harlem Renaissance, until Alice Walker, whose novel *The Color Purple* (1982) won a Pulitzer Prize for Fiction, renewed interest in Hurston's writings through her essay "In Search of Zora Neale Hurston" published in the magazine *Ms.* in 1975.[9] Later readers, especially women, have found the message of *Their Eyes were Watching God* empowering. Walker argues that Hurston's novel shows her love for people of color and her desire for them to have "a foundation in their own reality."[10]

In this way, rhetorical reading focuses on the writer, their audience, and how writers appeal to their audience to convey their message. It involves "constructing a rhetorical situation for the text, trying to account for author's purpose, context, and effect on the audience."[11] It accounts for a writer's motivations, the responses of readers, and the situational and historical context out of which the text grew. We recognize that texts are situated, just as we acknowledge our situatedness when we enter dialogues and difficult conversations. As we make meaning of texts, we draw on our prior knowledge, experience, and expectations, but we also recognize that texts and their writers may be situated quite differently than us. As Christina Haas and Linda Flower write, "The rhetorical reader understands that discourse is meant to engage us, to persuade us, to call us to action, but most of all to connect us—with writers and with other readers."[12] We understand reading as a social activity.

Close Reading

Close reading means carefully analyzing a text, investigating its particular words, sentences, and paragraphs.[13] When we read closely, we attend to the details of the text, opening ourselves to the images, metaphors, and imagination of others.[14] We participate in another way of seeing and interpreting the world. You may find yourself struck by what you consider to be key moments in a text, or you may be puzzled by other sections that seem obtuse or mysterious. Often such passages are opportune moments to engage in close reading, considering the relationship between language, style, and meaning, or reflecting on the author's tone and choice of words. As Martha Nussbaum writes,

> The telling itself—the selection of genre, formal structures, sentences, vocabulary, of the whole manner of addressing the reader's sense of life—all of this expresses a sense of life and of value, a sense of what matters and what does not, of what learning and communicating are, of life's relations and connections. Life is never simply *presented* by a text; it is always *represented as* something.[15]

A text represents life in a certain way, and when we attend to its concrete details, we strengthen our capacity of perception. We develop our "ability to miss less, to be responsible to more."[16] This has ethical implications: if we can imagine and experience the concrete lives of others, we become better equipped to notice and respond to their struggles.

For example, we might closely read a passage from *Their Eyes Were Watching God* that immediately follows an incident when Janie's second husband, Jody, slaps her for cooking a mediocre meal. Hurston writes,

> Janie stood where he left her for unmeasured time and thought. She stood there until something fell off the shelf inside her. Then she went inside there to see what it was. It was her image of Jody tumbled down and shattered.

But looking at it she saw that it was never the flesh and blood figure of her dreams. Just something she had grabbed to drape her dreams over. In a way she turned her back upon the image where it lay and looked further. . . . She found that she had a host of thoughts she had never expressed to him, and numerous emotions she had never let Jody know about. Things packed up and put away in parts of her heart where he could never find them.

A close reading of the passage might talk about how time seems to stand still ("unmeasured"), and how Janie's estimation of Jody has fallen to such an extent that its irreparably damaged ("shattered"). It might point out the imagery of something "falling off the shelf" or something "she had grabbed to drape her dreams over," which draws to mind china and shawls, reframed in the context of herself and her dreams. It might reflect on the use of the word "something" to refer to Jody, and how it captures the sense of alienation that Janie feels toward him: he is no longer a person but a thing. It might notice that in this moment of inner reflection ("she went inside"), Janie becomes aware of the ways she has safeguarded herself by keeping thoughts and emotions hidden from Jody. After her experience of domestic abuse, Janie discovers ("found") parts of her heart that she never revealed to him. It might also contrast the casual way she depicts draping her dreams over Jody with the more intentional way she "pulls in her horizon" and drapes it over her shoulder at the end of the novel.

In this way, close reading entails analyzing the significance of words and phrases, and how they impact our understanding of the text. It allows us to immerse ourselves in the imaginative worlds of others, giving ourselves over to the text. Close reading involves "reading with the grain," a phrase that David Bartholomae and Anthony Petrosky coined, which means "to read generously, to work inside someone else's system, to see your world in someone else's terms."[17] By contrast, critical reading entails working against the grain, questioning the text, considering what it overlooks or ways it might be extended.

Critical Reading

Although we may associate criticism with fault-finding or harsh opinions, critical reading means engaging fully with the text, examining not only what it says, but what it omits. Critical reading encourages us to raise questions about the text, to identify its underlying assumptions, and to consider ways we might extend its observations and insights. As Rita Felski notes, "To engage in critique is to grapple with the oversights, omissions, contradictions, insufficiencies, or evasions in the object one is analyzing. . . . The role of critique is not to castigate, but to complicate, not to engage in ideas' destruction but to expose their cultural construction."[18] Critical reading urges us to explore the complexity of the text, how it connects to its cultural, historical, and social contexts, and how it relates to the writer's body of work.

For example, we might critically analyze the role of spirituality in *Their Eyes Were Watching God*. Hurston portrays God as sustaining the world: "She knew that God tore down the old world every evening and built a new one by sun-up. It was wonderful to see it take form with the sun and emerge from the gray dust of its making."[19] She also suggests that God intervenes in people's lives, implying God played a role in Janie meeting her final love, Tea Cake: "Ah wuz fumblin' round and God opened de door."[20] She acknowledges that natural disasters and other experiences of suffering lead one to question God and wonder "if He meant to measure their puny might against His."[21] Viewing God as all-powerful and all-knowing, Janie struggles to account for why He would not alleviate such suffering, and she looks up to the sky for a sign. Hurston writes, "The sky stayed hard looking and quiet so she went inside the house. God would do less than He had in His heart."[22] She draws attention to the discrepancy between God's love and God's inaction in response to suffering. This is what Hurston says about God in her text.

However, reading critically, we might point out that Hurston does not portray God as good. Western religions traditionally characterize God as all-good (omnibenevolent), all-powerful (omnipotent), and all-knowing (omniscient), and they struggle to reconcile how an omnibenevolent God would allow for suffering and evil in the world. Although some equate goodness with love, Hurston depicts love more ambivalently. On the one hand, Hurston connects love with the spirit, as she describes how Janie's "soul crawled out from its hiding place" when she fell in love with Tea Cake.[23] On the other hand, in Jody's case, sometimes love includes violence, which resonates with Hurston's depiction of God tearing down the old world and failing to intervene in instances of suffering and disaster. At the end of the novel, Janie reflects on love, saying, "Love ain't somethin' lak uh grindstone dat's de same thing everywhere and do de same thing tuh everything it touch. Love is lak de sea. It's uh movin' thing, but still and all, it takes its shape from de shore it meets, and it's different with every shore."[24] Comparing love to the ocean, she notes that it moves and shifts with each person it meets.

A critical reading might also connect Hurston's vision of love and spirituality with the work of later writers such as Alice Walker. When Janie finds her voice in *Their Eyes Were Watching God,* she writes, "Sometimes God gits familiar wid us womenfolks too and talks His inside business."[25] Several decades later, Walker coined the term "womanist" and defined it in three ways: first, a Black feminist or feminist of color; second, a woman who appreciates women's culture, emotional flexibility, and strength; and third, one who "loves music. Loves dance. Loves the moon. *Loves* the Spirit. Loves love and food and roundness. Loves struggle. *Loves* the Folk. Loves herself. *Regardless.*"[26] A critical reading might trace continuities and discontinuities between Hurston's depiction of women's strength, love, spirituality, and personal autonomy with Walker's later vision of womanism.

Mindful Reading

We can apply mindfulness to these ways of reading—rhetorical reading, close reading, and critical reading—by being deliberate and reflective about why and how we choose each type of reading.[27] As we have seen, each reading approach enables you to address different aspects of the text. Mindful reading is a metacognitive framework for thinking about how you move among these reading approaches. When you read mindfully, you can identify those moments in a text when you might shift reading approaches to yield greater insight.[28] Different contexts and genres place different demands on our reading, and mindful reading involves "rhetorical adaptability" as you reflect on and practice a range of reading approaches for these different contexts.[29]

When you first encounter a text, preview it by scanning its title, author, introductory material (such as an abstract), and general structure to determine its genre. Once you have determined the genre or context, you can adapt your strategies to fit that context. As Ellen Carillo notes, as you read a text you might ask yourself,

> Which reading approach will I employ first and why?
> How far does this reading approach take me?
> What does this reading approach allow me to notice in the text?

What must I ignore?

What meanings does this approach allow me to construct and what meanings does it prohibit?[30]

We can reflect on the reading strategies we use for a particular text, and we can also reflect on the strengths and limitations of each approach within a particular context.

Academic Reading Strategies

Preview academic writing to identify whether it is a peer-reviewed work, a book review, or a popular piece of writing. Peer-reviewed articles and books have been reviewed by at least two experts in the field. These reviewers either reject the article, call for major revisions, or request minor revisions. Because of this vetting process, peer-reviewed scholarship is often—but not always—considered reliable. Book reviews briefly summarize the topic, argument, and purpose of a book, evaluate its persuasiveness, and identify audiences that might benefit from reading it. Popular writing, including newspaper articles, blogs, op-ed pieces, and popular books, have not been vetted by academic experts, and they are typically written for more general audiences.

When reading academic articles, first skim the abstract, introduction, and conclusion to identify its central argument and supporting evidence. In an academic book, you will often find the argument and a description of each chapter of the book in the introduction. As you read, annotate it by writing notes, comments, and questions in the margins. As Ellen Carillo notes, "These marginal notes represent the initial ways in which you are participating in the scholarly conversation with the author of the text."[31] If you don't own the book or have a digital file to annotate, you might write down its central argument, key passages, and questions it raised for you.

You might look over the literature review, which is also called a scholarly review, to get a sense of how the writer situates their work in the larger field of scholarship. It will give you a sense of how their arguments compare to those in the field. You may find that you want to read some of those scholarly works. You might also mark passages or points that you find difficult to understand. As you read, you can alternate between reading to understand the argument, evidence, and underlying assumptions, and reading to critique it, which might entail assessing its strengths and weaknesses, elaborating on its implications, comparing it to alternative arguments, or assessing whether an argument accomplishes what it claims to.[32] For problematic passages—those that puzzle you, or raise questions for you—you might consider trying to "unpack" them in your own words, articulating how you might interpret those sections in your own words.

Contemplative Reading

Contemplative reading encourages us to slow down and attend to what we are reading. The Christian contemplative practice of *lectio divina* ("divine reading") encouraged people to first carefully read a sacred or devotional text (*lectio*), then reflect on its deeper meaning (*meditatio*), listen within (*oratio*), and be still and meet God in the text (*contemplatio*).[33] A secular practice of contemplative reading might begin by reading a passage, staying with the words for several minutes, writing down first thoughts about the passage, but then revisiting the passage and allowing it "to percolate and produce associations and insights."[34] It could be followed by a brief mindfulness practice and freewriting activity about the meaning you made following that deeper reading. For example, you might read part of Mary Oliver's poem "The Summer Day":

> I do know how to pay attention, how to fall down
> into the grass, how to kneel in the grass,
> how to be idle and blessed, how to stroll through the fields,
> which is what I have been doing all day.
> Tell me, what else should I have done?
> Doesn't everything die at last, and too soon?
> Tell me, what is it you plan to do
> With your one wild and precious life?[35]

You could reflect on the poem as a whole or focus on one or two verses, letting them sit with you. When we read contemplatively, we create space for slow, attentive reading and reflection.

Notes

1. Hurston, *Their Eyes Were Watching God*, 183–84.
2. Miller, "On Digital Reading."
3. Carillo, *Teaching Readers*, 7.

4. Carillo, *Securing a Place for Reading in Composition*, 117.

5. Jory, "Rhetorical Situation."

6. Hurston, *Their Eyes Were Watching God*, 183.

7. Richard Wright, *The New Masses*, October 5, 1937, quoted in Book Marks, "First Reviews."

8. George Stevens, *The Saturday Review of Literature*, September 18, 1937, quoted in Book Marks, "First Reviews."

9. Walker, "In Search of Zora Neale Hurston."

10. "Alice Walker on Zora Neale Hurston's 'Spiritual Food.'"

11. Haas and Flower, "Rhetorical Reading Strategies," 176.

12. Haas and Flower, "Reply," 482.

13. Carillo, *Securing a Place for Reading in Composition*, 114.

14. Bartholomae and Petrosky, *Ways of Reading*, 3.

15. Nussbaum, *Love's Knowledge*, 5.

16. Nussbaum, *Love's Knowledge*, 164.

17. Bartholomae and Petrosky, *Ways of Reading*, 9.

18. Felski, "Critique and the Hermeneutics of Suspicion."

19. Hurston, *Their Eyes Were Watching God*, 24.

20. Hurston, *Their Eyes Were Watching God*, 151.

21. Hurston, *Their Eyes Were Watching God*, 151.

22. Hurston, *Their Eyes Were Watching God*, 169.

23. Hurston, *Their Eyes Were Watching God*, 122.

24. Hurston, *Their Eyes Were Watching God*, 182.

25. Hurston, *Their Eyes Were Watching God*, 70.

26. Walker, *In Search of Our Mothers' Gardens*, xii.

27. Carillo, *Securing a Place for Reading in Composition*, 118.

28. Carillo, *Securing a Place for Reading in Composition*, 123.

29. Carillo, *Securing a Place for Reading in Composition*, 19.

30. Carillo, *Securing a Place for Reading in Composition*, 136.

31. Carillo, *Writer's Guide to Mindful Reading*, xi.

32. Gallagher and Maguire, *Religious Studies Skills Book*, 94.

33. Barbezat and Bush, *Contemplative Practices in Higher Education*, 111.

34. Barbezat and Bush, *Contemplative Practices in Higher Education*, 121.

35. Oliver, "Poem 133: The Summer Day."

CHAPTER TWELVE

Writing

If you want to be a writer, you must do two things above
all others: read a lot and write a lot. There's no way around
these two things that I'm aware of, no shortcut.
—Stephen King[1]

I distinctly remember feeling my stomach sink after my First Year Seminar instructor handed me back my paper. His red ink flooded its pages, and at the top, next to my abysmal grade, he had written "Strunk & White." I later discovered this was referring to William Strunk and E. B. White, authors of *The Elements of Style*.[2] This book became an invaluable resource, finding its way on my shelf next to my *Oxford American Dictionary*. When I met with my peer mentor to go over my paper and the instructor's feedback, he patiently pointed out how my writing completely obscured my meaning. He recommended I write simply and directly, echoing the advice of Jacques Barzun in *Simple & Direct: A Rhetoric for Writers*: "Have a point and make it by means of the best word,"[3] "weed out the jargon,"[4] and "look for all fancy wordings and get rid of them."[5] I had written in a way that I thought academics should write—using sophisticated words—without paying attention to what I was trying to say. I soon began eliminating passive-voice constructions from my writing, and I tried to avoid hifalutin jargon—grandiose words that are deliberately difficult to understand.

Reading and writing are connected practices.[6] As a writer, you must first identify the audience and purpose for your writing, and then attend to other elements of a rhetorical situation, including genre, exigence, and context. Consider questions such as: Who are your intended readers, and how much do they already know? What is your purpose for writing? What do you want your readers to know, believe, or do after reading your work? What genre is most appropriate for your context, and what style, language, and document design does the genre require?[7] Once you develop these rhetorical thinking skills, you can more easily transfer these skills from one writing context to another.[8]

The more you read, the more writing styles you encounter. As Stephen King notes, "Every book you pick up has its own lesson or lessons, and quite often the bad books have more to teach than the good ones."[9] Bad writing gives examples of what to avoid, while good writing may inspire you to try out various writing styles until you develop a sense of your own. Voracious reading, King writes, "offers you a constantly growing knowledge of what has been done and what hasn't, what is trite and what is fresh, what works and what just lies there dying (or dead) on the page."[10] When it comes to academic writing, specialists largely agree that you should

Use clear, precise language, even when you are expressing complex ideas
Avoid opaque, vague, or imprecise words
Use active verbs and concrete nouns
Avoid passive verb constructions or use them sparingly
Keep sentences short, simple, and concise
Use examples, illustrations, and anecdotes to engage your reader's attention
Create a compelling narrative.[11]

These rules help ensure that you communicate your ideas clearly and directly. As Helen Sword observes, even scientists have largely abandoned the impersonal passive voice in favor of a personal voice.[12] She recommends that academic writers use plenty of concrete nouns and vivid verbs, especially when discussing abstract concepts, keep nouns and verbs close together, and avoid extraneous words or phrases that clutter writing.[13] As she notes, concrete nouns help the reader visualize objects, actions, and relationships.

You can use such suggestions as a guide, but they only go so far. Ultimately, you must develop your own writing style. You can use mindfulness to help do that, turning toward your thoughts, feelings, and sensations. As Peter Elbow observes, when you speak or write, you draw on inner sources: words and nonverbal "felt sense." He writes, "If we are trying to say something we've never said before or never figured out, something as yet unformulated in our minds, we have greater need to draw on felt sense."[14] He describes the following process for finding words for what we sense but cannot yet express:

Accept the words that just arrive in the mind and mouth. Welcome them.
But then pause and be comfortable about noticing if they are wrong or don't fit what we feel or intend. Ask, "Do these words get at what I'm aiming for?" That is, don't ignore or blot out the sense of wrongness or just blunder

onwards out of a feeling of, "Oh well, I'm just not a verbal, articulate kind of person."

Pause and pay attention not just to the wrongness or gap but to the felt sense or felt meaning or intention *behind* the wrong words. Try to listen to the felt sense—or, more precisely, try to feel it, even in the body.

From this attending or feeling for felt sense, invite new words to come.[15]

As Peter Elbow emphasizes, we are often unable to find the right words for what we want to say on the first round, but we uncover them eventually. Freewriting—writing words as they arise in our thoughts, writing without stopping or rushing—can help bridge our felt sense and language.[16] Natalie Goldberg encourages a process of deep listening and receptivity to the world around you: "You listen so deeply to the space around you that it fills you, and when you write, it pours out of you. . . . Listening is receptivity. The deeper you can listen, the better you can write. You take in the way things are without judgment, and the next day you can write the truth about the way things are."[17] Being receptive and open, you start noticing words on a page, people in conversation, and aspects of your environment; these become material for your writing.

Writing calls for creativity and critical thinking, and their opposing aims make the writing process challenging.[18] Peter Elbow proposes separating the process into two stages of creating and criticizing: "First be loose and accepting as you do fast early writing; then be critically toughminded as you revise what you have produced."[19] Mindfulness—attuning to our inner thoughts, feelings, and sensations, or opening ourselves to our environment—can help in the creative stage when you want to generate new thoughts and words. The revising stage calls for a corrective frame of mind, which can be counterproductive during the creative stage.[20] As Peter Elbow writes, "We see faults in ideas before we've had a chance to work them out, and we get distracted in our thinking by all the fixing and correcting at the surface level."[21] When we think of creating and criticizing as separate stages or mindsets, we can use both to enhance our writing, rather than undermine it. Although we often distinguish between "creative writing" (poems, stories, novels) and "expository writing" (essays, reports, and memos), Elbow emphasizes that both call for creativity and critical thinking—for intuition and critical discrimination.[22]

This chapter explores the writing process and various ways of writing, including freewriting, reflection, research papers, and literature reviews. Before you continue reading, you might stop and reflect on your previous writing experiences. What types of audiences have you written for? What topics have you addressed, why did you write about it (exigence), what did you seek from your audience (purpose), and what type of writing (genre) did you use to accomplish those aims? What strategies have you used in the writing process, and were they successful? If not, what might you have done differently? Thinking about these fundamental aspects of writing—audience, exigence, purpose, and genre—will help you transfer your prior knowledge to future writing projects.

Freewriting

Freewriting gets words down on a page, warms you up to writing, and gets thoughts flowing. Simply write continuously without stopping for ten minutes. Don't stop to correct errors or read what you have written. Just keep writing until you have reached the ten-minute mark. As Peter Elbow writes, "If you can't think of anything to write, write about how that feels. . . . If you get stuck in the middle of a sentence or thought, just repeat the last word or phrase till something comes along. The only point is to keep writing."[23] Natalie Goldberg advises not to cross out, think, or get logical: "The aim is to burn through to first thoughts, to the place where energy is unobstructed by social politeness or the internal censor, to the place where you are writing what your mind actually sees and feels, not what it *thinks* it should see or feel."[24] Freewriting helps overcome the initial inertia or reluctance to write, and it also resists the tendency to get caught up with your spelling, grammar, or punctuation. It cedes control to spontaneity. Poet Allen Ginsberg referred to it as the "spontaneous mind" that embraces the immediacy of first thoughts.[25] As Peter Elbow writes, "It helps you stand out of the way and let words be chosen by the sequence of the words themselves or the thought, not by the conscious self. In this way freewriting gradually puts a deeper resonance or voice into your writing."[26] You can also explore visual and oral alternatives such as free drawing, mind mapping, and verbal brainstorming.[27]

Reflection

Reflection involves turning back, thinking carefully about past experiences, and introspection.[28] You can reflect on new information and ideas, experiences, situations, and events, and how they impact your beliefs, values, attitudes, assumptions, and relationships. You not only reflect on what you learned, but how you learned it. One way to approach reflection is to first describe your experience in detail (who, what, where, when, and why), then examine what assumptions or expectations you brought to the experience, how you interpreted it, and how it impacted you, and finally, articulate what you learned, how you learned it, why it matters, and what you will do in light of it.[29] Another way to approach reflection is addressing the questions "What? So What? Now What?"[30] You describe in detail your experience, why it was significant, and next steps that you might take. The "What?" step involves describing what happened, what you learned from the experience, and what you found surprising or challenging. The "So What?" step reflects on critical questions that it caused, emotions that it evoked, how it connects to broader issues, conclusions you drew from it, how it impacted or changed your beliefs, values, and opinions, any new skills you learned, and what you learned about yourself or others as a result. The "Now What?" phase addresses how you might apply what you have learned, what you might want to learn more about, what you might do differently in the future, and where you go from here.[31]

Reflection promotes active learning and metacognition. You actively make meaning from your experiences and engage in transformational learning, which Jack Mezirow describes as "the process by which we transform our taken-for-granted frames of reference (meaning perspectives, habits of mind, mind-sets) to make them more inclusive, discriminating, open, emotionally capable of change, and reflective so that they may generate beliefs and opinions that will prove more true or justified to guide action."[32] Instead of solely following external authorities and their expectations, you develop a sense of "self-authorship," which Marcia Baxter Magolda defines as "the internal capacity to define one's beliefs, identity, and relationships."[33] Recognizing that many events or experiences fall beyond our control, but that we have ownership over how we respond to and make meaning of them, we learn to trust our internal voice, align our lives to our internal voice, and live our convictions.[34]

We can engage in brief forms of reflective writing, such as one-minute papers, or more extended forms of reflective writing in learning portfolios. After you attend class or do a reading, you can briefly reflect on what was the muddiest point and the most important idea, how you might relate topics or connect them to other ideas, and what important questions remain unanswered for you.[35] After participating in an experiential or service-learning activity, completing an internship, or studying abroad, you can reflect on your experience following the Describe, Explain, and Articulate Learning (DEAL) or What? So What? Now What? approaches. Finally, you might reflect on what you learned in a particular course, your major, your cocurricular activities, and your entire college experience through a learning portfolio which, as we mentioned in chapter 7, can be a digital ePortfolio. You can reflect on what you learned, how you learned it, how you might apply it to other contexts, how you might integrate it with other experiences or ideas, how it impacted you and others, and how your beliefs, values, or opinions changed as a result.[36]

Research Papers

Research starts with good questions—ones that fascinate you, puzzle or perplex you, and make you want to learn more. In college some of my research questions were: Why did the stories of slave conversions to Christianity differ so greatly from those of slave owners? How do post-colonial African authors criticize corruption and violence in their novels? How might people overcome the tendency toward self-deception?

Research-based writing involves developing research questions; analyzing, synthesizing, and documenting sources; and writing, editing, and revising your paper.[37] To develop research questions, conduct preliminary research so you can narrow your questions enough to be feasible in scope, precise, and significant. Once you have determined the questions you are trying to answer, you can identify your information needs and generate search terms for them. You will use these sources in different ways, as Joseph Bizup points out in his BEAM model:

Background: using a source to provide general information or factual evidence to provide context in your paper

Exhibit: using a source as evidence that you analyze or interpret in your paper

Argument: scholarly arguments that you will engage in conversation with (affirming, disputing, refining, or extending their argument)

Method: using a key concept, a particular procedure, or a general model from a source[38]

Some may distinguish between primary, secondary, and tertiary sources—primary sources such as historical documents, literature, or interviews, secondary sources that discuss the primary sources, and tertiary sources that summarize or synthesize discussions from secondary sources—but the advantage of the BEAM approach is that it focuses on what you *do* with sources. As Joseph Bizup emphasizes, "Writers *rely on* background sources, *interpret or analyze* exhibits, *engage* arguments, and *follow* methods."[39] You use background sources to provide a context for your own argument and counterargument, you use exhibits as evidence in support of those positions, and you use scholarly arguments in your review of the field. You know whether you have a viable argument if someone else can argue against it and provide persuasive evidence in support.

You will bring your own personal style to your research paper. Shigehisa Kuriyama, one of my teachers, recommends the mystery story format: a mystery, the obvious suspects, and the unexpected—yet convincing—solution. You begin by presenting a puzzle and persuading the reader it is an interesting one. He insists this is 80 percent of a successful paper: being able to identify a compelling problem and why the reader should care about it. Then, you explore possible explanations, anticipating the mental moves that your reader might make, as you would in a chess game. Finally, you present your solution to the problem. A good paper passes the test of, "So what? Why should I care?" Kuriyama recommends reading your paper aloud: if you can read it easily, and if you find it interesting and compelling, it passes the test.

Writing includes not only generating ideas and writing a draft of your paper, but also revising, editing, and polishing it. When you revise, you reconsider your ideas and the structure of your paper. You might reflect on the following questions and write one sentence in response to each:

Who is your intended audience?
What research questions do you aim to answer?
What new contribution(s) does your research make?
What is your overarching thesis or argument?
What evidence do you offer in support?[40]

Look at your paper's organization and structure. A scientific research paper conventionally has an introduction, method, results, and discussion structure.[41] Other research papers typically include an introduction, review of scholarship, supporting paragraphs for an argument and counterargument, and a conclusion. You can include section headings to give your paper structure, or even use questions as structuring devices: after raising the big question at the beginning, you can progress through smaller questions that address it, which helps the reader understand the sequence of ideas.

Keeping your audience and purpose in mind, read through what you wrote. Start with the title: does it engage and orient the reader to your topic? Continue with your introduction: does it have an opening "hook" such as a challenging question, anecdote, or surprising fact to engage the reader?[42] Does it provide a context for your paper, without oversimplifying or generalizing, and does it clearly articulate your argument, and ideally, your counterargument as well? Next, consider your supporting paragraphs: do they clearly connect with and contribute to your argument or counterargument? Consider making that connection explicit by beginning your supporting paragraphs with a "mini-thesis" where you, in your own words, state what you will argue in the paragraph to contribute to the overall argument, and ensure you have smooth transitions between paragraphs. Have you provided compelling evidence in support, thoroughly unpacking the quotations from your exhibit sources? Have you cited those sources and provided a list of works cited at the end? Have you defined terms that may be unfamiliar to your reader, and provided clear examples and images to illustrate abstract ideas? Finally, examine your conclusion: does it discuss questions raised but unexplored, or avenues of possible future research?

You can then engage in editing, making changes in your sentences and paragraphs. Pay attention to your choice of words and phrasing. Tighten and clean up your language, aiming for precision and energy, as Peter Elbow suggests: "The more you zero in on the precise meaning you have in mind, the more you can strip away unnecessary words and thereby energize your language."[43] Elbow recommends looking for places where you stumble or get lost mid-sentence and cutting out extra words, vagueness, and digression to recover the energy, vitality, and meaning of your words.[44] Finally, you can polish your paper by checking your spelling, grammar, punctuation, and formatting.

You can also solicit feedback from others. They approach your work with fresh eyes, and they experience it in new ways. Likewise, if you read other people's work, you become more attuned to the importance of transitions, threads of arguments, and simple and direct words. Mindfulness can help us to stay receptive to feedback and to avoid taking criticisms personally. Peter Elbow emphasizes the value of sharing your work with others without having them give suggestions for improvement or note strengths or weaknesses. He writes, "When we read our words to others, we learn about our writing with enormous efficiency simply by feeling the shapes of our words and sentences in our mouths and hearing them in our ears."[45]

Literature Reviews

Literature reviews, otherwise known as scholarly reviews, explore scholarly conversations that have already occurred about your research topic. They give readers a sense of the scholarly field: what scholars have argued, how their arguments compare to one another, and how your own argument contributes to the field of scholarship. As you construct and create your review of the field, you engage in creative inquiry and dialogue with the scholars whose arguments you discuss. Alfonso Montuori writes,

> Like any community, or any family, there are alliances, friendships, arguments, longstanding feuds, and so on. Some of the members of our community may have views we believe to be deeply misguided, whereas some we may be in complete agreement with. It is worth keeping in mind the inspirational potential of views we disagree with. Sometimes it is precisely an author whose work we detest and are in complete and utter disagreement with who may motivate us to go deeper into in an issue, write an article, challenge a position, and so on. We might view the literature review as our description of, and entry point into, our community, the beginning of our dialogue with "our people." This is how we see and describe them and how we describe ourselves and our participation in this community.[46]

In other words, the literature review marks your entry into this scholarly community, and your audience includes the very authors that you put yourself in dialogue with. It provides your survey of the field: you interpret it and decide which authors and positions to discuss. The ability to articulate other people's arguments in your own words and determine how various positions—including your own—relate to one another will be helpful as you participate in various communities (personal and professional) in your life. As you read through your argument sources, articulate in your own words what are they arguing and what other arguments they put themselves into dialogue with (either in agreement or opposition). How would you compare their argument with your other argument sources? How does your own argument compare to theirs? Write a literature review in which you give the reader a sense of the scholarly terrain ("lay of the land"). When you discuss a particular scholar's argument, be sure to include a parenthetical citation afterward so that you avoid plagiarizing, which is explored further in Appendix 4.

Mindful Writing

Mindfulness—paying attention to whatever is arising for you in this the present moment—can be used before, during, or after periods of writing. Allen Ginsberg, mentioned above, offered one of the first classes on mindful writing at Naropa University. An exercise he assigned to students instructed them to

1. Stop in tracks once a day, take account of sky, ground & self, write 3 verses haiku
2. Sit 5 minutes a day, & after, re-collect your thoughts
3. Stop in middle of street or country, turn in 360-degree circle, write what you remember[47]

These exercises engage us in mindful writing: writing a haiku about a moment in our day, a reflection on a brief mindfulness practice, or a recollection of an experience. Haiku is a form of poetry that originated in Japan during the late nineteenth and early twentieth centuries; it traditionally consisted of a pattern of five, seven, and five syllable verses. It also contains a special word describing the season in which it was set (such as colored leaves for fall, or snow for winter) and a pause at the end of the first or second verse. Matsuo Bashō (1644–1694), the most famous of all haiku poets, was influenced by Zen Buddhism and wrote a famous travel journal that incorporated haiku entitled *The Narrow Road to the Deep North* (*Oku no Hosomichi*) that includes the following haiku:

on a withered branch
a crow has settled—
autumn evening[48]

His haiku conveys a sense of loneliness and the Japanese idea of *mono no aware*, "the pathos of things," which alludes to the transience and impermanence of all things. An example of *mono no aware* in Japan today is love for the cherry tree, whose blossoms usually fall within a week of their appearance: "It is precisely the evanescence of their beauty that evokes the wistful feeling of *mono no aware* in the viewer."[49] Another haiku by Bashō reads:

old pond
a frog jumps in
water's sound[50]

This haiku captures another passing moment—the sound of splashing water as a frog jumps into a pond. As Ginsberg suggests, we might convey a particular moment from our own lives in haiku form as a form of mindful writing.

Journal Writing

Journal writing can also draw our attention to the present moment, fostering an awareness and appreciation of our lives.[51] As Daniel Barbezat and Mirabai Bush note, "A journal records the movement of one's inner experience. It differs from a diary, which usually records the unstructured events of a person's life. Journal entries are reflections of the mental, emotional, and imagistic occurrences within the writer."[52] As the contemplative Thomas Merton writes, "Journals take for granted that every day in our life there is something new and different."[53] Journals allow us to write about our field of awareness—sensations, emotions, thoughts, sounds, sights, insights—each day. You can keep a journal of your formal mindfulness practice, or you can attune yourself to experiences in your daily life that might otherwise pass unnoticed. For example, you can journal about movements through space—moments of "passage"[54]—during daily commutes, or your surrounding environment, as natural historians, ecologists, and travelers do in their journals.[55] As Andrew Schelling observes, when we consider the questions "Where am I?" and "When am I?", we consider ourselves in relation to time and space, interacting with "forces and dynamics and aspects of the ecosystem, bio-system, or watershed that [we're] in."[56]

Notes

1. King, *On Writing*, 145.
2. Strunk and White, *Elements of Style*.
3. Barzun, *Simple & Direct*, 20.

4. Barzun, *Simple & Direct*, 27.

5. Barzun, *Simple & Direct*, 35.

6. Carillo, *Securing a Place for Reading in Composition*, 137.

7. Bean, *Engaging Ideas*, 40.

8. Moore and Bass, *Understanding Writing Transfer*.

9. King, *On Writing*, 145.

10. King, *On Writing*, 150.

11. Strunk and White, *Elements of Style*, 66; Sword, *Stylish Academic Writing*, 27.

12. Sword, *Stylish Academic Writing*, 39.

13. Sword, *Stylish Academic Writing*, 49.

14. Elbow, *Writing with Power*, xviii.

15. Elbow, *Writing with Power*, xvi.

16. Elbow, *Writing with Power*, xviii.

17. Goldberg, *Writing Down the Bones*, 58.

18. Elbow, *Writing with Power*, 8.

19. Elbow, *Writing with Power*, 10.

20. Elbow, *Writing with Power*, xxv.

21. Elbow, *Writing with Power*, xxv.

22. Elbow, *Writing with Power*, 12.

23. Elbow, *Writing with Power*, 13.

24. Goldberg, *Writing Down the Bones*, 8.

25. Ginsberg, *Spontaneous Mind*, 406.

26. Elbow, *Writing with Power*, 16.

27. Sword, *Stylish Academic Writing*, 170.

28. "reflection, n.," *Oxford English Dictionary Online*, accessed March 12, 2022, https://www-oed-com.liblink.uncw.edu/view/Entry/160921?redirectedFrom=reflection.

29. Ash and Clayton, "Generating, Deepening, and Documenting Learning."

30. Rolfe et al., *Critical Reflection*.

31. University of Connecticut, "Reflection Models."

32. Mezirow, *Learning as Transformation*, 7–8.

33. Baxter Magolda, "Activity of Meaning Making," 631.

34. Baxter Magolda, "Three Elements of Self-Authorship."

35. Fink, *Creating Significant Learning Experiences*, 130.

36. Fink, *Creating Significant Learning Experiences*, 134.

37. Carillo, *Teaching Readers*, 182.

38. Bizup, "BEAM," 75-76.

39. Bizup, "BEAM," 76.

40. Sword, *Stylish Academic Writing*, 157–58.

41. Sword, *Stylish Academic Writing*, 123.

42. Sword, *Stylish Academic Writing*, 86.

43. Elbow, *Writing with Power*, 134.

44. Elbow, *Writing with Power*, 135.

45. Elbow, *Writing with Power*, xxii.

46. Montuori, "Literature Review as Creative Inquiry," 3.

47. Barbezat and Bush, *Contemplative Practices in Higher Education*, 132.

48. Barnhill, *Bashō's Haiku*, 25.

49. Parkes, "Japanese Aesthetics."

50. Barnhill, *Bashō's Haiku*, 54.

51. Barbezat and Bush, *Contemplative Practices in Higher Education*, 125.

52. Barbezat and Bush, *Contemplative Practices in Higher Education*, 125.

53. Quoted in Barbezat and Bush, *Contemplative Practices in Higher Education*, 125.

54. Barbezat and Bush, *Contemplative Practices in Higher Education*, 128.

55. Barbezat and Bush, *Contemplative Practices in Higher Education*, 130.

56. Barbezat and Bush, *Contemplative Practices in Higher Education*, 130.

CHAPTER THIRTEEN

Making Presentations

Your grandmother says you read a lot. Every chance you get. That's good,
but not good enough. Words mean more than what is set down on paper. It
takes the human voice to infuse them with the shades of deeper meaning.
—Maya Angelou, *I Know Why the Caged Bird Sings*[1]

Public speaking changed my life. Or rather, public preaching did. I
enrolled in Harvard Divinity School as a candidate for ordination in
the Lutheran church, meaning I was on track to become a Lutheran
minister. Every Sunday, I would commute to Lynn, Massachusetts, where I
served as a seminarian (i.e., minister-in-training), assisting with communion
and occasionally delivering sermons. One Sunday during Advent, the season
leading up to Christmas, I was preaching about the significance of stopping
and pausing. (In fact, I had entitled my sermon "Mind the Gap.") I myself
took a moment to pause, and I looked out at the congregation. It was a mix
of elderly white people and recent refugees from Sudan. I suddenly became
aware of all the gaps: between their life experiences and my own as a twenty-
five-year-old white American, and between their faith and my own, which
was wobbly at best and certainly veering from its Lutheran roots. At that very
moment, I experienced a profound sense of dissonance. I knew that my calling
lay elsewhere, and I eventually became a teacher instead of a preacher. You
might say my rhetorical situation unraveled: I felt a disconnect between my
purpose and my audience.

Speaking, like writing, requires us to think rhetorically about our topic,
purpose, and audience.[2] When we make presentations, we may seek to increase knowledge, foster understanding, or promote change in our listeners'
attitudes, values, beliefs, or behavior.[3] Making that purpose clear will help
us determine our central message—the main point or "takeaway" from our
presentation, which should be vivid and memorable. Our language will adapt
to fit our audience and topic, but our delivery techniques (posture, gestures,

eye contact, and vocal expressiveness) will remain largely consistent across contexts: we want to stand upright instead of slouching, look at our listeners more than our notes, and speak loudly enough to be heard, trying to avoid filler words such as "um," "uh," "like," and "you know." Our presentation should have a clear grouping and sequencing of ideas, so that our listeners can easily follow and understand our central message. Finally, we want to use relevant, credible material to support our central message: "explanations, examples, illustrations, statistics, analogies, quotations from relevant sources, and other kinds of information or analysis that supports the principal ideas of the presentation."[4]

This chapter explores various contexts in which you might make a prepared and purposeful presentation, including group discussions, meetings, and research conferences. Before you continue reading, you might stop and reflect on your previous speaking experiences. What types of audiences have you spoken for? What topics have you addressed, why did you speak about it (exigence), and what did you seek from your audience (purpose)? What strategies have you used when speaking publicly, and were they successful? If not, what might you have done differently? Thinking about these fundamental aspects of speaking will help you transfer your prior knowledge to future speaking engagements.

Discussions

Discussions provide opportunities for you to hone your speaking and listening skills and build your confidence in public speaking.[5] In discussions, you assess various perspectives and positions, or you explore possible solutions to a complex problem, and this ability to discuss conflicting interpretations of situations with civility will serve you in workplace environments. When you participate in classroom discussions, you ideally come prepared by doing the reading and generating a list of its key points and questions that it raised for you.[6] When you lead classroom discussions, you need to be even more prepared, because you cannot assume that others have done the reading. This means you need to provide a summary of the reading, highlight the key ideas, anticipate possible areas of confusion, *and* generate a list of questions for discussion.

When you present your summary or synopsis of the reading, make sure you clearly convey your main point or takeaway, and that you make eye contact with your listeners, speak expressively (varying your pitch, volume, speed, and sounds instead of speaking in a monotone voice), and use any supporting material that elucidates that central message. You may use a quotation from the reading, share a personal story tied to its main idea, or provide a handout. You may ask them to share any points of confusion or share those that you anticipated in advance. Ideally, your presentation will clearly convey your central message, trigger recall for those who did the reading, and equip those who came unprepared with a basic understanding so that everyone can participate in the discussion. If the group has not already generated ground rules for discussion, you might encourage them to actively listen, avoid interrupting others, criticize ideas instead of people, and not monopolize the discussion.

What makes for a good discussion question? You want to avoid questions that only have one correct answer, such as facts or terms, which some call "closed questions."[7] Instead, create questions with many valid responses, that call for further interpretation, application, or analysis. Open-ended questions work well because they invite a wide range of personal responses; they often start with "why" or "how" instead of "what," "who," or "when."[8] If you feel courageous enough to facilitate it, you can even invite participants to do a "question brainstorm" where you provide a passage from the reading that you feel might serve as a good basis for discussion, and then you invite the group to brainstorm as many questions as possible suggested by the passage, writing them down on the board.[9] As Stephen Brookfield and Stephen Preskill note, "There is no stopping for discussion, judgment, or criticism. Comments are turned into questions whenever possible."[10] Then, you narrow the group of questions to those considered most significant or compelling, and you use those as the basis for discussion.

During the discussion, you need to actively listen so that you can intervene if it strays too far off topic, or if it lags and stalls. If someone raises a compelling question or point that seems worthy of discussion, but it is met with silence, you might restate or rephrase what they said, to see if others may not have understood. You can redirect conversations by returning to the original thread of discussion, or even recast the topic of discussion by identifying other ways that it might be understood or analyzed. Brookfield and Preskill share an example: "Maybe A is not the real problem. Perhaps what's really behind this is B."[11] You might also bring back-up material for your discussion, such as a "hatful of quotes" containing slips of paper with key sentences or assertions from the reading on them. After drawing a slip and taking a moment to think about their quotation, each participant reads their quotation and comments on it. Because the same five or six quotations are used, participants who may be fearful or reluctant to speak will hear others comment, so that "even if they have little to say about their own interpretation of the quote, they can affirm, build on, or contradict a comment a peer has already made on that quote."[12]

Meetings

When you present in a meeting, you should have a clear sense of the audience and the purpose of the meeting, especially what they are expecting to learn from your presentation. Meetings often have agendas set in advance, which can give you a sense of where your presentation will fall during the meeting, other items that might be discussed, and the time allotted for your presentation. With unfamiliar audiences, you want to briefly establish a connection with them to increase their engagement. A meeting will often have a facilitator or chair who keeps track of time, keeps people on task, enables them to share their views, summarizes what has been considered and agreed upon, and discusses next steps.[13] If you are leading the meeting, you want to make sure that people know why they are there (their role) and what they will do in the meeting (its purpose), and then do that at the meeting (meet its purpose) and have someone report out what everyone will do going forward (next steps).[14]

Before convening a meeting, you should determine whether it is necessary to meet. As Caity Weaver writes, "The convening of meetings 'that could have been an email' is a popular tribulation in the modern office worker's lament."[15] Consider two criteria to decide if you should meet: "First, must all parties be present at the same time in the same space to exchange the information? Second, will the information be better understood through 'lean media' (which is text-based) or 'rich media' (which includes nonverbal context)?"[16] Text messaging allows for simple coordination, whereas in-person or synchronous video chats suit complex coordination and negotiation. If you do decide to meet, consider who needs to be at the meeting (more than six people increases the risk of social loafing), how long it will take to accomplish the task (rather than defaulting to an allotted meeting time), and during the meeting, welcome attendees at the beginning and ensure the meeting starts and ends on time.[17]

When you present at the meeting, begin by hooking your audience with a compelling question, personal story, or puzzle. Know your audience—what they know about your topic and how much they care about your topic—so that you can adjust your approach to meet their needs. Clearly convey your central message, making eye contact, speaking expressively, and offering examples, stories, or other material that might support your message. Use audiovisual aids if you need to show them images, statistics, or other data, otherwise focus on connecting with your audience and increasing their understanding or inspiring them to change.

Research Presentations

When presenting your research, you also want to hook your audience with a compelling question, tension, or puzzle underlying your inquiry into the topic. Focus on one or two takeaways rather than trying to cover everything that you encountered in your research. Make eye contact, speak expressively, and share any supporting material. Research presentations often include posters, handouts, or audiovisual materials because they involve the dissemination of research findings such as statistics and other data. Although you can easily present in discussions and meetings without using audiovisual aids such as Powerpoint, Prezi, or Google Slides, research presentations frequently call for these digital media.

Expectations and norms associated with public presentations are shifting because of our exposure to digital media, and people now tend to prefer engaging stories that incorporate multimedia images and personally connect with the audience, as exemplified in TED talks.[18] Because digital delivery includes both face-to-face and virtual audiences, speakers must create engaging narratives that connect with diverse audiences, and effective delivery includes successful interplay between the narrative, visuals, and vocal and physical techniques.[19] As April Kedrowicz and Julie Taylor note, "Delivery, then, is becoming less about vocal and physical polish and rehearsal and more about characteristics of electronic eloquence, including enthusiasm, passion, and connection."[20]

We can think about our presentations as stories and connect our storytelling with visuals and interpersonal connection. As Garr Reynolds suggests in *Presentation Zen*, we should attend to design, story, symphony, empathy, play, and meaning by

Focusing on the topic, key messages, and audience when we design our presentations

Incorporating illuminating and engaging stories

Sharing the patterns and big pictures

Attending and adjusting to nonverbal cues of the audience
Bringing in humor when appropriate
Focusing on meaning[21]

Garr argues that communication involves engaging both sides of the brain by appealing to your listeners' emotions but also providing them information. If you have a lot of data or information to share, he recommends using handouts since "it is difficult for audiences to process information when it is presented in spoken and written formats at the same time."[22]

Valuing simplicity in design, Seth Godin advises making Powerpoint slides that reinforce your words rather than repeat them. He writes, "No more than six words on a slide. EVER. There is no presentation so complex that this rule needs to be broken."[23] When you become adept at creating visuals that enhance your presentation—rather than distract and detract from it—you can use them more adeptly in future contexts. These might include investor pitches, corporate keynotes, or TED talks, which tend toward short formats, multimodal delivery, and often a "leveling out" between speaker and audience with the removal of speaker podiums.[24]

Grounding Techniques

Public speaking can induce feelings of fear and anxiety. Grounding techniques can help us anchor ourselves in our bodies and return to the present moment. You can bring mindfulness to your body while sitting or standing. Draw attention to feel the weight of your body sitting in the chair, letting yourself feel the heaviness of gravity pulling down. While standing, notice the weight in your left or right foot if you rock slightly side to side. You can also become aware of where your hands rest on your lap, where your feet contact the floor, or any other part of the body where you may feel sensations strongly.

You can engage your senses of sight, touch, sound, smell, and taste to orient to the surrounding environment, using the 5-4-3-2-1 technique. After drawing your attention to your breath and taking a few deep breaths, you slowly look around your environment, noticing: five things you can see, four things you can touch, three things you can hear, two things you can smell, and one thing you can taste.[25]

You can use your senses in other ways to ground you before, during, or after a presentation. You might hold an object to touch or feel your hands pressing together, eat a piece of candy that has a pleasant taste, use a lotion whose smells calm you, attend to the sounds around you, or notice and name objects that you see in your surrounding environment. Engaging your senses in these ways can help you feel grounded and supported in the present moment.

Letting Go of Regrets

Like any skill, speaking improves with practice, and you will inevitably have experiences of your presentations falling short. This might include (at least, it has for me): speaking too quickly to be understood, reading your notes instead of looking at your audience, stammering and using filler words ("um," "uh," "like"), completely forgetting your point, stumbling in response to a question, or even breaking down in tears (at the time, I blamed pregnancy hormones, but still). When we experience failure, our "inner critic" comes forward, and we can fixate on our shortcomings. We previously explored ways that you can mindfully approach judgments and critical thoughts, such as engaging in practices of kindness and self-compassion. Another way we might work with our inner critic is to engage in a practice that Mark Coleman describes as "letting go of regrets." Drawing to mind our presentation, we can reflect on why we acted the way we did. For example, being nervous because of someone we knew in the audience, feeling unprepared, forgetting to bring notes, failing to anticipate questions in advance, or having hormones surging through your body. Then, Coleman invites us to reflect on bits of wisdom, including,

> We can't undo the past.
> Everything always looks clearer with 20/20 hindsight.
> You always did the best you could, given the experience, knowledge, and information you had at the time.
> What was, was, and it cannot be changed.
> Peace comes from letting go of regrets about past actions.[26]

You then apply these insights to your own situation, and after you reflect, see if you can forgive yourself and let regret go.

Notes

1. Angelou, *I Know Why The Caged Bird Sings*, 82.
2. The National Communication Association identifies these factors as key in oral communication: that speakers compose and deliver messages using delivery methods and interpersonal skills suitable to the topic, purpose, context and audience. NCA,

"Speaking and Listening Competencies for College Graduates," accessed February 23, 2021, https://www.natcom.org/sites/default/files/pages/Assessment_Resources_Speaking_and_Listening_Competencies_for_College_Students.pdf.

3. Association of American Colleges and Universities, "Oral Communication VALUE Rubric."

4. Association of American Colleges and Universities, "Oral Communication VALUE Rubric."

5. Cornwall, "Failing Safely," 113.

6. Herman and Nilson, *Creating Engaging Discussions*, 12.

7. Brookfield and Preskill, *Discussion Book*, 72.

8. Brookfield and Preskill, *Discussion Book*; Herman and Nilson, *Creating Engaging Discussions*, 21.

9. Brookfield and Preskill, *Discussion Book*, 108.

10. Brookfield and Preskill, *Discussion Book*, 108.

11. Brookfield and Preskill, *Discussion Book*, 5.

12. Brookfield and Preskill, *Discussion Book*, 182.

13. Hopper, *Making Meetings Work*, 5–6.

14. Weaver, "Meetings."

15. Weaver, "Meetings."

16. Weaver, "Meetings."

17. Faust, "How to Lead Your Team to Peak Performance."

18. Kedrowicz and Taylor, "Shifting Rhetorical Norms and Electronic Eloquence."

19. Kedrowicz and Taylor, "Shifting Rhetorical Norms and Electronic Eloquence," 369.

20. Kedrowicz and Taylor, "Shifting Rhetorical Norms and Electronic Eloquence," 370.

21. Reynolds, *PresentationZen*, 16–19.

22. Reynolds, *PresentationZen*, 11.

23. Reynolds, *PresentationZen*, 20.

24. Rossette-Crake, "'New Oratory.'"

25. Pikörn, "5-4-3-2-1 Grounding Technique."

26. Coleman, *Make Peace with Your Mind*, 83.

CHAPTER FOURTEEN

Building Careers

When things are shaky and nothing is working, we might
realize that we are on the verge of something.
—Pema Chödrön[1]

I wanted to be a pediatrician when I was a teenager. My experiences of asthma attacks as a child fueled my conviction that I would empathize with my future young patients. Although I wasn't particularly enthusiastic about A.P. chemistry—I found lab reports much less interesting to write than literature papers—I told myself that was normal. After all, many premed students complain about their organic chemistry class. In my senior year of high school, I jumped at the opportunity to shadow a pediatric surgeon at Duke University. Soon thereafter I found myself in the Neonatal Intensive Care Unit, standing next to a group of medical students in front of an incubator as my mentor explained the baby's condition. The room felt warm. Struggling to follow the medical terminology she was using, I peered into the incubator. My vision started to blur, and my legs felt weak...

Needless to say, I did not pursue a career in pediatric medicine. Although that fainting spell was especially embarrassing, it was not anomalous. I had previously fainted at the sight of blood. By the time I went to college, my career sights had shifted to psychology. As a psychologist, I reasoned, I could help patients without needing to use syringes or surgical tools. However, while I found psychology courses fascinating, especially my social psychology course cotaught by Claude Steele (well-known for his idea of "stereotype threat") and Philip Zimbardo (famous for his 1971 Stanford prison experiment), I felt a greater pull toward studio art, literature, and the study of religion. In this way, I zigged and zagged my way through possible career trajectories, until I ultimately became a professor of East Asian religions.

As it turns out, my experience is the norm rather than the exception. Although some assume there is a linear path between college majors and careers—evidenced by the fact that people often ask "What are you going to do with that?"[2] when you tell them your major—most college graduates follow a nonlinear path where unplanned events and changing conditions lead them to their jobs.[3] As Katharine Brooks notes in *You Majored in What?*, "the job search seems chaotic and messy at best."[4] She advocates approaching your career as a chaos theorist might, allowing for "change and the unexpected," taking into account "your diverse interests and broad scope of knowledge," and giving yourself "permission to explore and let events unfold."[5] She outlines five basic tenets of chaos theory to apply to your career development:

> Assess what you know, cannot know, and can learn.
> Decisions are complex: don't base them on a single factor.
> Change is constant. Allow for the butterfly effect.
> Situations may appear chaotic, but an order will appear.
> Attractors will help to focus your attention.[6]

Several factors play into your career options, including the job market, your interests, and your skills, but as Brooks writes, "Your career is more improvisational than scripted. Be ready to handle the changes that come along. And say 'yes!' You never know when one small interaction, event, or experience will propel you in a whole new direction."[7] This holds true for my own experience, as I have shared in this book: shadowing a pediatric surgeon and preaching in a church led me in new directions, and my training in HTML coding equipped me for a job that I never anticipated. The fifth tenet encourages us to notice what energizes or excites us, as it can open us to new pathways and avenues for exploration. Although it may seem chaotic or meandering, if we bring intentionality and awareness to our journey, it can result in what Brooks calls "wise wanderings."[8] Drawing from the 4-D cycle of Appreciative Inquiry that we explored previously, she encourages you to discover your strengths, develop your vision, design your path, and deliver your talents. In this chapter, I focus mostly on the stage of "designing your path," in which Brooks encourages you to "create the necessary tools and actions to forge your path."[9] I would suggest a slight tweak, which in my mind makes all the difference: forge your *paths*. Allow for multiple possibilities and pathways and gather as many tools as possible. For you are often building *careers*, rather than a single career.

As Bill Burnett and Dave Evans point out in *Designing Your Life*, many dysfunctional beliefs persist and prevent people from designing the lives that they want. First and foremost, in agreement with Brooks, they identify the dysfunctional belief that your degree determines your career: "Three-quarters of all college grads don't end up working in a career related to their major."[10] They also note that people often erroneously think they need to plan and make the right choices: "If only they make the *right* choice (the *best, true, only* choice), they will have a blueprint for who they will be, what they will do, and how they will live. It's a paint-by-numbers approach to life, but in reality, life is more of an abstract painting—one that's open to multiple interpretations."[11] Mindfulness can open us to possibilities. If we overlook this multiplicity, we feel pressured, and we become cautious and averse to taking risks or exploring alternatives. We are frogs in a well. We lose our cognitive flexibility, and we feel constrained and constricted to one career path.

Instead, if we open our field of awareness, allowing for multiple possibilities and alternatives, we can approach our lives and careers with mindfulness. Burnett and Evans write, "There are many designs for your life, all filled with hope for the kind of creative and unfolding reality that makes life worth living into. Your life is not a thing, it's an experience; the fun comes from designing and enjoying the experience."[12] Life is about growth and change, and mindfulness allows us to become aware and open to such changes. When we think about life as an experience—better yet, a range of experiences—we can then identify tools and skills we want to develop to facilitate those experiences. Instead of pigeonholing ourselves into one career path, we can equip ourselves for multiple career trajectories. For example, we can be strategic in our general education courses, so that we target multiple pathways instead of taking courses solely within our major. Although we may not know what jobs or careers await us, we can explore a broad range of disciplines that interest and excite us, so that we can pivot and pursue other career trajectories in the future. We can think about developing competencies—not exclusively pursuing our major—including communication, critical thinking, equity and inclusion, leadership, professionalism, teamwork, and technology, all of which we have explored in this book.[13]

Designing Careers

Burnett and Evans recommend approaching your life as a designer to figure out what you want to grow into and create in your life. They write, "We all have lots of lives within us. We certainly have three at any particular moment. Of course, we can only live out one at a time, but we want to ideate multiple variations in order to choose creatively and generatively."[14] Just as you might employ design thinking to generate ideas in a collaborative space, you can approach your own life and career pathways in a similar vein. Burnett and Evans encourage you to create three different plans for the next five years of your life: the first being what you already have in mind, the second being what you would do if your first were no longer an option, and the third being what you would do if money or image were no object.[15] Then, map it out visually on a timeline, think of any questions or concerns it raises in your mind, and finally gauge four items:

- Resources (Do you have the objective resources—time, money, skill, contacts—you need to pull off your plan?)
- Likeability (Are you hot or cold or warm about your plan?)
- Confidence (Are you feeling full of confidence, or pretty uncertain about pulling this off?)
- Coherence (Does the plan make sense within itself? And is it consistent with you, your [view of work and your view of life?])[16]

In this way, you can envision different pathways for your life and career. They also encourage you to consider where you might live, what experience you might gain, the impacts of choosing that alternative, and what life would look like.[17] Finally, they recommend sharing the plan with a group of three to six people, telling them not to critique or advise but instead to "receive, reflect, and amplify."[18] "Tell me more about…" is one way to keep the inquiry appreciative and supportive.[19]

You can engage in this process of reflection and inquiry to clarify possible career pathways. As Burnett and Evans emphasize, "You aren't designing the rest of your life; you are designing what's next. Every possible version of you holds unknowns and compromises, each with its own identifiable and unintended consequences."[20] When you envision different career pathways, you invite curiosity about future possibilities. You open yourself to future careers that may not even exist yet: many jobs today, such as app developer, social media manager, and Uber driver, only emerged after smartphones appeared in 2007.[21] Instead of planning or predicting, you embrace chaos and uncertainty with a growth mindset. Once you have envisioned various pathways, you can continue by prototyping them—getting an understanding of what they might feel like—by shadowing and networking with people in those fields.

Shadowing and Networking

Shadowing someone means following them in their footsteps as they do their work. In my case, I followed a pediatric surgeon as she treated babies in the NICU and taught her residents. When you shadow someone, you get a sense of what their work entails. It enables you to experience what the career is like, which you can also gain from an internship.[22] Burnett and Evans also advocate reaching out to people who have experience and expertise in that career and asking if they might share their story of how they came to do what they do. In those meetings, they emphasize that you are *not* after a job, but instead listening to their story to find out if their career interests you.[23] These informal conversations, a form of informational interview, can give you an insider's perspective and expand your network of contacts in that field.

Networking—cultivating professional contacts—can lead to job opportunities that you would otherwise be unaware of. Although many of us do not enjoy networking, Burnett and Evans encourage us to think of it as asking for directions: it allows you to participate in a particular community or network that has its own conversations, relationships, and concerns.[24] Just as you put yourself in conversation with scholars in a literature review or research-based paper, you can interact and network with professionals in a career that interests you.

Résumés, Cover Letters, and Job Interviews

Although they point out that most employers do not even respond to half of their applicants, and they identify mining the internet for a job as a misguided approach, when applying for a job, Burnett and Evans recommend rewriting your résumé so it uses the same keywords as the job description in order to increase your likelihood of being interviewed.[25] If you do not yet have a résumé, create one! Your résumé should ideally be formatted in twelve-point font, one page in length, tailored to the job, and include:

Contact information: your name, address, email, and phone number
Education: your degrees, institutions, and year of graduation (or projected graduation) listed in reverse chronological order

Professional experience: including bullet points underneath that concisely describe your responsibilities, start with action verbs, and do not use personal pronouns

Leadership and extracurricular activities: spell out the names of organizations and include volunteering experiences

Skills: technical or field-specific certifications, rather than broad skills

Honors or awards: limited to collegiate and postgraduate experiences, in reverse chronological order

Try to design your résumé so that employers can easily read it, keeping it simple instead of cluttered, as you would design audiovisual slides. In your cover letter, you should address it to the hiring official or committee, introduce yourself in the opening paragraph, discuss your training and cite specific examples from previous experiences that speak to the job description, convey your interest in that specific position or company, and conclude by thanking them for their time and consideration.

If you do get an interview, be prepared to share a story that demonstrates how you fit the job description and expectations. If you have an ePortfolio, look through it and identify experiences that illustrate the skills and competencies sought in the job description. Research the organization or company, so that you can bring questions to your interview to show your knowledge and interest in the position.

Expanding Our Perspective

Building a career involves developing skills and competencies, exploring different pathways, and cultivating professional relationships. These inner and outer dimensions of career exploration call for cognitive flexibility and situational openness, which draw to mind Zhuangzi's philosophy. As we previously discussed, Zhuangzi described an inner emptying of the mind that enables an outer responsiveness to one's surroundings. Moving beyond social conventions and categories allows us to adopt a more expansive perspective. As Michael Puett and Christine Gross-Loh write, "All moments can be creative and spontaneous when we experience the entire world as an open and expansive place. We get there by constantly cultivating our ability to imagine transcending our own experience."[26] You can envision a future unlike the present, developing skills for a job that may not exist yet. Zhuangzi praises those who are fearless and unwavering in the face of change—even death. He writes,

Life, death, preservation, loss, failure, success, poverty, riches, worthiness, unworthiness, slander, fame, hunger, thirst, cold, heat—these are the alternations of the world, the workings of fate. Day and night they change place before us and wisdom cannot spy out their source. Therefore, they should not be enough to destroy your harmony; they should not be allowed to enter the storehouse of spirit. If you can harmonize and delight in them, master them and never be at a loss for joy, if you can do this day and night without break and make it be spring with everything, mingling with all and creating the moment within your own mind—this is what I call being whole in power.[27]

As you think about a potentially chaotic career trajectory, or the possibility of changing circumstances or unplanned events suddenly shifting your career path, what physical sensations, emotions, and thoughts surface for you? How might you preserve your sense of "harmony" amid such change? In what ways might you enable yourself to "mingle with all" the possible trajectories? What disciplines might you explore, or skills and competencies might you cultivate, to facilitate this kind of adaptability? What habits of mind—moments within your mind—might support your feeling empowered despite such uncertainty?

Notes

1. Chödrön, *When Things Fall Apart*, 8.
2. Brooks, *You Majored in What?*, 1.
3. Brooks, *You Majored in What?*, 7.
4. Brooks, *You Majored in What?*, 7.
5. Brooks, *You Majored in What?*, 7.
6. Brooks, *You Majored in What?*, 10–11.
7. Brooks, *You Majored in What?*, 10.
8. Brooks, *You Majored in What?*, 11.
9. Brooks, *You Majored in What?*, 15.
10. Burnett and Evans, *Design Your Life*, x.
11. Burnett and Evans, *Design Your Life*, 87.
12. Burnett and Evans, *Design Your Life*, xx.
13. "What Is Career Readiness?"
14. Burnett and Evans, *Design Your Life*, 91.
15. Burnett and Evans, *Design Your Life*, 92-94.
16. Burnett and Evans, *Design Your Life*, 96.
17. Burnett and Evans, *Design Your Life*, 97.

18. Burnett and Evans, *Design Your Life*, 104.

19. Burnett and Evans, *Design Your Life*, 104.

20. Burnett and Evans, *Design Your Life*, 104.

21. Hallett and Hutt, "10 Jobs That Didn't Exist 10 Years Ago."

22. Burnett and Evans, *Design Your Life*, 118.

23. Burnett and Evans, *Design Your Life*, 147.

24. Burnett and Evans, *Design Your Life*, 151.

25. Burnett and Evans, *Design Your Life*, 137–38.

26. Puett and Gross-Loh, *Path*, 152.

27. Zhuangzi, *Zhuangzi: Basic Writings*, 69.

CHAPTER FIFTEEN

Changing the World

Without the possibility of action, all knowledge comes to one labeled 'file and forget,' and I can neither file nor forget. Nor will certain ideas forget me; they keep filing away at my lethargy, my complacency.
—Ralph Ellison, *Invisible Man*[1]

During the summer after my sophomore year of college, I participated in a service-learning program volunteering full-time at a substance-abuse rehabilitation center in East Palo Alto. Each morning I would ride my bike down University Avenue, and I knew I had crossed the boundary into East Palo Alto when my handlebars started vibrating from the broken asphalt. I mainly performed clerical work for the clinic, and I attended weekly seminars reflecting on service. I learned that most successful social service nonprofits were faith-based organizations, and when I spoke with founders and directors of such programs, they emphasized the importance of relationships in their work: love served as the foundation of their service.

When I returned to the San Francisco Bay area after volunteering as an English teacher in China, I experienced reverse culture shock. From billboards on highways to conversations in hallways, everything revolved around the "dot.com" revolution that had taken the Bay area by storm. I felt overwhelmed by the materialism of American culture: the over-consumption, excess, and irresponsibility of it all. I witnessed gentrification and skyrocketing housing costs that forced low-income tenants from their homes. I gradually realized that my own country could appear just as alien and incomprehensible as any foreign country. I took a job at the Haas Center for Public Service at Stanford, whose mission was to respond to community needs as identified by community members, to develop in students the knowledge, skills, and commitment for a lifetime of public service, and to connect community needs to academic scholarship.

When you become aware of social injustice and inequality, you feel called to respond and to act to redress such injustice. In *Pedagogy of Freedom* Paulo

Freire, a Brazilian educator, writes, "Our being in the world is far more than just 'being.' It is a 'presence,' a 'presence' that is relational to the world and to others. . . . Insofar as I am a conscious presence in the world, I cannot hope to escape my ethical responsibility for my action in the world."[2] When we are fully present in the world, we become aware of the suffering of others, and we want to alleviate that suffering.

This chapter explores ways that you might change the world, from engaging in service-learning to social action projects. Before you continue reading, you might stop and reflect on your previous experiences trying to bring about social or political change. What sort of activism have you participated in? Have you petitioned local officials, or assisted in political campaigns, or joined in demonstrations such as rallies, street marches, or sit-ins? Have you been involved in other forms of collective action or social movements? What types of community service have you engaged in? Have you volunteered, done a field education project, or completed an internship in a community organization? Have you participated in advocacy work, or donated money to advocacy groups? You will have numerous opportunities to engage in activism, collective action, community service, and advocacy work in your life. We will discuss a few of them here, and how mindfulness can support your social justice efforts.

Service-Learning

Service-learning includes community service and learning from that service.[3] It involves action and critical reflection where you "participate in an organized service activity that meets identified community needs and reflect on the service activity in such a way as to gain further understanding of course content, a broader appreciation of the discipline, and an enhanced sense of civic responsibility."[4] In service-learning, your service activity is determined by those who run the community organizations and work in the community, as they know what they need.[5] You can reflect on your service through personal journals, experiential research papers, or case studies. Your personal journal might include entries about critical incidents that occur, why they are significant, what you learned from them, how they will influence your future behavior, and what actions you may take next time; or you might divide your journal entry into three parts to engage in description, analysis, and application so that you can describe some aspect of your community experience, analyze how course content relates to it, and reflect on how the experience and course content might be applied to your personal and professional life. Alternatively, you can write experiential research papers that identify and research a social issue you encountered at your service-learning site, and then make recommendations to the community partner for future action; or you could also write a case study about an ethical dilemma that you experienced at the community site.[6]

Your reflection might describe and examine your service experiences, and articulate what you have learned (DEAL), or explore what you learned, its significance, and next steps (What? So What? Now What?), but it should also consider larger power dynamics that create such needs and address the root causes of social problems. Otherwise, it falls short of social change, and it can even perpetuate inequality and reinforce established hierarchies of privilege and oppression.[7] As Robert Reich observes,

> Charity and justice are conceptually distinct. For me, justice represents the effort to provide a set of institutional arrangements to meet the basic needs of people, to ensure that people receive that to which they are entitled. And charity represents the effort to try and provide direct services to people. In that respect, charity is a good thing—it provides people things that they might deserve or need. But it doesn't get at the root source of the problem. For example, is donating money or volunteering at the soup kitchen going to bring an end to hunger? The two are completely separate things.[8]

A social justice approach understands service as a means of resolving social problems and effecting structural change, not solely addressing immediate needs.[9] As an agent of social change, you can contemplate "both personal and institutional contributions to social problems and measures that may lead to social change."[10]

A critical approach to service-learning encourages you to examine and address social problems. Robert Rhoads gives examples of questions that might guide such an approach: "Why do we have significant economic gaps between different racial groups? Why do women continue to face economic and social inequities? Why does the richest country on earth have such a serious problem with homelessness?"[11] As you engage in ongoing reflection, you examine the structural causes of community needs, and you reflect on the intersectional identities of yourself and those whom you serve. When we occupy a position of privilege relative to those we serve, this type of reflection is essential. Otherwise, we run the risk of reinforcing negative stereotypes, viewing complex problems in superficial ways, and overlooking underlying structural inequalities.[12] Instead, when we open our awareness to include systems and structures, and we recognize our situatedness in these systems. As Barbara Jacoby and Jeffrey Howard write, we can "expand [our] emotional comfort zones in dealing with difference, gain an increasing ability to view the world from multiple perspectives, and reflect on [our] own social positions in relations to others."[13]

Social Action Project

Social action projects analyze a problem, develop a solution, and implement a campaign to achieve that solution. They begin with issue development, in which you identify "a solution to a social problem that you and others in your group feel strongly about and whose demand is specific, simple, and winnable, with the result of the campaign being a positive, concrete change for the community."[14] The demand should be concrete, stated in one sentence, require a yes or no answer, and be made to your target—"the lowest ranking person that can meet your demand."[15] As Scott Myers-Lipton writes, "A general rule in social action is to have no more than three demands, otherwise the campaign loses focus."[16] Identifying an issue to work on can take several months, because it entails going out into the community, asking community members about pressing problems that they are facing, gathering information from surveys, individual interviews, and small group meetings, and exploring possible solutions with community feedback. Social action projects shorten this stage by identifying a policy change—some rule, law, or practice within an institution—that they would like to change. Then they frame the issue in a way that expresses the groups' values and connects to those of their allies and the public.[17]

After identifying the issue and developing a recruitment plan, you conduct research analyzing the history of the social issue, determining your target's position on the issue, and mapping out who has power in the community to move the target—either as allies or opponents.[18] Then you select strategies for your campaign, such as meeting with lawmakers or those who oversee policies, as well as building alliances and coalitions with other groups. You may use press and social media platforms to get your message out by speaking at rallies, marches, or public hearings, or you may engage in nonviolent public actions such as walkouts or occupying spaces, which disrupt the target's normal operations.[19] Ultimately, you hope to eventually secure a meeting with the target.

When you engage in this type of community organizing, you can develop a variety of skills including your listening skills, speaking skills, ability to work across differences, persistence, and leadership. Scott Myers-Lipton defines this last attribute as "someone who thinks about the group and helps it function effectively."[20] You effect social change by bringing people together to achieve a demand that improves their community.[21] You move beyond complacency, take responsibility for addressing injustice, and impact the larger community.

Mindfulness and Social Justice

When you start to attend to the root causes of social issues, and you realize the extent of social injustice, you may want to effect social change but feel powerless to do so. As Beth Berila writes, "This form of dissonance entails learning to live with a very real contradiction: holding both the awareness of intractable systems that are far bigger than individuals *and* recognizing that change has to start with individuals, even if that transformation is a limited one."[22] If we can sit with feelings of uncertainty or dissonance in the face of oppression, instead of shutting down or feeling overwhelmed, we can build our capacity for engaging in social justice work. Pema Chödrön writes, "When we protect ourselves so we won't feel pain, that protection becomes like armor, like armor that imprisons the softness of the heart."[23] Instead, she suggests breathing in pain to dismantle the armor and meet the heart, and breathing out spaciousness to open ourselves completely. As Berila writes,

> When the pain arises, we can breathe into our heart center, feel the pain, and use it to connect with others who have felt that pain. We can mourn the disastrous impacts of systematic oppression that robs all of us of our humanity, in different ways. Fierce compassion helps us connect with one another in a radical openness, offering us an alternative to hardening and cutting ourselves off.[24]

Instead of separating from others in an "us" versus "them" mentality, we can connect to others through our experiences of suffering, including systems of oppression that harm us all.

Deborah Eden Tull describes this sense of interconnection and non-separation as "relational mindfulness," an awareness of our relationships to ourselves, others, and the planet.[25] She describes a practice of first turning within ourselves, drawing to mind a challenge facing the world, and noticing the feelings that arise when you hold that topic in your awareness. She continues:

> Now consider two different parties affected by this situation. For instance, if the issue you picked is police brutality, pick the victims and the police. See if you can find compassion for both parties in regards to the brutality—for example, compassion for everyone whose lives have been taken so unjustly and violently and those who must be carrying around a tremendous amount of trauma and fear to act so unjustly in the world. And lastly, see if you can find compassion for yourself, as someone witnessing these atrocities occurring during your lifetime, feeling affected by them every day. . . . If it is difficult to access compassion for any of the parties, you might experiment with these words, "I see you. I see your pain. I see your suffering. I allow my heart to open to you."[26]

This practice encourages us to expand our awareness beyond narrow, polarized perspectives so we can see how all of us suffer in the wake of social injustice. Another technique that we can use in everyday life, when we encounter or experience difficult circumstances in our social justice work, is the STOP practice (Stop, Take, Observe, Proceed). As Rhonda Magee explains, you stop what you are doing, take a conscious breath, observe what is arising inside you and broaden your awareness to take in the circumstances, and proceed with intentionality. She writes, "It can help whenever you're feeling distress, creating space to observe and tame your feelings, and to access the deeper resources within you."[27] As she points out, mindfulness practice can serve as a helpful resource to support us through intense feelings, so that we can be responsive rather than reactive.

Notes

1. Ellison, *Invisible Man*, 579.
2. Freire, *Pedagogy of Freedom*, 25–26.
3. Stanton et al., *Service-Learning*, 2.
4. Bringle and Hatcher, "Service-Learning Curriculum for Faculty," 112.
5. Elon University, "Service-Learning."
6. Bandy, "Best Practices in Community Engaged Teaching."
7. Mitchell, "Traditional vs. Critical Service-Learning," 51.
8. Quoted in De Witte, "Is There Something Wrong with Philanthropy?"

9. Stanton et al., *Service-Learning*, 18.

10. Mitchell, "Traditional vs. Critical Service-Learning," 54.

11. Robert A. Rhoads, "Critical Multiculturalism," 45.

12. Jones, "Underside of Service Learning."

13. Jacoby and Howard, *Service-Learning Essentials*, 233.

14. Myers-Lipton, *Change! A Student Guide to Social Action*, 1.

15. Myers-Lipton, *Change! A Student Guide to Social Action*, 3.

16. Myers-Lipton, *Change! A Student Guide to Social Action*, 3.

17. Myers-Lipton, *Change! A Student Guide to Social Action*, 6.

18. Myers-Lipton, *Change! A Student Guide to Social Action*, 71.

19. Myers-Lipton, *Change! A Student Guide to Social Action*, 87–89.

20. Myers-Lipton, *Change! A Student Guide to Social Action*, 22.

21. Myers-Lipton, *Change! A Student Guide to Social Action*, 53.

22. Berila, *Integrating Mindfulness*, 124.

23. Chödrön, *When Things Fall Apart*, 89.

24. Berila, *Integrating Mindfulness*, 137.

25. Eden Tull, *Relational Mindfulness*, 288.

26. Eden Tull, *Relational Mindfulness*, 291.

27. Magee, *Inner Work of Racial Justice*, 262.

How to Manage Your Time

The things that matter most must never be at the
mercy of the things that matter least.
—Goethe[1]

When you develop skills of time management, you gain a sense of self-efficacy: "the degree to which you feel you are competent, capable, and productive, able to solve your problems, do your work, and achieve your goals."[2] Instead of allowing outside circumstances to dictate how you spend your time or immediately reacting to external deadlines as they arise, you can take control of your time, choose how you use it, and take charge of your life and responsibilities.

Time management began as an effort to increase the efficiency and productivity of workers in manufacturing during the early twentieth century. Today time management experts continue to emphasize the importance of efficiency but also recommend prioritizing tasks according to their urgency and importance, to ensure that you accomplish not only short-term tasks but also long-term goals. Time management, in other words, means not only controlling *how* you spend your time, but *what* you spend your time on.

First, clearly define your long-term goals. What do you want to accomplish? Once you decide upon your long-term goals, set short-term priorities within those goals. Identify obstacles that stand in the way, additional knowledge, skills, or information required, or people and resources that may help you achieve your goal. Similarly, you will have long-term projects and short-term tasks that you need to complete. A larger project—a "multitask job"—requires you to complete many smaller jobs.[3] To tackle projects effectively, write out a timeline of those smaller jobs in chronological order: start with the desired result and visually chart your way backward to determine the steps necessary to successfully complete the project. Once you have established the chronological order and broken it down into parts, you can set priorities on those items, so you stay focused on your key tasks and activities.

Next, make a daily plan, as well as a monthly or yearly plan for long-term goals and projects, which you can periodically review to see if you have made progress and to determine whether you still consider your goals important.[4] Experts also recommend creating a daily to-do list; Brian Tracy writes, "The best time to make a list is the night before, so your subconscious mind can work on your list while you sleep. When you wake up in the morning, you will often have ideas and insights to help you achieve some of the most important goals on your list."[5] Taking ten minutes to write out your tasks for the next day can save you time in the long run. On your to-do list, prioritize urgent and important tasks: "An *important* task is something that has long-term consequences for your career. An *urgent* task is something that cannot be delayed or put off."[6] These tasks are largely determined by external demands: they are responsibilities associated with your job or classes. Next, consider tasks that are important, but not urgent, which could be delayed for a bit, such as papers due in a month. Finally, identify tasks that are urgent but not important, such as emails, as well as tasks that are neither urgent nor important. For tasks such as checking email, time management experts recommend doing them once or twice a day, so that you allow greater time for focusing on important tasks. Brian Tracy advises,

> Plan your work and work your plan. Never do anything that is not on your list. If a new task or project comes up, write it down on your list and set a priority for it before you start work on it. If you don't write down new ideas and activities, and instead react and respond to the nonstop demands on your time, you will quickly lose control of your day and end up spending most of your time on activities of low or no value.[7]

When you have the chance to focus on an important task, solely work on that task and keep working on it until it is complete. Tracy recommends checking in with yourself to ask, "What is the most valuable use of my time right now?"[8] He notes that sometimes it may be prioritizing good sleep, or getting exercise, or spending time with friends or family. Whatever you determine to be the most important task (either urgent and important, or important but not urgent), discipline yourself so you do it from start to finish. In other words, concentrate on the task at hand. Practice what Alan Lakein refers to as "single-handling": concentrate single-mindedly on a task and stay on it until it is complete. Avoid multitasking, which shifts your attention from task to task, disrupts your rhythm and momentum, and forces you to review what you have previously done.[9] Avoid the "attraction of distraction" by closing the door, turning off devices, and putting everything aside.[10]

Although you may be tempted to start your day with easy, enjoyable, and usually unimportant tasks, experts recommend tackling difficult, unpleasant, but important tasks first.[11] They also advise eliminating things that waste your time, such as taking on too many responsibilities. They urge you to say no to some activities so that you have time to devote to those that you find valuable and meaningful. If you find yourself not making time for such activities, start to schedule them into your daily plan until they become routine habits.

Finally, they encourage separating administrative and creative tasks. Drawing from Daniel Kahneman's *Thinking, Fast and Slow*, they point out that administrative tasks involve fast, short-term thinking, while creative tasks often require slow thinking.[12] Fast thinking addresses short-term tasks, responsibilities, and situations where we need to act quickly and instinctively, whereas slow thinking entails stepping back and taking time to reflect and think through details of situations before we decide what to do. Brian Tracy recommends batching similar or identical tasks—for example, checking and responding to emails twice a day, instead of repeatedly throughout the day—and devoting unbroken blocks of sixty to ninety minutes to complex tasks. He urges you to engage in "slow thinking" on a regular basis and writes, "True greatness only emerges with introspection, retrospection, solitude, and contemplation."[13] You might start by reflecting on the question "What am I trying to do?"[14] When you take time to think about your long-term goals and whether your present activities are enabling you to reach those goals, you can make more intentional choices about how you spend your time.

Notes

1. Quoted in Tracy, *Time Management*, 26.
2. Tracy, *Time Management*, 4.
3. Tracy, *Time Management*, 29.
4. Tracy, *Time Management*, 27; Greshes, *Don't Count the Yes's*, 31.
5. Tracy, *Time Management*, 34.
6. Tracy, *Time Management*, 49.

7. Tracy, *Time Management*, 38.

8. Tracy, *Time Management*, 48.

9. Tracy, *Time Management*, 64.

10. Tracy, *Time Management*, 66.

11. Cockerell, *Time Management Magic*, 71; Tracy, *Time Management*, 28.

12. Tracy, *Time Management*, 72.

13. Tracy, *Time Management*, 21.

14. Tracy, *Time Management*, 16.

How to Not Procrastinate

When we procrastinate, we choose to delay doing a task, even though we know that it will negatively impact our performance and even our health by creating future stress.[1] Timothy Pychyl writes of procrastination, "There is nothing preventing us from acting in a timely manner *except our own reluctance to act*."[2] Our reluctance leads us to choose doing something else against our better judgment.[3] Pychyl notes, "When we procrastinate, we fail to regulate our behavior to achieve our own goals. We make an intention to act, but we do not use the self-control necessary to act when intended."[4] Before reading further, you might identify tasks, projects, and activities that often prompt you to procrastinate, and notice what thoughts and emotions come to mind when you think of them.[5] Also write down obstacles or interruptions that may have prevented you from completing those tasks, projects, or activities. Finally, reflect on how the procrastination impacted your later performance, well-being, and happiness.[6]

Charlotte Lieberman notes, "At its core, procrastination is about emotions, not productivity."[7] Specifically, we feel negative emotions—frustration, anxiety, boredom, insecurity, and guilt—which make us averse to doing the task, and to escape such emotions we seek short-term relief in activities that make us feel good.[8] Instead, if we bring mindfulness to our experience, we might recognize and acknowledge those negative emotions, examining where we feel those emotions physically in our bodies and inviting some space between ourselves and our emotions, so that we can respond with greater attention and awareness.

Another strategy is to "just get started."[9] Instead of staring at a blank computer screen wondering what to type, just get typing. (Such freewriting serves a creative and generative purpose for writing projects, as you can explore further in the chapter on writing.) As Brian Tracy recommends, "Whenever you find yourself procrastinating on an important task, repeat to yourself, with energy and enthusiasm, 'Do it now! Do it now! Do it now!'"[10] Pychyl suggests a variety of mantras to remind yourself to "just get started": "Prime the pump"; "A job begun is a job half done"; and "A journey of a thousand miles begins with a single step."[11] You can also break your larger task into "bite-size chunks" so that you focus only on the next step, rather than the entire project.[12] Keep those steps simple and concrete. Tracy calls this "salami-slicing" the task: slicing off one small part that you resolve to complete before going onto something else.[13]

Finally, experts advise minimizing distractions, anticipating possible interruptions and how you will respond to keep yourself on task, and avoiding getting derailed once you have started. You can strengthen your self-regulation—your ability to influence, modify, and control your behavior according to goals or standards[14]—by ensuring you are getting sufficient sleep, trying to tackle tasks earlier in the day, and focusing on the values and goals that underlie the task. Pychyl suggests asking yourself, "Why is it important to us? What benefit is there in making the effort now? How will this help us achieve our goal?"[15]

If you have developed a habit of procrastinating, consider ways you might cultivate a new habit of working on tasks and projects. As you can read in greater depth in chapter 6, cultivating habits requires establishing new routines with their own cues and rewards. What cue might you develop to inspire you to "just get started," and what reward can you give yourself for successfully completing your task? If you experience setbacks or frustration, give yourself some grace and forgiveness (perhaps engaging in a self-compassion practice). It takes time to establish new habits, and you may find that you still occasionally succumb to procrastination. Instead of getting caught up in self-judgment or criticism, focus on your new cues and rewards to further strengthen your new habit.

Alternatively, you might reflect on how you have managed your time. See if you can plan your time better, so that you procrastinate less. Revisit your list of prioritized tasks and your daily to-do list. Ensure that larger projects are broken down into "bite-size" tasks, hold yourself accountable to staying on important tasks until you complete them, and reward yourself when you do.

Notes

1. Pychyl, *Solving the Procrastination Puzzle*, 2.
2. Pychyl, *Solving the Procrastination Puzzle*, 3.
3. Lieberman, "Why You Procrastinate."

4. Pychyl, *Solving the Procrastination Puzzle*, 20.

5. Pychyl, *Solving the Procrastination Puzzle*, 5.

6. Pychyl, *Solving the Procrastination Puzzle*, 14.

7. Lieberman, "Why You Procrastinate."

8. Pychyl, *Solving the Procrastination Puzzle*, 21.

9. Pychyl, *Solving the Procrastination Puzzle*, 50.

10. Tracy, *Time Management*, 69.

11. Pychyl, *Solving the Procrastination Puzzle*, 58.

12. Lieberman, "Why You Procrastinate."

13. Tracy, *Time Management*, 70.

14. Freund and Hennecke, "Self-Regulation in Adulthood," 557–62.

15. Pychyl, *Solving the Procrastination Puzzle*, 75.

How to Write a Professional Email

When you write an email to a professor, a work colleague, or anyone with whom you have a professional relationship, write formally (as you might in a letter), as opposed to informally (as you might in a text message). Make sure that you have spelled words correctly, punctuated properly, and generally followed writing conventions of standard written English. Consider your audience, your purpose for writing, and your genre (a professional email), which constitute your rhetorical situation, which you can read about further in chapter 12, on writing. As Paul Corrigan and Cameron Hunt McNabb note, key writing conventions include:

1. Use a clear subject line
2. Use a salutation and signature
3. Use standard punctuation, capitalization, spelling, and grammar
4. Do your part in solving what you need to solve
5. Be aware of concerns about entitlement
6. Add a touch of humanity[1]

In other words, you should clearly indicate the purpose of your email in the subject line and use "Dear Dr. _____," or "Dear Professor _____," at the beginning and "Sincerely, [*your name*]" at the conclusion. Your email should clearly convey why you are writing to them and demonstrate that you tried to find the answer to your question using resources at your disposal, such as the syllabus and course website. In this way, "you present yourself as responsible and taking initiative."[2] You should send your email from a professional email address, such as your school or work address, or a Gmail address that closely resembles your name.

If you are making a request, instead of asking a question or raising a concern, indicate the circumstances surrounding that request. Often professors allow for students to request extensions on assignments or permit absences from class in the event of extenuating circumstances, such as a death in the family or serious illness. You need not go into detail, but writing, for example, that your grandmother passed away or that you are in the hospital will signal the severity of your situation to your professor or colleague. If you are emailing to ask for a letter of recommendation, make sure that you remind your professor of the courses that you took with them and if possible, the signature assignments or projects that you created for their courses, in addition to sharing details about the program, opportunity, or position you are applying for and attaching your résumé.

If you are reaching out to someone professionally whom you have never met, be sure to indicate who referred you to them, especially if they know that person. For example, I sent this professional email to John McLeod, Chief Operating Officer and Director of the Office of Scholarly Publishing Services at the University of North Carolina Press, when I was first seeking funds to publish this book as an open educational resource:

> Subject: Thomas W. Ross Fund Publishing Grant
> Dear Mr. McLeod,
> I am writing to request an application for the Thomas W. Ross Fund Publishing Grant. I have been in conversation with Lucy Holman about the possibility of publishing an open-access book through UNCW / UNC Press, and I would like to apply for the grant to offset the costs of publication.
> Thank you for your help,
> Beverley McGuire

I clearly indicated my purpose for writing in my subject heading and first sentence, and I also shared the name of the colleague who recommended that I contact him. Similarly, when you write to people about their programs or positions, you can clearly signal what you are writing about and, if applicable, who advised you to reach out to them.

Notes

1. Corrigan and McNabb, "Re: Your Recent Email to Your Professor."
2. Corrigan and McNabb, "Re: Your Recent Email to Your Professor."

How to Not Plagiarize

Plagiarism means presenting another person's writing, thoughts, or expressions as one's own work. It violates academic integrity—a commitment to honesty, trust, fairness, respect, responsibility, and courage[1]—as well as honor codes that seek to uphold academic integrity by addressing issues of academic dishonesty such as cheating and plagiarism. For example, the UNCW honor code gives the following examples of plagiarism, which it defines as "the copying of language, phrasing, structure, or specific ideas of another and presenting any of these as one's own work, including information found on the internet":[2]

1. Reproducing someone else's work without quotation marks or proper attribution and submitting it as your own.
2. Paraphrasing or summarizing another's work without attribution or acknowledgment of the source and submitting it as your own.
3. Deliberate attribution to a source from which the referenced material was not in fact derived.
4. Failing to cite a source for ideas or information.[3]

In other words, to avoid plagiarizing, you should attribute, acknowledge, and cite the source of your information.

Academics love citations. After all, when you cite a source, you provide your reader the chance to engage in further exploration, research, and discovery. You also show that you engaged in research and joined a scholarly conversation about your topic. Whenever you refer to a source in your writing, you either include the citation in a footnote or in parentheses. Then, after your essay or paper, you list all the sources that you cited in a section titled "References" or "Works Cited." Those citations typically include the author's name, the title of their article or book, the date it was published, the name of the publisher, and if it is an article or chapter, the title of the journal, the volume number, the issue number, and the page numbers for the article.

There are various styles for citing sources, and you typically choose the style according to the discipline in which you are writing, although your professor may indicate their preferred citation style. APA (American Psychological Association) is used by the natural sciences, as well as psychology and education; MLA (Modern Language Association) is used by the humanities and arts; and the *Chicago Manual of Style* is generally used by the social sciences such as history and business.[4] Here, I give some examples to show you the different expectations for each citation style, but I would encourage you to consult each citation style's "quick guides" and website for further information.[5]

Books

In 2014, I published a book called *Living Karma*, and the publisher was Columbia University Press in New York. If you referred to my book in your writing, in APA style afterward you would write: (McGuire 2014). If you quoted from it, you would also include the page number: (McGuire, 2014, 50) for page 50. For MLA style, you would use my last name and page number for all citations—quotations or otherwise: (McGuire 50). For Chicago style, you would write: (McGuire 2014, 50). Do you see how they vary slightly?

On your "References" or "Works Cited" page, you would cite the book as follows:

APA: McGuire, B. (2014). *Living Karma: The Religious Practices of Ouyi Zhixu*. Columbia University Press.
MLA: McGuire, Beverley. *Living Karma: The Religious Practices of Ouyi Zhixu*. New York: Columbia University Press.
Chicago: McGuire, Beverley. 2014. *Living Karma: The Religious Practices of Ouyi Zhixu*. New York: Columbia University Press.[6]

Articles

For articles, the in-text citations—meaning the citation that you put in parenthesis after you refer to it in your writing—would follow the same guidelines as above. In 2020, I published an article entitled "Gaming and Grieving: Digital Games as Means of Confronting and Coping with Death" in volume 9, issue 3, of the *Journal of Religion, Media, and Digital Culture*, on pages 326–346. On your References or Works Cited page, you would cite the article as follows:

APA: McGuire, B. (2020) Gaming and Grieving: Digital Games as Means of Confronting and Coping with Death. *Journal of Religion, Media, and Digital Culture,* 9(3), 326–346.
MLA: McGuire, Beverley. "Gaming and Grieving: Digital Games as Means of Confronting and Coping with Death." *Journal of Religion, Media, and Digital Culture,* vol. 9, no. 3, 2020, pp. 326–46.
Chicago: McGuire, Beverley. 2020. "Gaming and Grieving: Digital Games as Means of Confronting and Coping with Death." *Journal of Religion, Media, and Digital Culture* 9, no. 3 (2020): 326–46.

Chapters

For chapters in edited volumes, the in-text citations would follow the same guidelines as above. In 2020, I published a chapter entitled "Instant Karma and Internet Karma: Karmic Memes and Morality on Social Media" in a volume entitled *Believing in Bits* edited by Diana Pasulka and Simone Natale, which was published by Oxford University Press on pages 107–24. On your "References" or "Works Cited" page, you would cite the chapter as follows:

APA: McGuire, B. (2020). Instant Karma and Internet Karma: Karmic Memes and Morality on Social Media. In D. Pasulka & S. Natale (Eds.), *Believing in Bits* (pp. 107–124). Oxford University Press.
MLA: McGuire, Beverley. "Instant Karma and Internet Karma: Karmic Memes and Morality on Social Media." *Believing in Bits,* edited by Diana Pasulka and Simone Natale, Oxford University Press, 2020, pp. 107–24.
Chicago: McGuire, Beverley. 2020. "Instant Karma and Internet Karma: Karmic Memes and Morality on Social Media." In *Believing in Bits,* edited by Diana Pasulka and Simone Natale, 107–24. New York: Oxford University Press.

Webpages

On November 15, 2021, I published an essay entitled "How to Hone Moral Attention—and Why It's So Important" in *Tricycle Magazine,* which they posted on their website. When you cite newspaper or magazine articles, blog posts, or websites, in-text citations follow the same guidelines above, and the citation on the "Reference" or "Works Cited" page would be:

APA: McGuire, B. (2021, November 15) *How to Hone Moral Attention—and Why It's So Important.* Tricycle Magazine. https://tricycle.org/trikedaily/moral-attention/

MLA: McGuire, Beverley. "How to Hone Moral Attention—and Why It's So Important." *Tricycle Magazine,* 15 Nov. 2021, https://tricycle.org/trikedaily/moral-attention/.

Chicago: McGuire, Beverley. 2021. "How to Hone Moral Attention—and Why It's So Important." *Tricycle Magazine,* November 15, 2021. https://tricycle.org/trikedaily/moral-attention/.

However, some citation styles such as Chicago say that you may not need to include a citation for a website on the "References" or "Works Cited" page, you could simply state that "As of May 1, 2017, Yale's home page listed . . . " They also note that, in the event there is no date available for a website, you can use *n.d.* (for "no date") instead of the year, and simply include the date that you accessed the website if you cite it on a "References" or "Works Cited" page.

In conclusion, to avoid plagiarism, pick a citation style—whether it is APA, MLA, or Chicago style—and cite all your sources of information.

Notes

1. "Fundamental Values of Academic Integrity."
2. University of North Carolina Wilmington, "Student Academic Honor Code."
3. University of North Carolina Wilmington, "Student Academic Honor Code."
4. "Citation Styles: APA, MLA, Chicago, Turabian, IEEE."
5. American Psychological Association, "APA Style 7th Edition Reference Guide"; Modern Language Association, "Works Cited: A Quick Guide"; "Chicago-Style Citation Quick Guide."
6. This is the format given in Chapter 15 of *The Chicago Manual of Style;* the format used in this book follows the format of Chapter 14, which varies slightly.

How to Identify and Regulate Your Emotions

I t is natural and normal to experience emotions ranging from dejection to elation. As Oren Jay Sofer writes, "All emotions are okay to feel. It's how we respond, what we do with them, that matters. When we're not aware of our emotions, or when we become flooded or allow them to take over, they can cause harm. What's problematic is *not the emotion itself* but rather our reactive expression of a feeling or our habitual suppression of it."[1] Because of societal pressure to be happy and positive—especially on social media—we may criticize ourselves when we experience sadness or depression. But we are all human, and we inevitably have life experiences that may make us feel forlorn or depleted, such as illness, break-ups, and death of loved ones.

Mindfulness can help us identify and regulate our emotions. It begins with noticing and naming what we are feeling. We can heighten our sensitivity and awareness of our emotions by drawing attention to where we feel them in the body. For example, if we feel anger, we may notice ourselves clenching our jaw or furrowing our eyebrows. If we experience joy, we may feel a warmth in our chest or notice our eyes are wide open. As Sofer observes, "The more clearly we begin to sense the somatic experience of our emotions, the more alert and skilled we become at identifying what we are feeling."[2] We can experience a wide range of emotions. When our human needs are met, we may feel:

Affectionate: friendly, loving, openhearted, sympathetic, warm
Confident: empowered, open, proud, safe, secure
Engaged: absorbed, alert, curious, engrossed, interested, intrigued
Excited: amazed, animated, eager, energetic, enthusiastic, giddy, lively, passionate, surprised
Exhilarated: blissful, ecstatic, elated, enthralled, radiant, thrilled
Grateful: appreciative, moved, thankful, touched
Hopeful: expectant, encouraged, optimistic
Joyful: amused, delighted, glad, happy, pleased
Inspired: amazed, awed, wonder

Peaceful: calm, clearheaded, centered, content, fulfilled, quiet, relaxed, relieved satisfied, serene, still, tranquil

Refreshed: rejuvenated, renewed, rested, restored, revived[3]

By contrast, when our needs are not met, we may experience:

Afraid: apprehensive, dread, frightened, mistrustful, panicked, scared, suspicious, worried

Annoyed: aggravated, dismayed, disgruntled, displeased, frustrated, impatient, irritated

Angry: enraged, furious, indignant, irate, livid, outraged, resentful

Aversion: animosity, contempt, disgusted, dislike, hate, horrified, hostile, repulsed

Confused: ambivalent, baffled, bewildered, dazed, hesitant, lost, mystified, perplex, puzzled, torn

Disconnected: alienated, aloof, apathetic, bored, cold, detached, distant, distracted, indifferent, numb, removed, withdrawn

Disquiet: agitated, alarmed, discombobulated, disconcerted, disturbed, perturbed, rattled, restless, shocked, startled, surprised, troubled, uncomfortable, uneasy, unnerved, unsettled, upset

Embarrassed: ashamed, flustered, mortified, self-conscious

Fatigue: burnt-out, depleted, exhausted, lethargic, listless, sleepy, tired, worn-out

Pain: agony, anguished, bereaved, devastated, grief, heartbroken, hurt, lonely, miserable, regretful, remorseful

Sad: depressed, dejected, despair, despondent, disappointed, discouraged, disheartened, forlorn, gloomy, hopeless, unhappy

Tense: anxious, cranky, distressed, distraught, edgy, fidgety, frazzled, irritable, jittery, nervous, overwhelmed, restless, stressed-out

Vulnerable: fragile, guarded, helpless, insecure, leery, reserved, sensitive, shaky

Yearning: envious, jealous, longing, nostalgic, pining, wistful[4]

As we become more adept at identifying nuanced emotions, we gain a better sense of the range and depth of our emotional life.

After identifying the emotion that we are feeling, we can then try to regulate it or balance it out. As we have learned, every sensation, emotion, and thought has a corresponding feeling tone—pleasant, unpleasant, or neutral—that it evokes within us. Oftentimes, we simply react based on these feelings. We cling to what we like, we push away what we dislike, or we pass over what is neutral. Mindfulness encourages us to rest our attention on our emotions. As Sofer writes, "Rather than clamping down or cutting ourselves off from our emotions, emotion regulation invites us to feel them fully. We develop the patience, strength, and spaciousness to let these waves of tone and energy wash through us without getting toppled by them."[5] We experience them with mindfulness: instead of identifying with our emotions and getting caught up in stories tied to them, we invite some space between ourselves and our emotions, so that we can observe them with curiosity and care. We allow them to surface, and we notice where they arise in our body. We also appreciate that emotions come and go. In this way, we develop our capacity to identify and regulate our emotions, so that rather than reacting blindly to them, we can choose how to respond to them.

Notes

1. Sofer, *Say What You Mean*, 141.
2. Sofer, *Say What You Mean*, 143.
3. Bay NVC, "Feelings/Emotions—Partial List."
4. Bay NVC, "Feelings/Emotions—Partial List."
5. Sofer, *Say What You Mean*, 144.

How to Take Reading Notes, by Erica Noles

An essential aspect of college success is the development of strong reading and note-taking skills. The collegiate learning environment will require you to tackle lots of reading assignments and to take comprehensive notes to retain that information. To give you a bit of information about the importance of reading and taking notes for learning, I want to briefly explain how memory works. When we need to learn new information through reading, we must first pay attention to the information, and then we have to encode this new information in our brains. Encoding happens when we understand the new information and make sense of what it means. Through this encoding process, we can take information from the outside world and move it inside our brains. Unfortunately, attending to the information and encoding (i.e., understanding what you read) isn't the end of the process. The trickier parts of learning involve storing this information in our brains and being able to accurately recall the content later.[1] Across our lives, we have learned countless facts, dates, and information, but they may not have been stored in a meaningful way that lets us retrieve the information when we need it. Fortunately, research has some key insights that can help us become better at encoding, storing, and retrieving this information.[2]

One of the best ways to learn new information is to constantly quiz yourself; this process helps your brain to practice retrieving the information it has stored. If you quiz yourself as you learn, you are practicing the important step of recalling the information you have already read. Your upcoming test does not measure the information you stored, it can only measure the stored information you can retrieve, so practicing information retrieval is crucial. Another great trick is to spread your studying sessions over a larger period (i.e., distribute your learning across multiple days instead of trying to cram it all in right before a test). Students who spread their learning across multiple days instead of cramming right before a test have better long-term retention of the material.[3] But what should you be quizzing yourself on and studying?

This is where taking good notes can be a lifesaver. I created a notes template for taking notes on your readings:

Name:

Title and Author of the Reading:

List five important points from the reading. Give enough detail that you will understand it if you go back and read it in a few months:

Explain two ideas that made you stop and think while reading. Alternatively, explain how the topic relates to your own life or things happening in society:

Provide two detailed critical thinking questions to guide class discussion about the topic:

This template encourages you to read the information and look for the main points of the reading; it asks you to determine what information was relevant to your life, and to examine any questions you have about the content. Though each class you take in college will require you to learn different types of content using various strategies, research demonstrates that if you can make the content personally relevant to you or connect it to knowledge you already have, then you will create a stronger and more durable memory for this information.[4] Using this knowledge may help you break the less effective habit of using a highlighter and quickly reading (and sometimes rereading) the content. Rereading and highlighting are not as effective as reading to determine the meaning of the material and to connect it to information you already know about the topic. With this knowledge, I have hopefully started to convince you that trying to rush through a reading assignment armed with a highlighter to quickly cram a bunch of words into your brain is not the best use of your time. Though using a highlighter while reading has not been shown to improve memory, using a pen or pencil to take notes is an excellent strategy. Notably, it has also been found that students who handwrite their notes tend to recall information significantly better than those who type their notes.[5] If this seems counterintuitive, let's consider what you now know about memory related to making information meaningful to help store and recall it at a later date. Even though taking notes on a computer allowed the students to record more words and take longer notes, the quality of handwritten notes was higher because students had to slow down and actually determine what content was important and meaningful. Based on this experiment and other research studies, if you want to remember information at a later date, it's important that you make the information meaningful instead of going as quickly as possible. If you can spend a bit more time initially learning and encoding information, you won't have to waste as much time rereading the content in the hope that you are storing it in your memory. The debate about computers in the classroom and how they impact learning and memory is ongoing. Research is constantly being published to help us understand this relatively new practice; but based on what we currently know across many studies, data suggests that relying on pen-and-paper notes is a more effective way to learn and remember information.

Notes

1. Grison and Gazaniga, *Psychology in Your Life.*
2. Dunlosky et al., "Improving Students' Learning"; Dunlosky et al., "What Works, What Doesn't."
3. Dunlosky et al., "Improving Students' Learning"; Dunlosky et al., "What Works, What Doesn't."
4. Grison and Gazaniga, *Psychology in Your Life.*
5. Mueller and Oppenheimer, "Pen Is Mightier Than the Keyboard."

Abrams, Abigail. "Yes, Imposter Syndrome Is Real. Here's How to Deal with It." *Time*, June 20, 2018. https://time.com/5312483/how-to-deal-with-impostor-syndrome/.

"Alice Walker on Zora Neale Hurston's 'Spiritual Food.'" *NPR Morning Edition*, April 26, 2004. https://www.npr.org/templates/story/story.php?storyId=1849395.

Ambrose, Susan A., Michael W. Bridges, Michele DiPietro, Marsha C. Lovett, and Marie K. Norman. *How Learning Works: 7 Research-Based Principles for Smart Teaching*. San Francisco: Jossey-Bass, 2010.

American Psychological Association. "APA Style 7th Edition Reference Guide for Journal Articles, Books, and Edited Book Chapters." Accessed March 19, 2022. https://apastyle.apa.org/instructional-aids/reference-guide.pdf.

American Psychological Association. "Key Terms and Concepts in Understanding Gender Diversity and Sexual Orientation." *American Psychological Association*. 2015. https://www.apa.org/pi/lgbt/programs/safe-supportive/lgbt/key-terms.pdf.

Association of American Colleges and Universities. "Oral Communication VALUE Rubric." 2009. Accessed March 13, 2022. https://www.aacu.org/initiatives/value-initiative/value-rubrics/value-rubrics-oral-communication.

Aylward, Martin. *Awake Where You Are: The Art of Embodied Awareness*. Somerville, MA: Wisdom Publications, 2021.

Bailenson, Jeremy N. "Nonverbal Overload: A Theoretical Argument for the Causes of Zoom Fatigue." *Technology, Mind, and Behavior* 2, no. 1 (February 23, 2021). DOI: 10.1037/tmb0000030.

Banaji, Mahzarin R., and Anthony G. Greenwald. *Blindspot: Hidden Biases of Good People*. New York: Delacourte Press, 2013.

Barzun, Jacques. *Simple & Direct: A Rhetoric for Writers*. New York: Quill, 2001.

Batchelor, Stephen. The Art of Solitude: A Meditation on Being Alone with Others in This World. New Haven, CT: Yale University Press, 2020.

Baxter Magolda, Marcia B. "The Activity of Meaning Making: A Holistic Perspective of College Student Development." Journal of College Student Development 50, no. 6 (November/December 2009): 621–39.

Baxter Magolda, Marcia B. "Three Elements of Self-Authorship." Journal of College Student Development 49, no. 4 (July/August 2008): 269–84.

Berila, Beth. Integrating Mindfulness into Anti-Oppression Pedagogy. New York: Routledge, 2016.

Betton, Victoria, and James Woolard. Teen Mental Health in an Online World: Supporting Young People around their Use of Digital Media, Apps, Gaming, Texting and the Rest. Philadelphia: Jessica Kingsley Publishers, 2019.

Bizup, Joseph. "BEAM: A Rhetorical Vocabulary for Teaching Research-Based Writing." Rhetoric Review 27, no. 1 (2008): 75–76.

Blumenfeld, Warren J. "Christian Privilege and the Promotion of 'Secular' and Not-So 'Secular' Mainline Christianity in Public Schooling and in the Larger Society." Equity & Excellence in Education 39 (2006): 195-210.

Book Marks. "The First Reviews of Their Eyes Were Watching God Ranged from Positive to Hostile." LitHub, September 18, 2020. https://lithub.com/the-first-reviews-of-their-eyes-were-watching-god-ranged-from-positive-to-downright-hostile/.

boyd, danah. It's Complicated: The Social Lives of Networked Teens. New Haven, CT: Yale University Press, 2014.

Brentano, Franz. "Über ein optisches Paradoxon." Zeitschrift für Psychologie und Physiologie der Sinnesorgane 3 (1892): 349.

———. "Radical Compassion-Loving Ourselves and Our World Into Healing." Tarabrach.com. Accessed February 26, 2022. https://www.tarabrach.com/part-1-radical-compassion/.

Bringle, Robert G., and July A Hatcher. "A Service-Learning Curriculum for Faculty." Michigan Journal of Community Service Learning 2, no. 1 (1995): 112–22.

Carbado, Devon. "Privilege." In Black Queer Studies: A Critical Anthology, edited by E. Patrick Johnson and Mae G. Henderson, 190–212. Durham, NC: Duke University Press, 2005.

Carillo, Ellen C. A Writer's Guide to Mindful Reading. Boulder, CO: University Press of Colorado, 2017.

———. Securing a Place for Reading in Composition: The Importance of Teaching for Transfer. Logan: Utah State University Press, 2014.

———. Teaching Readers in Post-Truth America. Logan: Utah State University Press, 2018.

Catalano, D. Chase J., Warren J. Blumenfeld, and Heather W. Hackman. "Sexism, Heterosexism, and Trans* Oppression." In Adams et al., Readings for Diversity and Social Justice, 341–53.

Caulfield, Mike. "Building a Fact-Checking Habit By Checking Your Emotions." Web Literacy for Student Fact-Checkers. Accessed February 21, 2022. https://webliteracy.pressbooks.com/chapter/building-a-habit-by-checking-your-emotions/.

———. "Information Literacy for Mortals." Project Information Literacy: Provocation Series, December 14, 2021. https://projectinfolit.org/pubs/provocation-series/essays/information-literacy-for-mortals.html.

Centers for Disease Control and Prevention. "Dietary Guidelines for Alcohol." Accessed April 23, 2022. https://www.cdc.gov/alcohol/fact-sheets/moderate-drinking.htm.

Centers for Disease Control and Prevention. "Improving Your Eating Habits." Accessed February 16, 2022. https://www.cdc.gov/healthyweight/losing _weight/eating_habits.html.

Centers for Disease Control and Prevention. "Mental Health." Accessed February 18, 2022. https://www.cdc.gov/mentalhealth/.

"Chicago-Style Citation Quick Guide." *The Chicago Manual of Style Online*. Accessed March 19, 2022. https://www.chicagomanualofstyle.org/tools_citationguide .html.

Chödrön, Pema. When Things Fall Apart: Heart Advice for Difficult Times. Boulder: Shambala, 2000.

Coleman, Mark. Make Peace with Your Mind: How Mindfulness and Compassion Can Free You From Your Inner Critic. Novato, CA: New World Library, 2016.

Confucius. The Analects (Lun yü). Translated by D.C. Lau. New York: Penguin Books, 1979.

Covey, Steven. The 7 Habits of Highly Effective People: Powerful Lessons in Personal Change. New York: Simon & Schuster, 2004.

Covey, Steven, A. Roger Merrill, and Rebecca R. Merrill. First Things First: To Live, to Love, to Learn, to Leave a Legacy. New York: Free Press, 1994.

Csikszentmihalyi, Mihaly. Flow: The Psychology of Optimal Experience. New York: HarperPerennial, 1990.

De Witte, Melissa. "Is There Something Wrong with Philanthropy?" Greater Good Science Center, December 19, 2018. https://greatergood.berkeley.edu/article /item/is_there_something_wrong_with_philanthropy. Duhigg, Charles. *The Power of Habit: Why We Do What We Do in Life and Business*. New York: Random House, 2012.

Duckworth, Angela. *Grit: The Power of Passion and Perseverance*. New York: Scribner, 2016.

Dunlosky, John, Katherine A. Rawson, Elizabeth J. Marsh, Mitchell J. Nathan, and Daniel T. Willingham. "Improving Students' Learning With Effective Learning Techniques: Promising Directions From Cognitive and Educational Psychology." *Psychological Science in the Public Interest* 14, no. 1 (2013): 4–58.

———. "What Works, What Doesn't." *Scientific American Mind* 24, no. 4 (2013): 47–53.

Dvořáková, Kamila, Moé Kishida, Jacinda Li, Steriani Elavsky, Patricia C. Broderick, Mark R. Agrusti, and Mark T. Greenberg. "Promoting Healthy Transition to College through Mindfulness Training with First-Year College Students: Pilot Randomized Controlled Trial." *Journal of American College Health* 65, no. 4 (2016): 259–67.

Dweck, Carol. *Mindset: The New Psychology of Success*. New York: Ballentine Books, 2006.

Eck, Diana. *A New Religious America: How a "Christian Country" Has Become the World's Most Religiously Diverse Nation*. New York: HarperOne, 2001.

Elbow, Peter. *Writing with Power*. New York: Oxford University Press, 1998.

Ellison, Ralph. *Invisible Man*. New York: Vintage International, 1990.

Elon University. "Service-Learning." *Center for Engaged Learning*. Accessed March 14, 2022. https://www.centerforengagedlearning.org/resources/service -learning/#:~:text=References-,Definition,Universities%20(AACU)%20in%20 2007.

Escalante, Alison. "New Science: Why Our Brains Spend 50 Percent of the Time Mind-Wandering." *Forbes*, January 28, 2021. https://www.forbes.com/sites /alisonescalante/2021/01/28/new-science-why-our-brains-spend-50-of-the -time-mind-wandering/?sh=1d2b3874854e.

Eyal, Nir. *Hooked: How to Build Habit-Forming Products*. New York: Penguin, 2014.

Eyler, Joshua R. *How Humans Learn*. Morgantown: West Virginia University Press, 2018.

Faust, Katrina. "How to Lead Your Team to Peak Performance with Dr. Steven Rogelberg." *Leadx*, January 28, 2019. https://leadx.org/articles/science -meetings-performance-team-steven-rogelberg/.

Feldman, Christina. *Boundless Heart: The Buddha's Path of Kindness, Compassion, Joy and Equanimity*. Boulder, CO: Shambala, 2017.

Felski, Ritz. "Critique and the Hermeneutics of Suspicion." *Media/Culture Journal* 15, no. 1 (2011). https://doi.org/10.5204/mcj.431.

Fink, L. Dee. *Creating Significant Learning Experiences: An Integrated Approach to Designing College Courses*. San Francisco: Jossey-Bass, 2013.

Freire, Paulo. *Pedagogy of Freedom: Ethics, Democracy, and Civic Courage*. New York: Rowman & Littlefield, 1998.

Freund, Alexandra M., and Marie Hennecke. "Self-Regulation in Adulthood." In *International Encyclopedia of the Social and Behavioral Sciences*, 2nd ed., edited by James W. Wright, 557–62. Amsterdam: Elsevier, 2015.

Friedman, Stewart D. *Leading the Life You Want: Skills for Integrating Work and Life*. Boston: Harvard Business Review Press, 2014.

"Fundamental Values of Academic Integrity." *International Center for Academic Integrity*. Accessed March 19, 2022. https://academicintegrity.org/resources /fundamental-values?highlight=WyJzaXgiLCJ2YWx1ZXMiLCJ2YWx1ZXMnIiw ic2l4IHZhbHVlcyJd.

Gallagher, Eugene V., and Joanne Maguire. *The Religious Studies Skills Book: Close Reading, Critical Thinking, and Comparison*. New York: Bloomsbury, 2019.

Gardner, Howard, and Katie Davis. *The App Generation: How Today's Youth Navigate Identity, Intimacy, and Imagination in a Digital World*. New Haven, CT: Yale University Press, 2014.

Ginsberg, Allen. *Spontaneous Mind: Selected Interviews, 1958-1996*. New York: Harper Collins, 2001.

Goldberg, Natalie. *Writing Down the Bones: Freeing the Writer Within*. Boulder, CO: Shambala, 2016.

Google. "How Google Search Works." *Youtube*, October 24, 2019. https://www.youtube.com/watch?t=33&v=0eKVizvYSUQ&feature=youtu.be.

Gordinier, Jeff. "Mindful Eating as Food for Thought." *New York Times,* February 7, 2012. https://www.nytimes.com/2012/02/08/dining/mindful-eating-as-food-for-thought.html.

Grant, Richard. "Do Trees Talk to Each Other?" *Smithsonian Magazine*, March 2018. https://www.smithsonianmag.com/science-nature/the-whispering-trees-180968084/.

Greshes, Warren. *Don't Count the Yes's, Count the No's and Time Management Skills that Work*. N.p.: Gildan Media, 2018.

Grison, Sarah, and Michael S. Gazaniga. *Psychology in Your Life*. New York: W.W. Norton, 2019.

Grossnickle, Emily M. "Disentangling Curiosity: Dimensionality, Definitions, and Distinctions from Interest in Educational Contexts." *Educational Psychology Review* 28, no. 1 (2016): 23–60

Haas, Christina, and Linda Flower. "Rhetorical Reading Strategies and the Construction of Meaning." *College Composition and Communication* 29, no. 2 (1988): 176.

———. "Reply." *College Composition and Communication* 40, no. 4 (December 1989): 482.

Hallett, Rachel, and Rosamond Hutt. "10 jobs that didn't exist 10 years ago." *World Economic Forum,* June 7, 2016. https://www.weforum.org/agenda/2016/06/10-jobs-that-didn-t-exist-10-years-ago/.

Hamblin, James. "Buy Experiences, Not Things." *The Atlantic*, October 7, 2014. https://www.theatlantic.com/business/archive/2014/10/buy-experiences/381132/.

Han, Byung-Chul. *The Scent of Time*. Medford, MA: Polity Press, 2017.

Hanh, Thich Nhat. *Peace Is Every Step: The Path of Mindfulness in Everyday Life*. New York: Bantam Books, 1991.

Hanh, Thich Nhat. *Silence: The Power of Quiet in a World Full of Noise*. New York: HarperOne, 2015.

Hanh, Thich Nhat, and Lilian Cheung. *Savor: Mindful Eating, Mindful Life*. New York: HarperOne, 2011.

Hanson, Rick. "Let It R.A.I.N." *Rick Hanson, Ph.D.* Accessed December 12, 2021. https://www.rickhanson.net/let-it-recognize-accept-investigate-not-identify/.

———. "Take in the Good." *Rick Hanson, Ph.D.* Accessed March 5, 2022. https://www.rickhanson.net/take-in-the-good/.

Harris, Dan. "Why Mindfulness Is a Superpower." *Youtube,* December 7, 2015. https://www.youtube.com/watch?v=w6To2g5hnT4.

Harris, Russ. *The Confidence Gap: A Guide to Overcome Fear and Self-Doubt.* Boston: Trumpeter Books, 2011.

Harro, Bobbie. "The Cycle of Socialization." In Adams et al., *Readings for Diversity and Social Justice,* 27–34.

Heilbron, John L. "Bohr's First Theory of the Atom." *Physics Today* 38, no. 10 (October 1985): 28–36. https://doi.org/10.1063/1.881014.

Herman, Jennifer H., and Linda B. Nilson. *Creating Engaging Discussions: Strategies for "Avoiding Crickets" in Any Size Classroom.* Sterling, VA: Stylus Publishing, 2018.

Higdon, Hal. "Half Marathon Training: Novice 1." *HalHigdon.* Accessed December 13, 2021. https://www.halhigdon.com/training-programs/half-marathon -training/novice-1-half-marathon/.

"Honor Native Land: A Guide and Call to Acknowledgment." U.S. Department of Arts and Culture. Accessed November 6, 2021. https://usdac.us/nativeland.

hooks, bell. *all about love: new visions.* New York: William Morrow, 2000.

———. *Yearning: Race, Gender, and Cultural Politics.* Boston: South End Press, 1990.

Hoover, Stewart. *Religion in the Media Age.* New York: Routledge, 2006.

Hopper, Richard. *Making Meetings Work: The Art of Chairing.* New York: Routledge, 2021.

Hudson, Simon. "Why Video Conferencing Is So Tiring and What You Can Do about It." *IT Pro,* February 3, 2020. https://www.itpro.com/software/video -conferencing/358488/why-videoconferencing-is-so-tiring-and-what-you -can-do-about-it.

Hurston, Zora Neale. *Their Eyes Were Watching God.* New York: Harper & Row, 1937.

"Implicit Association Test." *Project Implicit.* Accessed December 17, 2021. https://implicit.harvard.edu/implicit/takeatest.html.

Inbal, Miki, and Arnina Kashtan. "Universal Human Needs—Partial List." *Bay NVC.* Accessed February 23, 2022. https://thefearlessheart.org/nvc-reference -materials/list-of-needs/

Insight Timer. "Insight Timer." Accessed November 7, 2021. https://insighttimer .com/.

Irving, Zachary C. "Mind-Wandering Is Unguided Attention: Accounting for the 'Purposeful' Wanderer." *Philosophical Studies* 173 (2016): 547–71.

Jabr, Ferris. "How Does a Caterpillar Turn into a Butterfly?" *Scientific American,* August 10, 2012. https://www.scientificamerican.com/article/caterpillar -butterfly-metamorphosis-explainer/.

Jacoby, Barbara, and Jeffrey Howard. *Service-Learning Essentials: Questions, Answers, and Lessons Learned*. New York: John Wiley & Sons, 2014.

Jalāl al-Dīn Rūmī. *The Essential Rumi*. Translated by Coleman Barks. New York: HarperOne, 2004.

James, William. *Principles of Psychology*. Vol. 1. New York: Henry Colt, 1890.

Jastrow, Joseph. *Fact and Fable in Psychology*. New York: Houghton Mifflin Company, 1900.

Jones, Susan R. "The Underside of Service Learning." *About Campus* (September-October 2002): 10–15.

Jory, Justin. "The Rhetorical Situation." *Open English @ SLCC*. Accessed March 10, 2022. https://openenglishatslcc.pressbooks.com/chapter/the-rhetorical -situation/.

Karmapa. "Understanding Emptiness & Interdependence." *Lion's Roar*, May 5, 2013. https://www.ionsroar.com/it-starts-from-zero-may-2013/.

Kaur, Valarie. *See No Stranger: A Memoir and Manifesto of Revolutionary Love*. New York: One World, 2020.

Kedrowicz, April A., and Julie L. Taylor. "Shifting Rhetorical Norms and Electronic Eloquence: TED Talks as Formal Presentations." *Journal of Business and Technical Communication* 30, no. 3 (2016): 352–77.

Kendi, Ibram X. *How to Be an Antiracist*. New York: One World, 2019.

Keltner, Dacher, and Jonathan Haidt, "Approaching Awe, a Moral, Spiritual, and Aesthetic Emotion." *Cognition and Emotion* 17, no. 2 (2003): 297–314.

King, Stephen. *On Writing: A Memoir of the Craft*. New York: Scribner, 2000.

Kitchener, Caroline. "What It Means to Be Spiritual but Not Religious." *The Atlantic*, January 11, 2018. https://www.theatlantic.com/membership/archive/2018/01 /what-it-means-to-be-spiritual-but-not-religious/550337/.

Kuriyama, Shigehisa. *The Expressiveness of the Body and the Divergence of Greek and Chinese Medicine*. New York: Zone Books, 2002.

LaBarre, Denise. *Issues in Your Tissues: Heal Body and Emotion from the Inside Out*. Haiku, HI: Healing Catalyst Press, 2010.

Learning Center, University of North Carolina at Chapel Hill. "Metacognitive Study Strategies." Accessed February 20, 2022. https://learningcenter.unc.edu/tips -and-tools/metacognitive-study-strategies/.

Leary, Mark R., Kate J. Diebels, Erin K. Davisson, Katrina P. Jongman-Sereno, Jennifer C. Isherwood, Kaitlin T. Raimi, Samantha A. Deffler, and Rich H. Hoyle. "Cognitive and Interpersonal Features of Intellectual Humility." *Personality and Social Psychology Bulletin* 43, no. 6 (2017): 793–813.

Lee, Jena. "A Neuropsychological Exploration of Zoom Fatigue." *Psychiatric Times*, November 16, 2020. https://www.psychiatrictimes.com/view/psychological -exploration-zoom-fatigue.

Lee, Jung. "Finely Aware and Richly Responsible: The Daoist Imperative." *Journal of the American Academy of Religion* 68, no. 3 (September 2000): 511–36.

Levine, Arthur, and Diane R. Dean. *Generation on a Tightrope: A Portrait of Today's College Student.* San Francisco: Jossey-Bass, 2012.

Levy, David M. *Mindful Tech: How to Bring Balance to Our Digital Lives.* New Haven, CT: Yale University Press, 2016.

Lieberman, Charlotte. "Why You Procrastinate (It Has Nothing to do with Self-Control)." *New York Times,* March 25, 2019. https://www.nytimes.com/2019/03/25/smarter-living/why-you-procrastinate-it-has-nothing-to-do-with-self-control.html.

Loewus, Liana. "What Is Digital Literacy?" *Education Week,* November 8, 2016. https://www.edweek.org/teaching-learning/what-is-digital-literacy/2016/11.

Lorber, Judith. *Paradoxes of Gender.* New Haven, CT: Yale University Press, 1994.

Lyubomirsky, Sonja. *The How of Happiness: A New Approach to Getting the Life You Want.* New York: Penguin, 2007.

Magee, Rhonda. *The Inner Work of Racial Justice: Healing Ourselves and Transforming Our Communities through Mindfulness.* New York: TarcherPerigee, 2019.

Mantsios, Gregory. "Class in America." In Adams et al., *Readings for Diversity and Social Justice,* 173–82.

Marche, Stephen. "Is Facebook Making Us Lonely?" *The Atlantic,* May 2012. https://www.theatlantic.com/magazine/archive/2012/05/is-facebook-making-us-lonely/308930/.

McHaney, Roger. *The New Digital Shoreline: How Web 2.0 and Millennials are Revolutionizing Higher Education.* Sterling, VA: Stylus, 2011.

McIntosh, Peggy. "White Privilege: Unpacking the Invisible Knapsack." *Peace and Freedom Magazine* (July/August 1989): 10–12. https://nationalseedproject.org/Key-SEED-Texts/white-privilege-unpacking-the-invisible-knapsack.

McKeown, Greg. *Essentialism: The Disciplined Pursuit of Less.* New York: Crown Business, 2014.

McMahan, Ethan A., and David Estes. "Hedonic versus Eudaimonic Conceptions of Well-Being: Evidence of Differential Associations with Experienced Well-Being." *Social Indicators Research* 103 (2011): 93–108. https://doi.org/10.1007/s11205-010-9698-0.

Menakem, Resmaa. *My Grandmother's Hands: Racialized Trauma and the Pathway to Mending Our Hearts and Bodies.* Las Vegas: Central Recovery Press, 2017.

Mezirow, Jack. *Learning as Transformation: Critical Perspectives on a Theory in Progress.* San Francisco: Jossey-Bass, 2000.

Miller, Barbara Stoler, trans. *Yoga Discipline of Freedom: The Yoga Sutra Attributed to Patanjali.* New York: Bantam Books, 1998.

Miller, Richard E. "On Digital Reading." *Pedagogy* 16, no. 1 (January 2016): 153–64.

Mitchell, Tania D. "Traditional vs. Critical Service-Learning: Engaging the Literature to Differentiate Two Models." *Michigan Journal of Community Service Learning* 14, no. 2 (Spring 2008): 50–65.

Modern Language Association. "Works Cited: A Quick Guide." *MLA Style Center.* Accessed March 19, 2022. https://style.mla.org/works-cited/works-cited-a-quick-guide/.

Montuori, Alfonso. "Literature Review as Creative Inquiry: Reframing Scholarship as a Creative Process." *Journal of Transformative Education* 3 (2005): 374–93.

Moore, Jessie L., and Randall Bass. *Understanding Writing Transfer: Implications for Transformative Student Learning in Higher Education.* Sterling, VA: Stylus, 2017.

Moses, Jemma, Graham L. Bradley, and Frances V. O'Callaghan. "When College Students Look After Themselves." *Journal of Student Affairs Research and Practice* 53, no. 3 (2016): 346–59. https://doi.org/10.1080/19496591.2016.1157488.

Mueller, Pam A., and Daniel M. Oppenheimer. "The Pen Is Mightier than the Keyboard: Advantages of Longhand Over Laptop Note Taking." *Psychological Science* 25, no. 6 (April 2014): 1159–68. https://doi.org/10.1177/0956797614524581.

Muir, John. *Our National Parks.* Boston: Houghton Mifflin, 1901.

Muller, A. Charles, trans. "Daode jing," *Resources for East Asian Language and Thought.* Last modified April 26, 2021. http://www.acmuller.net/con-dao/daodejing.html#div-12.

Myers-Lipton, Scott. *Change! A Student Guide to Social Action.* New York: Routledge, 2018.

Nadeau, Randall. *Asian Religions: A Cultural Perspective.* Malden, MA: Wiley Blackwell, 2014.

National Communication Association. "Speaking and Listening Competencies for College Graduates." Accessed February 23, 2021. https://www.natcom.org/sites/default/files/pages/Assessment_Resources_Speaking_and_Listening_Competencies_for_College_Students.pdf.

Neff, Kristin. *Self-Compassion: The Proven Power of Being Kind to Yourself.* New York: HarperCollins, 2011.

———. "Self-Compassion Guided Practices and Exercises." *Self-Compassion.* Accessed February 26, 2022. https://self-compassion.org/category/exercises/#exercises.

Neimeyer, Robert, and Diana Sands. "Meaning Reconstruction in Bereavement: From Principles to Practice." In *Grief and Bereavement in Contemporary Society: Bridging Research and Practice,* edited by Robert A. Neimeyer, Darcy L. Harris, Howard R. Winokuer, and Gordon F. Thornton, 9–22. New York: Routledge, 2011.

Nield, David. "How to Get Google Search Results That Are Actually Useful." *Wired*, October 3, 2021. https://www.wired.com/story/how-to-useful-google -search-results/.

Noble, Safiya Umoja. *Algorithms of Oppression: How Search Engines Reinforce Racism*. New York: New York University Press, 2018.

Noddings, Nel. *Educating Moral People: A Caring Approach to Character Education*. New York: Teachers College Press, 2002.

Nouwen, Henri. *Spiritual Formation: Following the Movements of the Spirit*. New York: HarperOne, 2010.

Nouwen, Henri. *The Way of the Heart: Connecting with God through Prayer, Wisdom, and Silence*. New York: Ballantine Books, 1981.

Novak, Joseph D., and Alberto J. Cañas. "The Theory Underlying Concept Maps and How to Construct and Use Them, Technical Report of the Institute for Human and Machine Cognition." *Cmap*. Accessed February 20, 2022. https:// cmap.ihmc.us/docs/pdf/TheoryUnderlyingConceptMaps.pdf.

Nussbaum, Martha. "'Finely Aware and Richly Responsible': Moral Attention and the Moral Task of Literature." *Journal of Philosophy* 82, no. 10 (October 1985): 516–29. https://doi.org/10.2307/2026358.

———. *Love's Knowledge: Essays on Philosophy and Literature*. New York: Oxford University Press, 1990.

Odell, Jenny. *How to Do Nothing: Resisting the Attention Economy*. Brooklyn: Melville House, 2019.

Oliver, Mary. "Poem 133: The Summer Day." *Library of Congress*. Accessed March 11, 2022. https://www.loc.gov/programs/poetry-and-literature/poet-laureate/poet -laureate-projects/poetry-180/all-poems/item/poetry-180-133 /the-summer-day/.

Oliveros, Pauline. *The Roots of the Moment*. New York: Drogue Press, 1998.

Ostiguy-Finneran, Benjamin, and Madeline L. Peters. "Ableism." In Adams et al., *Readings for Diversity and Social Justice*, 467–74.

Parkes, Colin Murray. "Bereavement as a Psychosocial Transition: Processes of Adaption to Change." *Journal of Social Issues* 44, no. 3 (1988): 53–65.

Parkes, Graham. "Japanese Aesthetics." *Stanford Encyclopedia of Philosophy*, December 4, 2018. https://plato.stanford.edu/entries/japanese-aesthetics /#MonoNoAwarPathThin.

Pauk, Walter, and Ross J. Q. Owens. *How to Study in College*. 11th ed. Boston: Wadsworth, Cengage Learning, 2014.

Paul, Richard, and Linda Elder. *Critical Thinking: Tools for Taking Charge of Your Personal and Professional Life*. 2nd ed. Upper Saddle River, NJ: Pearson Education, 2014.

Pew Research Center. "Most Americans Say There Is Too Much Economic Inequality in the U.S., but Fewer Than Half Call It a Top Priority." January 9, 2020. https://www.pewresearch.org/social-trends/2020/01/09/trends-in-income-and-wealth-inequality/.

———. "In U.S., Decline of Christianity Continues at Rapid Pace: An Update on America's Changing Religious Landscape." October 17, 2019. https://www.pewforum.org/2019/10/17/in-u-s-decline-of-christianity-continues-at-rapid-pace/.

———. ""Nones" on the Rise." October 9, 2012. https://www.pewforum.org/2012/10/09/nones-on-the-rise/.

———. "The Global Religious Landscape." December 18, 2012. https://www.pewforum.org/2012/12/18/global-religious-landscape-exec/.

Perry, Bruce, and Oprah Winfrey. *What Happened To You? Conversations on Trauma, Resilience, and Healing.* New York: Flatiron Books, 2021.

Pétrement, Simone. *Simone Weil: A Life.* New York: Pantheon Books, 1976.

Phillips, Katherine. "How Diversity Works." *Scientific American* (October 2014): 43–47.

———. "Why Diversity Matters." *Talks@ Columbia on Youtube.* December 11, 2015. https://www.youtube.com/watch?v=lHStHPQUzkE.

Pikörn, Isabelle. "The 5-4-3-2-1 Grounding Technique: Manage Anxiety by Anchoring in the Present." *InsightTimer Blog.* Accessed March 13, 2022. https://insighttimer.com/blog/54321-grounding-technique/.

Pluralism Project of Harvard University. "What Is Pluralism?" *Pluralism Project.* Accessed December 9, 2021. https://pluralism.org/.

Price, Catherine. *How to Break Up with Your Phone.* New York: Ten Speed Press, 2018.

Powers, Richard. *The Overstory.* New York: W.W. Norton, 2019.

"Public Theologies of Technology and Presence." Institute of Buddhist Studies. Accessed November 6, 2021. https://www.shin-ibs.edu/luce/.

Puett, Michael, and Christine Gross-Loh. *The Path: What Chinese Philosophers Can Teach Us about the Good Life.* New York: Simon & Schuster, 2016.

Pychyl, Timothy A. *Solving the Procrastination Puzzle: A Concise Guide to Strategies for Change.* New York: Jeremy P. Tarcher, 2010.

Reynolds, Candyce, and Judith Patton. *Leveraging the ePortfolio for Integrative Learning: A Faculty Guide to Classroom Practices for Transforming Student Learning.* Sterling, VA: Stylus, 2014.

Reynolds, Garr. *PresentationZen: Simple Ideas on Presentation Design and Delivery.* 2nd ed. Berkeley, CA: New Riders, 2012.

Rhoads, Robert A. "Critical Multiculturalism and Service Learning." In *Academic Service Learning: A Pedagogy of Action and Reflection,* edited by Robert A. Rhoads and Jeffrey Howard, 39–46. San Francisco: Jossey-Bass, 1998.

Roediger, Henry L., III, Mark A. McDaniel, and Peter C. Brown. *Make It Stick: The Science of Successful Learning*. Cambridge, MA: Belknap Press, 2014.

Rolfe, Gary, Dawn Freshwater, and Melanie Jasper. *Critical Reflection for Nursing and the Helping Professions: a User's Guide*. Basingstoke, UK: Palgrave Macmillan, 2001.

Rosenberg, Marshall B. *Nonviolent Communication: A Language of Life*. Encinitas, CA: PuddleDancer Press, 2015.

Ross, Jen. "Engaging with 'Webness' in Online Reflective Writing Practices." *Computers and Composition* 34 (2014): 96–109.

Rossette-Crake, Fiona. "'The New Oratory': Public Speaking Practice in the Digital, Neoliberal Age." *Discourse Studies* 22, no. 5 (2020): 571–89.

Runner's World. "This Plan Will Take You from Beginner to 5K in Just Six Weeks." *Runner's World*, December 9, 2021. https://www.runnersworld.com/uk/training/5km/a760067/six-week-beginner-5k-schedule/.

Salmons, Janet. *Learning to Collaborate, Collaborating to Learn: Engaging Students in the Classroom and Online*. Sterling, VA: Stylus, 2019.

Salzberg, Sharon. *Lovingkindness: The Revolutionary Art of Happiness*. Boston: Shambala, 2002.

Samuel, Sigal. "It's Hard to Be a Moral Person. Technology Is Making It Harder." *Vox*, August 3, 2021. https://www.vox.com/the-highlight/22585287/technology-smartphones-gmail-attention-morality.

School of Thought. "Yourbias.is." *Yourbias.is*. Accessed February 2, 2022. https://yourbias.is/

Schwartz, Barry. *The Paradox of Choice: Why More Is Less*. New York: Harper Perennial, 2004.

Shaer, Matthew. "What Emotion Goes Viral the Fastest?" *Smithsonian Magazine*, April 2014. https://www.smithsonianmag.com/science-nature/what-emotion-goes-viral-fastest-180950182/?no-ist.

Shāntideva. *The Way of the Bodhisattva: A Translation of the Bodhicaryāvatāra*. Boulder: Shambhala, 2006.

Singleton, Glenn E., and Cyndie Hays. "Beginning Courageous Conversations about Race." In *Everyday Antiracism: Getting Real about Race in School*, edited by Mica Pollock, 18–23. New York: New Press, 2008.

Sofer, Oren Jay. *Say What You Mean: A Mindful Approach to Nonviolent Communication*. Boulder: Shambala, 2018.

Sperry, Rod Meade. "'Right Now, It's Like This': How to Make This Popular Buddhist Phrase Work for You." *Lion's Roar*, April 20, 2017. https://www.lionsroar.com/right-now-its-like-this/.

Stanton, Timothy K., Dwight E. Giles Jr., and Nadinne I. Cruz. *Service-Learning: A Movement's Pioneers Reflect on Its Origins, Practice, and Future*. San Francisco: Jossey-Bass, 1999.

Staples, Brent. "Black Men and Public Space." *Harper's Magazine* (December 1986): 19–20.

Steele, Claude. *Whistling Vivaldi: How Stereotypes Affect Us and What We Can Do.* New York: W.W. Norton, 2010.

Stone, Linda. "Continuous Partial Attention." Keynote speech at the Idea Conference 2007. Accessed March 26, 2017. https://www.csmedia1.com /paseodelrey.org/continuous-partial-attention.pdf.

"Structured Liberal Education." Stanford University. Accessed November 6, 2021. https://sis.stanford.edu/structured-liberal-education-sle.

Strunk, William, Jr., and E. B. White. *The Elements of Style.* Boston: Allyn & Bacon, 2000.

Styron, William. *Darkness Visible: A Memoir of Madness.* New York: Vintage Books, 1990.

Suni, Eric, and Abhinav Singh. "How Much Sleep Do We Really Need?" *Sleep Foundation*, March 10, 2021. https://www.sleepfoundation.org/how-sleep-works /how-much-sleep-do-we-really-need.

Suni, Eric, and Alex Dimitru. "Circadian Rhythm: What It Is, What Shapes It, and Why It's Fundamental to Getting Quality Sleep." *Sleep Foundation,* January 20, 2022. https://www.sleepfoundation.org/circadian-rhythm.

Suni, Eric, and Nilong Vyas. "Sleep Hygiene: What It Is, Why It Matters, and How to Revamp Your Habits to Get Better Nightly Sleep." *Sleep Foundation*, November 29, 2021. https://www.sleepfoundation.org/sleep-hygiene.

Suzuki, Shunryu. *Zen Mind, Beginner's Mind: Informal Talks on Zen Meditation and Practice.* Boston: Shambala, 2011.

Sword, Helen. *Stylish Academic Writing.* Cambridge, MA: Harvard University Press, 2012.

Tanner, Kimberly D. "Promoting Student Metacognition." *CBE-Life Sciences Education* 11, no. 2 (Summer 2012): 113–20. https://doi.org/10.1187/cbe.12 -03-0033.

Tatum, Beverly Daniel. *Why Are All the Black Kids Sitting Together in the Cafeteria? And Other Conversations about Race.* New York: Basic Books, 2017.

Thera, Nyanaponika. *The Heart of Buddhist Meditation: The Buddha's Way of Mindfulness.* San Francisco: Weiser Books, 1996.

Tracy, Brian. *Time Management.* New York: Harper Collins, 2014.

Treleaven, David. *Trauma-Sensitive Mindfulness: Practices for Safe and Transformative Healing.* New York: W.W. Norton, 2018.

Turkle, Sherry. *Alone Together: Why We Expect More from Technology and Less from Each Other.* New York: Basic Books, 2011.

UCLA Block Learning and Forgetting Lab. "Research: Applying Cognitive Psychology to Enhance Educational Practice." Accessed February 20, 2022. https://bjorklab.psych.ucla.edu/research/.

University of Connecticut. "Reflection Models." *Center for Excellence in Teaching and Learning.* Accessed March 12, 2022. https://edtech.uconn.edu/multimedia-consultation/portfolios/reflection-models/#.

University of North Carolina Wilmington. "Mindful UNCW." Accessed November 6, 2021. https://uncw.edu/mindful/.

———. "Seahawk Respect Compact." Accessed March 19, 2022. https://uncw.edu/diversity/src.html.

———. "Student Academic Honor Code." Accessed March 19, 2022. https://uncw.edu/odos/honorcode/documents/student-academic-honor-2021-22.pdf.

USC Annenberg. "Algorithms of Oppression: Safiya Umoja Noble." *Youtube,* February 28, 2018. https://www.youtube.com/watch?v=6KLTpoTpkXo&feature=youtu.be.

U.S. Department of Health and Human Services. *Physical Activity Guidelines for Americans.* 2nd ed. Washington, DC: U.S. Department of Health and Human Services, 2018.

U.S. Department of Justice. "Introduction to the Americans with Disabilities Act." *ADA.gov.* Accessed December 9, 2021. https://beta.ada.gov/topics/intro-to-ada/.

Vaccaro, Annemarie. "Building a Framework for Social Justice Education." In *The Art of Effective Facilitation: Reflections from Social Justice Educators,* edited by Lisa M. Landreman, 23–44. Sterling, VA: Stylus, 2013.

Vallor, Shannon. *Technology and the Virtues: A Philosophical Guide to a Future Worth Having.* New York: Oxford University Press, 2016.

Walker, Alice. *In Search of Our Mothers' Gardens.* New York: Harcourt, 1983.

———. "In Search of Zora Neale Hurston." *Ms. Magazine* (1975): 74–89.

Wang, Frances Kai-Hwa. "How Violence Against Asian Americans Has Grown and How to Stop It, According to Activists." *PBS News Hour,* April 11, 2022. https://www.pbs.org/newshour/nation/a-year-after-atlanta-and-indianapolis-shootings-targeting-asian-americans-activists-say-we-cant-lose-momentum.

Weaver, Caity. "Meetings. Why? Does this Conversation Need to Be a Meeting? Does Anything?" *New York Times,* June 24, 2021. https://www.nytimes.com/2021/06/24/business/work-meetings-zoom.html.

Weil, Simone. *Waiting for God.* New York: Harper Perennial Modern Classics, 2009.

West, Cornel. "Courage." In Adams et al., *Readings for Diversity and Social Justice,* 635–37.

Weston, Linda Yaron. "Mindfulness in Class and Life: Mental Health and Emotional Resilience Alongside Academic Studies." *Liberal Education* 106, no. 3 (2020). https://www.aacu.org/article/mindfulness-in-class-and-in-life-mental-health-and-emotional-resilience-alongside-academic-studies

"What Is Career Readiness?" *NACE: National Association of Colleges and Employers.* Accessed November 15, 2021. https://www.naceweb.org/career-readiness/competencies/career-readiness-defined/.

Whitney, Diana D., and Amanda Trosten-Bloom. *The Power of Appreciative Inquiry: A Practical Guide to Positive Change.* 2nd ed. San Francisco: Berrett-Koehler Publishers, 2010.

Williams, Florence. *The Nature Fix: Why Nature Makes Us Happier, Healthier, and More Creative.* New York: W.W. Norton, 2017.

Wineburg, Sam, and Sarah McGrew. "Lateral Reading and the Nature of Expertise: Reading Less and Learning More When Evaluating Digital Information." *Teachers College Record* 121, no. 110302 (November 2019): 1–40.

Wingert, Jason R., Jeffrey C. Jones, Robert A. Swoap, and Heather M. Wingert. "Mindfulness-Based Strengths Practice Improves Well-Being and Retention in Undergraduates: A Preliminary Randomized Controlled Trial." *Journal of American College Health* 70, no. 3 (2020): 1–8. https://doi.org/10.1080/07448481.2020.1764005

Wittgenstein, Ludwig. *Philosophical Investigations.* 3rd ed. Translated by G. E. M. Anscombe. New York: Macmillan Publishing, 1958.

Yang, Chia-Chen, Sean M. Holden, Mollie D.K. Carter, and Jessica J. Webb. "Social Media Social Comparison and Identity Distress at the College Transition: A Dual-Path Model." *Journal of Adolescence* 69 (December 2018): 92–102. https://doi.org/10.1016/j.adolescence.2018.09.007.

Yearley, Lee. "Selves, Virtues, Odd Genres, and Alien Guides: An Approach to Religious Ethics." *Journal of Religious Ethics* 25, no. 3 (1997): 127–55.

Yeskel, Felice, and Betsy Leondar-Wright. "Classism Curriculum Design." In *Teaching for Diversity and Social Justice: A Sourcebook,* edited by Maurianne Adams, Lee Anne Bell and Pat Griffin, 231–60. New York: Routledge, 1997.

Zajonc, Arthur. *Meditation as Contemplative Inquiry: When Knowing Becomes Love.* Great Barrington, MA: Lindisfarne Books, 2009.

Zhuangzi. *Zhuangzi: Basic Writings.* Translated by Burton Watson. New York: Columbia University Press, 2003.

Zomorodi, Manoush. *Bored and Brilliant: How Spacing Out Can Unlock Your Most Productive and Creative Self.* New York: Picador, 2017.

Page locators in italics indicate figures

Printed in the USA
CPSIA information can be obtained
at www.ICGtesting.com
LVHW102041280823
756457LV00029B/70